China: The Impact
of Revolution

China: The Impact of Revolution

A survey of twentieth century China

Edited by
Colin Mackerras

Contributors
Ian Davies
Edmund S.K. Fung
Bruce McFarlane
Colin Mackerras
Wang Gungwu
Ian Wilson

Longman

Longman Australia Pty Limited
Hawthorn Victoria Australia

Associated companies, branches, and
representatives throughout the world

First published 1976

ISBN 0 582 68669 5 (limp)
ISBN 0 582 68685 7 (cased)

Filmset in Hong Kong by
T.P. Graphic Arts Services
Printed in Hong Kong by
Sheck Wah Tong Printing Press

Acknowledgement
We are grateful to Joseph Waters
for permission to reproduce the
photographs in this book.

Contents

List of maps

Notes on contributors

Ian Davies was formerly Research Scholar, Centre of Asian Studies, Hong Kong University (1969). He obtained his PhD from the Department of Geography, Sydney University, in January 1974. Since 1972 he has worked in the Australian Government Public Service.

Edmund S.K. Fung is a Lecturer in the School of Modern Asian Studies, Griffith University, Brisbane. He holds a BA and an MA from the University of Hong Kong, and a PhD from the Australian National University. He has taught modern Chinese history at Monash University, Melbourne, and the University of Singapore.

Bruce McFarlane is a Reader in the Department of Politics, University of Adelaide. He has worked mainly on the strategy of economic development in a number of socialist countries which have experienced rival models of social progress. In 1968 he was a guest of the Chinese Academy of Science to carry out a study of Chinese economic planning. The results of this were published in the book *The Chinese Road to Socialism* (Penguin, 1970) which has been translated into Spanish, Dutch, Norwegian, and Italian.

Colin Mackerras is Foundation Professor in the School of Modern Asian Studies, Griffith University, Brisbane. He taught English in Peking from 1964 to 1966. His principal publications include *The Rise of the Peking Opera* (Clarendon Press, 1972) and *The Uighur Empire According to the T'ang Dynastic Histories* (Australian National University Press, 1972).

Wang Gungwu is a Fellow of the Australian Academy of the Humanities and Head of the Department of Far Eastern History, Australian National University, Canberra. His principal publications include *A Short History of the Nanyang Chinese* (Eastern Universities Press, Singapore, 1959) and *The Structure of Power in North China during the Five Dynasties* (University of Malaya Press, 1963).

Ian Wilson is a Senior Lecturer in the Department of Political Science at the Australian National University. He has taught courses in Chinese politics and modern Chinese history since 1961.

He first visited China in 1957 as a student and has been there twice since. He is editor and contributing author of *China and the World Community* (Angus and Robertson, 1973).

Preface

The purpose of this book is to trace China's twentieth century development from the overthrow of the monarchical system by Sun Yat-sen's revolution in 1911 through Mao Tse-tung's Communist victory in 1949 and down to the present. It aims to provide an account which is both thematic and chronological, as well as both informative and interpretative.

To approach half a century or more of a people's history by detailing events and trends in chronological order is a traditional and legitimate method of study. In some respects it is even a necessary one. However to deal with a people by themes is just as productive an approach. This makes for greater interest and more depth, and it relates facts and insights to each other more readily, thus making them easier to remember. In this book we have chosen to use a combination of both approaches. There are five sections, each devoted to a separate theme or discipline and each affording a different way of looking at China. At the same time the chronological approach is preserved in some chapters. In particular, the dual method is maintained in the two appendices, the glossary and the chronology. Readers who come across unfamiliar terms or wish to be reminded of some date or other may wish to use these sections for reference purposes.

It is worth pointing out that there is considerable overlap among some of the themes. For instance, in contemporary China politics has a much broader meaning than in the West and encompasses virtually every aspect of life. For this reason political aspects are tightly related to economic or social aspects. There is thus some common ground covered in the chapters on 'Political Development since 1949' and on 'The Economy of the Chinese People's Republic'. We believe this to be desirable, although it involves a little repetition, because it emphasizes the point that knowledge can never be neatly split up into unconnected categories. Another example of an interdisciplinary chapter is that on 'Economic Geography'. This could easily have been placed in a section labelled 'Geography'. On balance, however, it was decided that the chapter added more light when placed in conjunction with those on economic matters. What needs emphasis is that the thematic divisions of the five sections cannot be and are not intended to be more than approximate guides. They are not tight classifications; understanding of China—or, for that matter, anything, anyone, or anywhere else—simply does not work that way.

Returning to the chronological aspect, it will not escape the reader that we have made a clear dividing point in the year 1949, that is the year in which the Communists set up the People's Republic of China. Although we refrain from implying that no aspect of China survived the year unchanged, it does, nevertheless, remain a vital watershed in Chinese history. Indeed the coming to power of the Communists has probably caused a more radical transformation of China's society than any other single event in the thousands of years of her history. The Communists have been the first government to demand of the Chinese people changes in their basic attitudes and values, a break with long-standing traditions. They have shattered once and for all the popular image of the unchanging and unchangeable Chinese.

Our other concern in writing this book has been to preserve a fair balance between the twin aspects of scholarship—information and interpretation. It is obvious that there can be no understanding of a people without detailed and accurate information. But this is certainly not enough. Information without interpretation easily becomes meaningless and dull. On the whole, facts and information are susceptible enough to demonstration that agreement among reasonable people about their validity is possible, although it needs to be said that value judgments will affect *what* facts are considered important and *how* they are told. Interpretations are much more difficult to establish and much less susceptible to proof. Usually they are based on particular value systems, an implicit set of assumptions. Consequently people argue more about them. Professor Wang, in his chapter on 'Nationalism in China before 1949', brings out the disagreements among China-scholars over the role played by the vital component of nationalism in twentieth-century Chinese history and gives his own view of it. Other chapters also put forward interpretations of events, and it will be obvious to readers where they are in conflict with those espoused by conventional wisdom.

China is nothing if not controversial. Its way of life, so different from that of the West, has aroused both strong hostility and great admiration. This is especially true of the period since the Communists came to power in 1949. In Australia, China was for years held up as a threat and excoriated by governments as a consequence. There were also people who disagreed radically with this official view and instead saw in China a challenge or even a model. Even though Australia and China established diplomatic relations in December 1972 and trade and exchanges have broadened since that time, the controversy surrounding China remains sharp and there are still proponents of the 'threat' view. On the whole, however, attitudes have changed somewhat, and it is no longer fashionable to view China with implacable enmity. Certainly the contributors to the present work make no apology for approaching contemporary China without hostility.

This book has been designed principally for students, both at senior high school and university level. On the other hand its authors hope to interest also any general reader. After all China is important enough to be of concern to everybody, and its present stage is more or less inseparable from its modern history.

Finally the technical question of romanization. There are several accepted systems at present. Possibly the one most often used in English-speaking countries is the standard postal romanization for place-names and the Wade-Giles transcription for other technical terms or proper names. We have followed this system throughout the present book.

Part 1
The geographical setting

Chapter 1
Physical geography

Ian Davies

China occupies a dominant position in Asia in terms of land area, population, resources, and location. China is situated in the mid-latitudes (or temperate zone—corresponding closely to the United States), and from south to north her territory stretches 4000 kilometres (2500 miles) from tropical Hainan Island to subarctic northern Heilungkiang Province.

Centrally located in East Asia, the country borders on virtually all of the mainland nations of Asia—twelve in all. They are North Korea, the Soviet Union, Mongolia, Afghanistan, Pakistan, India, Nepal, Sikkim, Bhutan, Burma, Laos, and North Vietnam. Also part of China's international boundary are the two short segments separating Portuguese-controlled Macao and British-controlled Hong Kong from the mainland. Across the sea, to the south and the southeast, China faces Japan, the Philippines, and Indonesia.

In the past, however, the inhospitable nature of China's border-land areas has greatly hindered the free flow of trade and cultural exchange with her neighbours. Consequently China has long been an isolated country, and the Chinese have traditionally called themselves *Chung-kuo*, which means the Middle Kingdom. Nevertheless her central and strategic location is an important factor in China's current world power status.

With a total area of 9 560 000 square kilometres, China's territory is larger than that of the United States and third in the world, after the Soviet Union and Canada. The total length of China's land boundary is nearly 22 000 kilometres. The longest, with the Soviet Union, is 6640 kilometres; the shortest, with Afghanistan, is only 75 kilometres. The Pacific coastline extends 14 000 kilometres.

Off the eastern and southern coasts stretch the Pohai, the Yellow, the East China, and the South China Seas, all of which join the Pacific. Over 3400 islands dot these seas, of which 96 per cent are continental islands (continuations of coastal hills which remain above sea level). The remainder are ocean islands (usually coral reefs), and are located mostly in the South China Sea. Of these islands, Taiwan is the largest followed by Hainan. Other island groups are the Penghu Islands off Taiwan, the Choushan Archipelago off Chekiang Province, and the island of the South China Sea, that is the Tungsha, Sisha (Paracel), Chungsha, and Nansha Islands. The Chinese government has set China's territorial sea limit at twelve nautical miles and declared that the entire Pohai Sea and the Chiungchou Straits, separating Hainan Island from the mainland, are China's inland seas. The waters east of the Chinese mainland cover a broad continental shelf, and are for the most part less than 200 metres deep—consequently they are ideal fishing grounds.

Although most of China's boundaries have been affirmed by treaties concluded during the early 1960s, there still remain certain disputed frontier regions, notably sections of the Sino-Indian and Sino-Soviet borders, both of which are products of what China regards as 'unequal treaties' imposed by strong imperialist nations on a weak China in the nineteenth century. China's claim to certain coral reefs in the South China Sea and the Tiaoyu Islands off Taiwan have also been challenged. The territories held by the Chinese Nationalist government of Taiwan are regarded as integral parts of China's territory, but as these areas are at present outside the control of the People's Republic of China, they will not be covered in this chapter.

Because China's territory is so large, it encompasses great variations in topography, climate, and land use. Large areas, mainly in the west, are unproductive because they are too dry, too cold, or too rugged. More than one half of China exceeds two kilometres in elevation, and much of this is cut by a host of river valleys which carry fast streams during the summer rains. Two-thirds of the land is arid and only 15 per cent of it can be considered arable. Most of this arable land is located in the eastern segment of China which is made up of the eighteen provinces south of the Great Wall, known as China Proper, plus Manchuria or Northeast China. This area contains 96 per cent of the population and is the commercial and agricultural heart of the country because it is favoured with a temperate climate, rich productive soils, and usually adequate rainfall. The remaining half, often known as Outer China, is made up of the Mongolian, Sinkiang, and Tibetan topographical areas, but plays only a minor role in the life of the country.

Topography

Extending over 4000 kilometres from the Pacific coast to the Pamir Plateau in Central Asia, China has great variety in topographical relief. Physically, China falls into three main divisions, the outlines of which follow roughly a three step west-east staircase. These divisions are the lofty mountain massifs, extensive plateaus, and basins of the west, the hill country of the southeast, and the plains of the north and northeast. This west-east inclination can be seen in the cross-section and relief map on page 4.

Both diagrams also clearly depict the dominance of the mountain ridges running eastwards from Tibet like fingers of a spread right hand. However physical diversity also characterizes each of these regions, particularly the western sector where some of the Himalayan mountain peaks reach over 8000 metres in altitude, in contrast to the Turfan Basin depression in Sinkiang, which extends to 154 metres below sea level.

The Major Mountain Systems

Five major mountain systems are present in China, all of which rise in western China and gradually descend eastward, some actually extending as far as the hills and plains of China Proper. It is in these mountain systems and the high Chinghai-Tibet Plateau that are found the headstreams of most of China's major rivers.

The Altai and Tienshan mountain systems are found in northern Sinkiang, the former with an elevation over 3000 metres and the latter with elevations over 4000 metres above sea level. The Kunlun mountain system runs from the Pamirs in the far west and extends eastward at a decreasing elevation to the western edge of the Szechwan Basin. Averaging 5000 metres high, these ridges divide the Tarim Basin of Sinkiang from the high Tibetan Plateau.

The Himalayan mountain system and the associated Karakoram and Kangkar-Tesi Ranges rise abruptly above the southern and western fringe of the Tibetan Plateau and run eastward to join the north-south Hengtuan Mountains which run into western Szechwan and Yunnan. These eastern chains are also known as the Great Snow Mountains and the Cloudy Peak Range and are sometimes collectively known as the Chinese Alps. The Himalayas consist of three gigantic highly folded parallel mountains, of which the central range is the highest, with many peaks over 8000 metres. Mt Everest (or Mt Jolmo Lungma as it is known to the

3

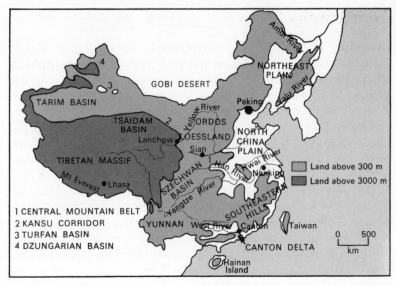

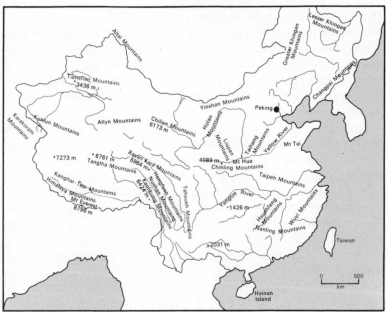

Above—Landform regions of China

Below—China's mountains

4

Chinese) is the world's highest at 8882 metres and is located on the Sino-Nepalese border. The entire system has a perpetual snowline and many glaciers among its peaks. The northern slopes, facing the Tibetan Plateau, are dry with sparse vegetation because the peaks block moist air currents blowing up from the Indian Ocean. In contrast the southern slopes (facing India and Nepal) have a lush vegetation cover and an abundant rainfall.

The major mountain system within China Proper is the Chinling mountain range. Averaging 2000–3600 metres above sea level, this range forms the most important geographic boundary in China. Extending across central China from southern Kansu to the lower reaches of the Hwai and Yangtze Rivers, it functions as the watershed between the Yangtze and Yellow River Valleys. It also acts as a major climatic barrier to monsoon rainfall from the south and dust-laden desert winds (and cold air) from the north, thereby forming a natural dividing line between China's temperate and subtropical zones. Not only does it determine the distribution of soils and vegetation, but also cultivated crops, customs, and dialects.

Other smaller mountain chains exist in northeast and southeast China, close to the Pacific coast. The southern Nanling Mountains of Kwangsi, Hunan, Kwangtung, and Kiangsi separate the valleys of the Yangtze and Pearl Rivers. Although averaging over 1000 metres above sea level, they are sufficiently high to block northern cold waves, so that to the south the climate is warm and the fields green all year round. The Nanling geographic boundary is second only to the Chinling in importance in China, as it defines the tropical parts of China (the region of two or more successive rice harvests a year) and the Cantonese language area.

To the north, a mountain chain extends from the Taihang Range of Shansi-Hopei through to the Greater Khingan Mountains of Heilungkiang Province. This chain stands squarely in the path of the southeastern monsoon, weakening its inland penetration and thus functioning as a dividing line between the moist east and the arid west.

Plateaus, Basins, and Hilly Regions
Plateaus claim up to 26 per cent of China's total area. The most important of them are the Chinghai-Tibet, Inner Mongolian, Yunnan and Kweichow, and Loess Plateaus. The Chinghai-Tibetan Plateau is the world's most extensive tableland, and covers an area of over 1 500 000 square kilometres at an altitude of 4000 metres. The western sector is largely desolate, whereas the

A doctor and nurse travelling in the mountains of Kansu Province. In contemporary China it is a prime duty of those in the professions to give assistance to rural people and to leave the cities at regular intervals

eastern and southern sectors are drained by large rivers and are suitable for livestock grazing.

The Inner Mongolian Plateau is bounded on the south by the Great Wall, on the east by the Greater Khingan Mountains, and on the west by the Chilien Range. It is a desert and steppe plain over 1000 metres in altitude. The western section extends into the Gobi Desert, while the eastern and southern grassland steppes, in contrast, are largely rich pastoral areas.

The Yunnan and Kweichow Plateaus stand between 1000 and 2000 metres in altitude, but decline in elevation from west to east. They are composed largely of limestone which has been deeply cut by many streams, with the result that the plateau has a very undulating topography dotted by numerous limestone pinnacles. Small fertile plains have been converted to paddy fields while hill slopes have been extensively terraced.

The Loess Plateau of north China is located in Shansi, Shensi, southeastern Kansu, and northwestern Hopei, and is roughly bounded by the Great Wall on the north, the Chinling Mountains on the south, and the Taihang Range in the east. Averaging 1000 metres above sea level, this plateau is covered by a thick layer of fertile loess (fine silt), which in many places is more than 100 metres deep. As the sparseness of vegetation leaves the fine loess open to wind and water erosion, immense efforts have been made since 1949 to check this loss through terracing and the planting of grass and trees over the undulating loess ridge formations. This in time has brought about a marked improvement in farming in this area, although many decades of consistent effort will be required in the future to solve the erosion problem completely.

Basins and depressions occupy somewhat less of China's total land area than plateaus—about 20 per cent. The five largest are the Szechwan, Tarim, Turfan, Dzungarian, and Tsaidam Basins. With the exception of the Szechwan Basin, all are located in the western hinterland and are characterized by a dry climate. They consist largely of tracts of desert and grasslands, interspersed with numerous fertile oases. They are also well endowed with valuable deposits of oil, coal, and metallic ores.

Even less extensive than the basins are the hilly regions, which occupy about 10 per cent of the total area of China, and are largely located in the southeastern section below the Yangtze Valley. Other hilly areas can be found in the Liaotung and Shantung Peninsulas further north, where the general elevation is below 400 metres.

The Southeastern Hills account for three-quarters of China's total hilly area. They average 400 metres above sea level, although some higher areas exceed 1000 metres. These hills include the entire area south of the Yangtze, with the exception of the coastal plains, the Nanling Mountains, and the Yunnan-Kweichow Plateau. Erosion is responsible for the low elevation of these hills, while their gentle slopes, interspersed by fluvial plains and small basins, make them ideal terrain for terracing and the cultivation of a wide variety of crops.

The Plains of China

Like the hilly regions, China's plains are distributed mainly in the eastern coastal regions and, while only accounting for 12 per cent of China's total area, they measure over 1 000 000 square kilometres, or more than four times the size of the British Isles. In general they are flat or gently undulating and do not rise more than 200 metres above sea level. In most cases the plains consist of flood or river deposits which have rich, easily worked soils. The working of these soils over thousands of years by the Chinese has made these plains among the world's great centres of agricultural production. The four most important plains are the Northeast, the North China, the Middle and Lower Yangtze Plain, and the Canton Delta region.

The Northeast Plain is an immense flat plain, roughly 350 000 square kilometres in area, stretching from northern Heilungkiang to the Pohai Gulf, and is drained by the Liao, Nun, and Sungari Rivers. Fertile black soil in the northern sector has, together with ample rainfall, resulted in this region becoming one of China's major granaries.

The North China Plain embraces the greater part of Hopei Province, eastern Honan, and western Shantung. With an area of 300 000 square kilometres, it is China's largest and earliest cultivated area, consisting largely of soils formed by the Yellow, Hai, and Hwai Rivers. It is uniquely flat and low—50 metres and less in most places above sea level. Brown soils cover most of the plain and are fertile and easily cultivated, in contrast to the saline-alkaline soils of the low-lying and coastal areas. Adequate drainage on the plain has long been a problem, while floods have been a constant phenomenon. To overcome this threat, the plain has been the scene of much effort over the past two decades in the construction of a number of large-scale water conservancy projects. It is an important producer of winter wheat, *kaoliang* (sorghum), maize, and industrial crops such as cotton.

The Middle and Lower Yangtze Plain adjoins the North China

Plain along the Hwai River, and stretches along the banks of the Yangtze (apart from the upper reaches). The Middle Yangtze Plain is centred on the Tungting and Poyang Lakes of Hunan and Kiangsi and is very level, with the bulk of the area below 50 metres above sea level. Rich soils and good irrigation contribute to the fact that the entire Yangtze Plain ranks as China's main producer of rice. The Lower Plain takes in the regions along the Yangtze in Anhwei and the Yangtze Delta in Kiangsu. It is very low in elevation, the delta region being less than 10 metres above sea level. Lakes and rivers abound in this plain, and rural inhabitants of the delta region use boats as often as their counterparts in the north use carts. The accumulation of silt deposited by the Yangtze at its mouth has gradually extended seawards at an average rate of 25 metres a year.

The Canton Delta, also known as the Pearl River Delta, is a small fertile coastal plain of 11 000 square kilometres, lying at the estuary of the Pearl River in Kwangtung Province. As in the case of the Yangtze Delta, the Canton Delta is elevated barely above river level and has a highly developed agricultural economy, supporting a very dense population of 1000 persons per square kilometre.

River Patterns and Water Conservancy Projects

Just as important as the mountains, plateaus, and plains are the waterways which flow through them. All of China's great rivers flow eastward to the Pacific, the pattern being determined by the east-west structural trend of the country's topography.

The Yangtze River system is by far the largest in China, draining 60 per cent of China Proper and carrying over twenty times the annual runoff of the great north Chinese river, the Hwang Ho or Yellow River. In terms of annual runoff, however, the larger Pacific drainage basin rivers are the Yangtze, followed by the Si Kiang (West River), the Heilung (Amur) and Sunghua (Sungari) Rivers (both of which are frozen for five or six months of the year), the Mekong (Lantsang, which flows into Laos), the Yellow River, the Min River (at Foochow), and the Hai River (at Tientsin).

The Salween (Nu) and Tsangpo (Yalutsangpo or Brahmaputra) Rivers have their sources in the mountains of Tibet and Yunnan, and flow into the Indian Ocean. The Irtysh River in the extreme north of Sinkiang is the only river in China with an outlet

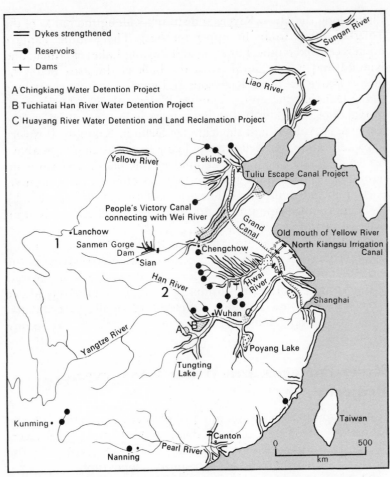

Major water conservancy works. This map shows the large-scale flood-control schemes and some of the more important hydroelectric schemes completed or under way.
1 Liuchia Gorge—volume 4900 million cubic metres, power 1·05 million KW
2 Tanchiangkou Dam—volume 51 600 million cubic metres, power 0·9 million KW

(via the Ob) in the Arctic Sea. The Tarim River in Sinkiang is the largest river among China's large and arid interior drainage basins; it is fed by melting snow on the Tienshan and Kunlun Ranges.

In general China's rivers have the greatest volume of water in summer as most rain falls in summer while snow melts on the mountains in the west. In winter water levels are low and in areas from the Yellow River northward, rivers are frozen. Except for the Amur, all northern rivers (in particular the Yellow River) are great silt carriers and have in the past been subject to frequent and devastating flooding along their lower courses. In the main these rivers are not navigable. In contrast the Yangtze and its tributaries and the West River carry heavy volumes of water, little sediment, are ice free and navigable, and are not liable to flood as often.

The Yangtze River System

With a total length of 5800 kilometres, the Yangtze is China's and Asia's largest river, and accordingly is known to the Chinese as *Ch'ang-chiang* or 'long river'. Originating in the Chinghai-Tibet Plateau, the Yangtze flows through gorges into the Szechwan Basin, where it abruptly turns eastward, cutting through the famous Yangtze gorges (The Three Gorges) on the Szechwan-Hupei border, until it enters the large Middle and Lower Yangtze Plain at Ichang. It then flows eastward for 1700 kilometres, emptying into the East China Sea near Shanghai.

It drains a basin of 1 800 000 square kilometres or 19 per cent of China's total area which is inhabited by 300 000 000 people or one-third of China's population. In its lower reaches it has an average annual flow of 30 000 cubic metres per second, which earns it third place among the rivers of the world after the Amazon and the Congo, although at high water (in summer) the flow exceeds 80 000 cubic metres per second.

The river does not usually flood, since its lower course is marked by a series of lakes of which the Tungting, Poyang, and Tai are the largest. These periodically fill up with flood waters which are slowly released back to the river as the river level falls. Nevertheless disastrous floods have been known, such as the 1931 catastrophe when an area (the Hunan and Hupei Plains) the size of Britain was flooded and 3 000 000 people drowned or starved to death.

In 1954 floods occurred on a similar scale in the same region, although the loss of life was far less due largely to the efficiency of government relief measures. Since then the flood danger along critical sections has been greatly reduced as a result of the completion of a series of large water conservancy works. Two flood detention basins were constructed in Hupei Province to accommodate excess flood waters: in 1954 the Chingkiang project, south of Shasi in Hupei, and the Tuchiatai, near Wuhan, in 1956. This second one not only regulated flood waters from the Yangtze but also those of the Han River. Associated with these projects was the strengthening of dykes totalling 180 kilometres in the same region by millions of peasant workers during the mid-1950s.

The gentle flow of the river over the Yangtze Plains (dropping at a rate of only 4 centimetres per kilometre compared with 1·5 metres per kilometre in western Szechwan) provides excellent conditions for navigation. The Yangtze system accounts for over two-thirds of China's inland waterway transportation, indicating the size and importance of this transport artery.

The Hwai River

The Hwai, the largest river between the Yangtze and the Yellow Rivers, is unique in that it is the only long river without a natural outlet. Hence it is particularly susceptible to floods, which have occurred quite often and have caused much serious damage. Originating in the Tungpo Mountains of Honan Province, it flows eastward for 1000 kilometres through Anhwei and Kiangsu, into the Hungtse Lake, and eventually into the Yangtze and through canals to the sea. The drainage basin of the Hwai system covers 260 000 square kilometres inhabited by 120 000 000 people.

Since 1194 AD the Hwai's former outlet to the sea has been blocked as a result of the Yellow River's overflowing into the Hwai and silting the outlet. The Hungtse Lake was created by the trapped flood waters, which were forced to flow into the Yangtze via the Grand Canal. Although the area has long been susceptible to disastrous floods, the situation worsened between 1938 and 1947, following the shifting of the Yellow River channel back to the Hwai as a result of the blowing up of the southern dykes in Honan by Nationalist troops.

In 1951 the new Communist government embarked upon an ambitious programme of flood control for the Hwai system. This involved the construction of detention reservoirs on upstream tributaries (for example the Futseling and Paisha dams), the dredging of the main channel, the strengthening of dykes, the construction of flood diversion dams, and the digging of a new outlet to the Yellow Sea from Hungtse Lake. During the late

1950s further river outlets were built, while recently new canals were dug to divert water from numerous tributaries into the Hungtse Lake, thus relieving the load on the Hwai during the summer flood period. The entire scheme, which has so far involved the removal of earth equivalent to the construction of twenty Suez Canals, is now nearing completion and has resulted in the region becoming a large and reliable producer of grain and cotton.

The Yellow River System

The Yellow River is the largest in north China, and is so called because of the colour of the silt that it carries. Rising at a height of 4000 metres in the Tibetan highlands, it runs 4845 kilometres through the easily eroded loess formations of the great bend around the Ordos Plateau and between Shansi and Shensi, into the North China Plain, where its gradient is greatly reduced. The silt-laden river is no longer able to carry its load at this stage, resulting in extensive deposition. Over time this deposition has raised the level of the river bed to such an extent that the channel is now several metres above the level of the surrounding country-side. The river's natural levees have had to be raised by the construction of embankments to prevent flooding.

In the past, however, the embankments were frequently breached, resulting in widespread devastation (in 1853 and 1938, for example) and the spreading of alluvium over the North China Plain. This has often resulted in the complete changing of the main channel and the position of the mouth of the river. The latter has changed twenty-six times in two thousand years, while nine major changes in the entire channel have occurred, resulting in the river reaching the Pohai north of the Shantung Peninsula some-times and south of the peninsula at other times. The flatness of the North China Plain meant that Yellow River floodwaters were slow to be led off, resulting in widespread famine and prolonged economic hardship for the inhabitants. With a flood frequency every two years, it is little wonder that the Yellow River was called 'China's Sorrow'.

The new Communist government set to work to plan the regulation of the river, and by 1953 had strengthened the dykes along the lower course and diverted water for irrigation in such projects as the People's Victory Canal on the north bank near Chengchow in Honan Province. In 1955 an overall water resource development programme was announced, covering half a century of work. It includes the building of forty-six large dams,

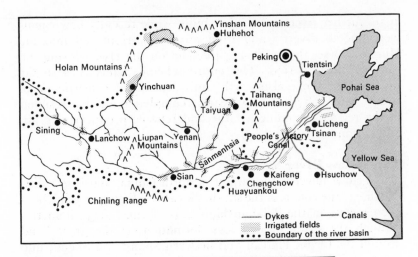

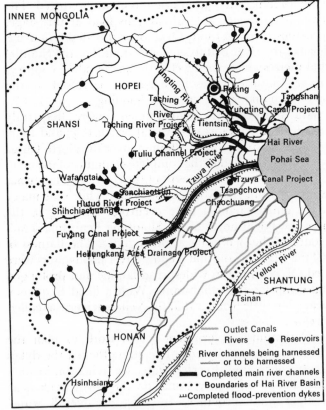

Above—The Yellow River

Below—The Hai River Control Project

the erection of hydroelectric stations, the creation of navigable reaches, and work on soil conservation and irrigation and drainage projects.

The first phase of the programme included the construction of the Sanmen Gorge reservoir, and the Liuchia Gorge dam and hydroelectric plant, and the Yenkuo dam and hydroelectric plant (with a designed capacity of 1 050 000 kilowatts and 600 000 kilowatts respectively) both of which are near Lanchow. Although these projects were interrupted in 1960 by the departure of Soviet technicians, the position today is that two of the dams (Sanmen and Yenkuo) have been completed but only 1 300 000 kilowatts of generating capacity is in operation. During the 1960s efforts were mainly channelled into the expansion of irrigation facilities along the river and the improvement of alkaline soils in areas subject to waterlogging. The erection of the Sanmen dam between 1958 and 1962 has basically solved the flood problem of the Lower Yellow River Valley, but a tremendous amount of work is still required (particularly in the soil conservation area) before the silt problem can be checked.

The Hai River System

The Hai River is the 70 kilometre long outlet of five major tributaries (Pai, Yungting, Taching, Tzuya, and Wei) that drain the North China Plain and converge fan-like at Tientsin, causing a flood problem. This region receives nearly three-quarters of its annual rainfall in three months during summer, with the result that during heavy rains these rivers pour into the Hai River at Tientsin at high velocity. Like the Yellow River, the lower reaches of the five tributaries follow a bed raised constantly by deposits, and require protection by dykes. Unable to take the increased flow following heavy rains, the river frequently burst its banks, extensively flooding the surrounding area.

In the 1950s an attempt was made to reduce this threat by constructing flood control reservoirs—notably the Kuanting reservoir northwest of Peking (1954) and the Miyun reservoir northeast of Peking (1959). However the greatest flood recorded for two centuries occurred in 1963 around Tientsin. As a result the Chinese government initiated the Hai River water conservancy project, which involved the reorganization of almost every river system north of the Yellow River. Basically completed in 1973, the scheme has greatly reduced the dangers of flood, and reclaimed an enormous area of irrigated farmland which gives high and stable yields from what were formerly waterlogged fields

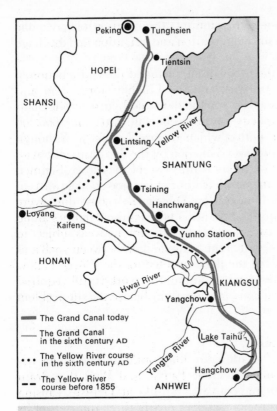

The Grand Canal today

The Grand Canal
in the sixth century AD

• • • The Yellow River course
in the sixth century AD

- - - The Yellow River
course before 1855

Above—The Grand Canal

Below—This section of the ancient Grand Canal, between the Yangtze and
Hwai Rivers, is now a busy navigation route

16

of alkaline soil. More than 50 000 000 people in the area have benefited directly from this project which included the construction of over twenty new outlets to the sea, the erection of fourteen dykes, and the building or enlargement of many reservoirs in the upper reaches of the tributaries.

The huge scale of this scheme can be seen clearly when one considers that, in terms of the amount of earth moved, the project was equivalent to the construction of seven Panama Canals or four Suez Canals.

The Si Kiang System

The Si Kiang or West River is 2100 kilometres long and is the largest in south China. Rising in the Yunnan-Kweichow Plateau, the river flows through Kwangsi and western Kwangtung Province. Because of its location in a high rainfall area, the river carries an enormous flow equivalent to over six times that of the Yellow River. The West River meets the Tung (East) and Pei (North) Rivers south of Canton to form a big estuary consisting of many channels separated by numerous islets and alluvial bars, and is known as the Pearl River or Canton Delta. Flooding along the West River is possible during the typhoon season and consequently the channels are protected by dykes, which are continuously being strengthened. The river is an important transport artery, as river steamers can proceed 370 kilometres upstream to Wuchow.

The Grand Canal

Known to the Chinese as Tayun Ho, the Grand Canal stretches for 1782 kilometres from Peking to Hangchow, and to this day remains the world's largest. It was built section by section between 486 BC and 1292 AD, although the bulk of the large-scale work on it was done in the Sui (581–618 AD) and Yüan (1280–1368) dynasties. The purpose of the canal was to simplify the transport of grain (the basis of taxation) from the Yangtze Valley to Peking, and to improve imperial communication between north and south China. The canal played an important role until 1855 when navigation on the Shantung section became difficult following the change in the course of the Yellow River. By the late nineteenth century the canal fell into disrepair and lost much of its usefulness because of siltation, the development of sea transport, and the building of the Tientsin-Shanghai Railway. The canal's condition deteriorated during the first half of this century.

Beginning in 1950, however, efforts were initiated to restore the navigation and irrigation functions of the canal by strengthening dykes and constructing water regulation gates along 330 kilometres of the north Kiangsu section, in conjunction with the Hwai River scheme. Later projects deepened and widened the canal, straightened meandering sections, and enlarged the discharge capacity of the northern section around Tientsin. However, though navigation on the canal today is still hindered by siltation in the vicinity of the Weishan Lake, river steamers only can freely ply the Peking-Yellow River-Tsining section and the Hangchow-Hsuchow section. Although a considerable amount of improvement work is still in progress, it appears that the original plans for a canal capable of serving barges and ships of up to 2000 tonnes is still a long way off.

Climate

The great extent of China, together with the great diversity of topographical conditions, has given the country wide variations in climate, while its location puts most of the country under strong monsoon influence. Although most of China lies inside the temperate belt, it has hot wet summers and cold dry winters, with temperatures decreasing rapidly from south to north in winter in contrast to the more uniform temperature prevailing over the whole country during summer. For instance, during January (winter) there exists a gap of more than 30°C between temperatures in Canton and Harbin, but during July (summer) the difference is only 4°C.

In addition, the length of seasons also varies. Some places have prolonged winters and practically no summers (the Chinghai-Tibet Plateau), while others are hot all the year round and have no real winters (the areas south of the Nanling). Rainfall is more seasonal than temperature in China, being highly concentrated during the summer months and dominated by winds known collectively as the winter and summer monsoons. Furthermore rainfall shows an even greater regional contrast than temperature.

Rainfall is the chief climatic factor differentiating north and south China. Precipitation in areas south of the Chinling Range (or the Yangtze) vary between 1000 and 2000 millimetres, but in moving north and west this decreases to 600 millimetres in the North China Plain and Northeast China, to less than 100 in the Gobi Desert and only 25 in the Turfan Basin in Sinkiang. For the purpose of comparison, it may be of interest to note that the average rainfall in the Australian cities of Sydney, Canberra, and

Perth is 1100, 610, and 900 millimetres respectively, although precipitation is less seasonal than in China.

As climatic conditions, and in particular rainfall, directly influence the farming pattern and agricultural productivity in China, the lives of millions of its inhabitants are directly and often dramatically affected. For centuries millions of Chinese have lived in areas of climatic uncertainty, in zones where climatic conditions may fluctuate greatly—and disastrously—from year to year. One such critical area is the North China Plain, where the annual rainfall variability exceeds 30 per cent in what is considered a relatively low rainfall zone, compared with the more manageable 15 per cent variability in the relatively high rainfall areas of Szechwan and southern China.

The fluctuations in northern China have in past centuries caused disastrous drought-flood famines, which have decimated the peasant populations of entire regions. In 1878–79 famine in the loess region resulted in over 9 000 000 deaths, while the drought of 1920–21 in north China made some 20 000 000 people destitute and brought about the death of 500 000 people. Over 2 000 000 people perished through drowning or from starvation as a result of the flooding of the Yellow River in Honan Province in 1887.

The peasants of China of this early era were helpless when confronted by the variability of China's climate, as they lacked the necessary degree of organization, the technology, and the resources to overcome these calamities. Although man cannot change the climate, he can reduce, and possibly eliminate, the climate's disastrous impact, for example through afforestation which controls runoff or through irrigation in areas of uncertain rainfall. It has only been during the past two decades, following major social and political changes, that a new relationship has been created between man and climate in China, in which man has been striving to increase his technological competence and organizational ability to combat the effects of climate fluctuations.

Monsoons

As mentioned above, China's climate is very strongly influenced by the wet summer and the dry winter monsoons. During summer warm and moist sea air masses invade China from the southeast (the summer monsoon) and prevail over eastern China. Heavy rains fall over much of the area when this air mass is lifted by either mountains or cold front wedges. Hot oppressive summer weather is typical of eastern China, with the Yangtze Plains being

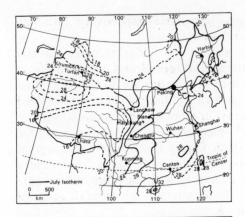

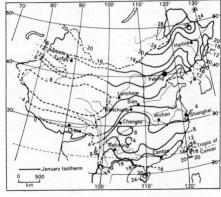

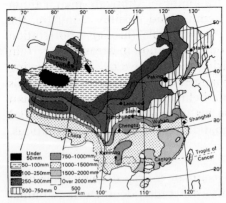

Above—July temperatures (in degrees Centigrade)—the broken lines are drawn according to incomplete data

Centre—January temperatures (in degrees Centigrade)

Below—Mean annual rainfall

20

notoriously hot and humid.

The winter monsoon is followed by cold and dry air masses from Siberia which move successively into China and often penetrate—though greatly modified—to the southern provinces. Little rain falls during the colder months; clear days with low temperatures and very low humidities are normal. During late winter and spring strong northerly winds sweep across north China and hazy days caused by dust storms are common. In general the cold dry polar air affects a much greater area of China for a longer period than do the warm moist winds of the summer monsoon.

Superimposed on the monsoons are the destructive typhoons and cyclones, and the intermittent polar cold waves. The latter often cause the temperature to drop by 10°C or more within twenty-four hours, and can affect the entire country with the exception of the Szechwan Basin and the Yunnan-Kweichow Plateau. The resultant frost can cause a lot of harm to crops and fruit orchards, while the danger is particularly great at the time of the spring sowing or before the autumn harvest.

Mid-latitude cyclones moving eastward through the Yangtze Valley and across the North China Plain during summer produce most of the rain throughout China. However much of it (particularly between June and August) is related to the passage of tropical typhoons, which usually strike the southern Chinese coast three or four times a year and sweep northward to the Shantung Peninsula. These storms cause great damage to crops in the coastal regions, and in the past resulted in flooding which killed many people.

Temperature and Rainfall
Seasonal temperatures vary greatly because of the monsoonal circulation pattern. The greatest annual temperature range is found in Heilungkiang Province (see Harbin's temperature pattern on page 22) where the January average drops to –21°C, while that of July averages 20°C. The annual temperature range decreases gradually towards the south—in tropical Hainan Island it is only 8°C. From the centre map opposite it can be seen that the January isotherms (that is lines of equal temperature) are all aligned from east to west. The 0°C isotherm follows the Hwai River, the Chinling Range, and then curves around the western rim of the Szechwan Basin into southern Tibet. Temperatures in the North China Plain are mostly between 0°C and –8°C during winter, compared with the much colder (–8°C to

-20°C) Northeastern Plain; both areas experience frequent snowfalls, while the earth is often frozen in the northeast.

Temperature (°C) and Rainfall (millimetres) Comparisons

	Canton	Wuhan	Shanghai	Peking	Harbin
Annual rainfall	1575	1250	1130	620	565
January temperature	13·2	3·9	4·0	−4·6	−20·9
July temperature	28·6	28·8	26·5	26·1	24·0

During July temperatures are warm to hot and are more uniform, with an average of 20°–30°C prevailing throughout most of China. The highest summer temperatures are found in Hainan Island and the Turfan and Tarim Basins of Sinkiang Province, while the lowest average July readings occur in the Tibetan Highlands and the Altai Mountains.

Like temperature, rainfall is seasonal in its distribution and has a direct relationship with the monsoons, agricultural pattern, and crop harvests. Atmospheric moisture comes mostly from the Pacific, so that there is less and less rainfall as one moves from the south and east towards the north and west (see rainfall map). Although most of China's rainfall occurs during the summer monsoon, south China receives some rain throughout the year. In contrast, north China has virtually none in winter, apart from a few snowfalls, because of the influence of the cold dry air of the northerly monsoon.

These contrasting conditions of humidity exercise a direct influence on land utilization and the processes of soil formation. The hot wet summers that prevail over the greater part of the country provide adequate moisture for the growing of high yield crops, and usually fall at a time when crops are in their most vigorous period of growth.

Widespread double cropping and paddy rice cultivation usually extend as far north as the 30th parallel, roughly in line with the Chinling Range and the Hwai River. This is also where the 15°C average annual temperature isotherm, the average winter 0°C isotherm, and the 1000 millimetre rainfall line occur. This important dividing line also separates the growing season of 220–280 days in northern China from that of 300–340 days in the southern areas.

The longer springs, warmer weather, and more reliable and heavier rainfall of southern China make possible the growing of tropical crops such as sugarcane, rubber, coffee, coconuts, oil palm, sisal, and bananas. Broad leaved evergreens (oak, laurel, and magnolia) and bamboo groves provide the major forest cover, although dense jungle exists in river valleys of southwestern Yunnan Province. More recently reafforestation projects have introduced pine, poplar, and eucalyptus trees to this region.

Mineral Resources

China is relatively well endowed with most minerals. They are distributed in large and small deposits all over the country, but since large-scale prospecting has in the past been concentrated in eastern China, most of the known deposits are located in this area. In general China's mineral base is sufficiently diversified for the country to become a first-rate industrial power.

In particular China has large reserves of coal, iron ore, tungsten, wolfram, molybdenum, manganese, magnesite, tin, antimony, mercury, salt, gypsum, and aluminium-bearing clays. Her reserves of antimony (concentrated in Hunan), tungsten (in Kiangsi and Kwangtung), and magnesite (on the Liaotung Peninsula) are the world's largest. China ranks second in molybdenum reserves (Liaoning, Fukien, Kwangtung, and Hunan), third in coal resources (located largely in northern China) and fourth in iron ore reserves (distributed in all major regions). Recently, as a result of extensive prospecting, China has claimed it has the world's third largest potential crude oil reserves. These include newly discovered off-shore reserves in the Pohai Gulf, and the vast reserves of the Taching oil basin in Heilungkiang Province. Her tin deposits are located in the far southwest in Yunnan Province, manganese deposits are concentrated in Hunan and south China, uranium is found in Kiangsi and Sinkiang, while gold is mined in the northeast and in Sinkiang.

Iron ore deposits are the key to a country's industrial potential and, in China, determine the location of major steel works. They are widely distributed, with the largest workable deposits located at and around Anshan, Penchi, Tayeh, Paiyunopo (Inner Mongolia), Hsuanhua, Peking, Maanshan, Wuan, Chichiang, Hainan Island, Chingtiehshan (Kansu), and western Hupei. The last deposit has not as yet undergone exploitation. Overall reserves, however, are not of a high quality. Few deposits have iron contents exceeding 60 per cent, whereas the average iron content is only in the vicinity of 40 per cent.

China's copper, lead, and zinc assets are modest, but are able to fulfil most domestic requirements. However it is known that China is deficient in deposits of chromium, nickel, silver, cobalt, and platinum. Northeast China has the most balanced, fairly abundant, and accessible array of minerals in the country; these have undergone large-scale exploitation for the past two generations and are only partially depleted. China's non-ferrous metals are mostly located south of the Yangtze River, while her mineral fuel deposits are located largely in the north.

Select Bibliography

Institute of Geography, USSR Academy of Sciences *The Physical Geography of China*, Moscow, translated in the US Government publication, *Joint Publication Research Service*, No. 32 119 (1965). A very comprehensive study of all aspects of China's topography.

Jen Yu-ti *A Concise Geography of China*, Foreign Languages Press, Peking, 1964. Contains a brief account of China's physical features, climate, rivers and lakes, soils and vegetation.

Tregear, T.R. *A Geography of China*, London University Press, London, 1972. A useful reference book covering all aspects of China's physical environment.

Wang Chun-heng *A Simple Geography of China*, Foreign Languages Press, Peking, 1958. An earlier version of Jen Yu-ti's book; useful but not very comprehensive.

Part 2
Political history

Chapter 2
Political development in the republican period.

Ian Wilson

In October 1911 forces hostile to the ruling Manchu Ch'ing dynasty staged a successful uprising in the city of Wuchang[1], touching off a revolution which quickly overthrew the last emperor of all China. Thus ended 267 years of Manchu rule in China and a far longer period of imperial government, the main features of which had emerged during the Han dynasty (206 BC–AD 220). However one suspects that the old order would have collapsed without this impromptu revolution, which was so lacking in planning that the leader of the revolutionary movement, Sun Yat-sen, was raising funds in America at the time and learnt of its success only through a St Louis newspaper. The new Republic of China was proclaimed early in 1912 but the search for new forms of political and governmental organization and for a new ideology had only just begun. The quest was to take another forty years of hardship and suffering for the Chinese people in whose name the infant nation had been brought into being.

Republican Revolution, Ideology and Impact

A major problem lay in the fact that although the emperor, his chief advisers, and his massive entourage had been swept away, little else had been changed by the events of late 1911. Political power at the local level still remained in the hands of the landlords and gentry, the traditional social order survived the crisis intact in its essential elements, and at the provincial level regional military figures quickly assumed power from the old imperial army and Manchu governors. Indeed, because he was thought to be the only person capable of protecting the government against these warlords, the former imperial Commander-in-Chief, Yüan Shih-k'ai, was made the first President of the Republic. So little was he in sympathy with the ideals of Sun Yat-sen and his followers that he soon set about having himself enthroned as emperor, thus attempting to betray his republican allies as he had earlier betrayed his Manchu ruler. Yet the popular reaction to this attempt to restore the dynastic system did indicate that the people of China, particularly the students and the soldiers, were looking for something more from the brief battles of 1911 and would not accept a return to imperial rule.

Sun Yat-sen had tapped strong anti-Manchu sentiments and also feelings that China needed a radical break with the past if she was to be strong in the new international system. Amongst a powerful group of intellectuals there was the belief that the Confucian political philosophy which had been the basis of imperial rule must be replaced with a modern, broadly democratic approach to government. Others were even more critical of the entire Confucian philosophical system. They claimed that its survival would prevent China from properly adopting the modern scientific and technological methods from the West which alone would enable China to compete effectively with Europe, America, and Japan, where these adaptations had been made so successfully. On the other hand, some scholars claimed that Confucianism could be made relevant to the modern world, but by 1911 these men found themselves in a minority. Since the last quarter of the nineteenth century, increasing numbers of young Chinese had been sent abroad to study and had come in contact with what they saw to be more effective ways to organize society. After 1911 these young men flocked back to their homeland, anxious to participate in the process of nation building and to contribute their experience in the search for a new social and political order. The young republic owed much to these men but its ideology was drawn from the earlier writings of Sun Yat-sen and this was to prove a poor base from which to build a new society.

During his efforts to 'revive' and 'regenerate' China at the turn of the century, Sun enunciated his *San-min-chu-i* or 'Three Principles of the People' and this hurriedly assembled collection of ideas became the official ideology of the Kuomintang or Nationalist Party, which he founded on the basis of earlier groupings in 1912, and of the Republic of China. The first and most important of the principles was nationalism (see also chapter 3). Sun called for an end to foreign control and influence, rights of extraterritoriality, and all the evils he believed flowed from these practices which had been imposed on the Chinese nation.

The second principle, 'People's Rule', was not in fact a call for democracy in China. Sun's view was that the very low standards of education and cultural development in China made it necessary first to institute a period of political 'tutelage' during which the masses would be educated into the ways of democratic government by their enlightened leaders, presumably the Kuomintang. Full self-government would come only later in this benevolent but highly paternalistic political programme.

The third principle, 'People's Livelihood', was even vaguer than the other two and called for a reorganization of economic life to remove grave inequalities, particularly in land, thus hoping to save China from the dangers of class struggle. The state was to have a major economic role in this reorganization, but the plan could not be described as socialist in form. As it was, Sun and the Kuomintang were so dependent on the very groups in the cities and the countryside most likely to suffer from such a reorganization that little was done to spell out these aspects of the official ideology, let alone put them into practice. Land reform, the most pressing of China's economic needs, was not tackled in a head-on fashion for another three decades.

To Sun and his followers the nationalist question appeared to be the most important in 1911. Sun was often to complain that the Chinese people were like a loose heap of sand, lacking the cement to create a strong and integrated nation. The foreigners, who had done so much to bring down the old order and make the revolution possible, once again obliged and provided a cause which gave the nationalist movement the bonding cement it required. Until 1919 the main impact of republicanism and nationalism had been amongst the educated urban population and the students of China's high schools, universities, and military academies.

After the death of Yüan Shih-k'ai in 1916, the power base of Sun Yat-sen and the party he led moved to the south, although their authority was far from unchallenged there, while the north remained under the control of various political and military cliques. China's participation in the First World War had not been of great military significance but she had contributed labour teams to the allied cause in the expectation that the high principles of United States President Woodrow Wilson on the question of national self-determination would be honoured after the war and those parts of China alienated by the Germans would be returned to China. But Japan, which had made a greater contribution, put in a claim for these territories and it was upheld. The popular reaction to this betrayal at Versailles erupted in the May Fourth Movement. Street demonstrations were held, Japanese goods were boycotted, and there were longer-term results in the vernacular literary movement, which also had its origins at about the time of these events. The response to the Versailles decision and to the infamous 'Twenty-one Demands' made by Japan against China was still restricted to the intellectual élite of China, but by 1920 it had involved a much wider urban group and the popular phase of the nationalist movement can be said to have commenced. However nationalism did not spread effectively to the countryside until somewhat later (see chapter 3).

The republican movement had suffered numerous reverses under Yüan Shih-k'ai and the subsequent development of warlord rule but the national humiliation of China at Versailles discredited the ruling clique and gave Sun Yat-sen a second opportunity to reunite the country. Sun Yat-sen reorganized the Kuomintang (KMT) on a mass basis with advice from Joffe and Borodin, two agents of the Comintern or Communist International which had been founded in March 1919 in Moscow. Sun had some misgivings about the correctness of Lenin's policies but was most impressed by the political organization he had welded together to pursue the revolution in Russia. The Russians, with the exception of Leon Trotsky, saw no prospect of a proletarian revolution in China and thought a period of nationalist democratic rule under bourgeois leadership was necessary first. The KMT under Sun seemed to have the best chance of carrying out this phase, uniting the country, and limiting foreign influence in China which could threaten the security of the new Soviet state along the thousands of miles of the border of China. For his part, Sun welcomed the arrangement since he was provided with a strong party structure made up of numerous cells, each subordinate to the party committee immediately above them and ultimately to him as the leader. However the KMT was not to be his sole weapon and Sun Yat-sen was engaged in fruitless negotiations with northern warlords and political cliques in Peking, hoping once again to make an alliance which would bring about unification. His plans were abruptly brought to an end when he died on 12 March 1925. He was quickly transformed into a national hero and in the same year one of his lieutenants, Chiang Kai-shek, assumed control of the KMT which now enjoyed a prestige and reputation it had never had under its founder.

At the same time as the KMT was being reorganized as the mass movement of the Chinese nationalist revolution, a much smaller political grouping was formed. The ideas behind the

Russian revolution of 1917 were much slower to make an impact in China than were its organizational lessons but small socialist and Marxist discussion groups were formed in Peking and amongst Chinese youths studying abroad in Paris after the First World War. The Comintern was also interested in the propagation of Marxism in China and sent another agent, Voitinsky, to provide some instruction during 1920 but it was not until mid-1921 that the Chinese Communist Party (CCP) was formed.

For the next four years the CCP remained a small collection of enthusiastic but not always very practical revolutionaries, many of them students and intellectuals from the major cities of China. The leaders were openly scornful of the narrow nationalism of Sun Yat-sen and instead adopted a cosmopolitan outlook which further limited their appeal within China. Their hopes were centred on a massive conflagration in the developed states of Europe and North America which would then spread to China. Until this took place it was difficult to see a useful role for the small CCP because the much larger KMT was in clear command of the national revolution and Sun, who had rejected the Russian course of class war and proletarian revolution, was justifiably suspicious of any Chinese claiming to be followers of Lenin. However in 1923 it was agreed that members of the CCP would be allowed to join the mainstream of the national movement as individuals rather than as Communists. The CCP members retained their own organization and tight discipline within the KMT, which gave them an influence out of proportion to their numerical strength, but in return some of them worked extremely hard to make the KMT a much more effective movement. This was particularly true of the KMT units attempting to carry the nationalist message to the peasantry where a young Hunanese proved such a good organizer that he was elected to the KMT Central Executive Committee as an alternate delegate. His name was Mao Tse-tung and he was also a member of the Central Committee of the CCP.

Chiang Kai-shek versus Mao Tse-tung, 1926–37

In 1926 the KMT under Chiang Kai-shek launched the Northern Expedition, a military campaign to bring the warlords of the north under Republican control and thus unite China. The campaign gathered considerable mass support and the CCP members, some of whom like Chou En-lai held important posts in Chiang Kai-shek's army, actively participated in the struggle to unite China under KMT rule, even though Chiang Kai-shek had begun to suspect the intentions of the CCP and their links with the Russians. Before the Expedition set out he staged a *coup* in Canton, the capital of Kwangtung Province, to eliminate Communist influence but after Wuhan was taken and Chiang moved off at the head of his National Revolutionary Army, a group of left-wing KMT members and CCP elements established a rival government in Wuhan, thus further arousing Chiang Kai-shek's suspicions. He received information which showed that the Russians were trying to direct the CCP towards increasing their influence and forcing the adoption of an even closer pro-Soviet policy on the government.

Despite the obvious tension between Chiang and the CCP and the experiences in Canton, the Comintern agents continued to urge co-operation with the KMT and a large group of Communists, including Chou En-lai, managed to organize the workers of Shanghai and seize control of the city before Chiang Kai-shek's army arrived. They handed over control to the National Revolutionary Army but were then ordered to surrender their weapons, which most of them did. Chiang Kai-shek then struck on 12 April and within hours thousands of Communists and trade unionists had been shot or arrested. Further *coups* quickly followed in the other coastal cities and the rival government in Wuhan also fell. Chiang Kai-shek managed to regain sole control of the KMT and nearly managed to smash the CCP completely. By early 1927 membership had grown to over 56 000 but after the bloody *coups* of April only a bare 10 000 survived, either underground in the cities or scattered in the countryside.

The leadership of the CCP was still largely an intellectual one, even though urban workers had begun to be recruited as ordinary members after 1925. They still had the traditional scholar's attitude to the peasantry, which saw them as useful but socially inferior, and to this they added the approaches of Karl Marx and, to a lesser extent, Lenin who saw the peasants as backward, conservative, and opposed to both democracy and socialism. The revolution in China was seen in terms of Marxist theory and European experience as being based on the advanced industrial workers under Communist leadership and as being centred in the cities. Mao Tse-tung, with his background in a rich peasant family and his experience in peasant organization for the KMT as head of the Peasant Training Institute in Canton, was an exception. So was P'eng Pai, who organized the peasants of

Hailufeng in Kwangtung into an efficient fighting force which overthrew the local authority of the landlords and established strong peasant unions which forced the remaining landlords to reduce rents by 25 per cent.

Mao was aware of P'eng Pai's success and early in 1925 spent some time in his home province of Hunan observing developments amongst the peasants and helping to organize some associations and unions. He returned briefly at the beginning of 1927 and then wrote his important study, 'A Report of an Investigation into the Peasant Movement in Hunan'. In it he criticized those Communists and KMT leaders who deplored the rural disorder and chaos as the peasants rose up against the landlords and local gentry in advance of the arrival of the National Revolutionary Army on its Northern Expedition. He said such disorder was a good thing and was the inevitable consequence of the revolutionary process. To attack what the peasants were doing spontaneously and of their own accord as 'an awful mess' showed a lack of political realism. He wrote:

> A revolution is not the same as inviting people to a banquet or writing an essay or painting a picture or embroidering a flower; it cannot be anything so refined, so calm and gentle, or so 'mild, kind, courteous, restrained and magnanimous'. [These were said to be the attributes of Confucius.] A revolution is an uprising, an act of violence whereby one class overthrows the authority of another.

Prophetically Mao reported that within 'a very short time several hundred million peasants... will rise up like a tempest or tornado —a force so extraordinarily swift and violent that no power, however great, will be able to suppress it'. The CCP could either 'follow in their rear, gesticulating and critizing them', or it could provide the leadership and organization necessary if their rebellion was not to waver and collapse like so many other peasant rebellions in the past. These had failed through lack of a coherent programme and proper co-ordination with peasants throughout the rest of the country.

Mao Tse-tung's analysis was not accepted with much enthusiasm by the urban-oriented leadership of the CCP and the Comintern agents, but following the massacre of Communists and their supporters in the cities in April 1927 there was a hurried attempt in August to test the revolutionary strength of the peasantry. Known as the Autumn Harvest Uprising, this attempt was crushed along with the scheme to seize Nanchang city in Kiangsi Province and a later one based on Canton. The remnants of Mao's forces joined with those of Chu Te, a gifted military leader with a bandit background and warlord pretentions before he was recruited to the Communist cause. Together they established a rural base for their forces in the inaccessible hill region of Chingkangshan in Kiangsi, cut off from the CCP headquarters and in disagreement with many of its policies.

At this point, with the Communist movement smashed, scattered, and divided, China's destiny seemed to lie with Chiang Kai-shek. His Northern Expedition gained enough support for him to negotiate with the various warlord groups from a position of strength and he managed to bring the larger part of the country under unified government, although not without having to make some concessions to local power-holders. Chiang's party, the KMT, aimed to build the strong, united, and prosperous China that Sun Yat-sen, had envisaged. The economic model to be followed was broadly a Western one, although it was hoped that many of the pitfalls of European capitalism would be avoided, and there was a particularly strong commitment to remove the last vestiges of imperialism from China, for it was imperialism that was blamed for reducing China to her weakened state. Chiang Kai-shek's later dependence on the United States for military and economic aid should not obscure his earlier opposition to imperialism and his book, *China's Destiny*, is a trenchant attack on foreign influence.

Yet the dreams of the KMT idealists were not to be realized. The nature of the movement and the conditions under which it gained political power made this difficult. The structure of the party machine, borrowed from the Russians, tended to concentrate power at the top at least as much as had happened in the Communist Party of the Soviet Union under Lenin and particularly Stalin, who was able to use the authoritarian aspects of democratic centralism to subdue and eliminate his opponents. Furthermore, the role of the army had been such that it found little difficulty in retaining its power after China had been unified. Regional commanders soon carved out power bases for themselves and resisted attempts from the central government and the civil administration either to bring them under control or to demobilize many of the troops. By 1929 the cost of maintaining the various armies was consuming more than three-quarters of the national budget after the foreign debts had been serviced. After 1931, when Japan attacked China and gained control of the northeast naming it Manchukuo, it was even more difficult to disband some of the armies, even though they were poor fighters and had done little to deter the Japanese. Finally it became obvious that reform was not the force guiding many of the prominent KMT leaders and it was not high on the president's list of priorities.

The factional rivalries, the corruption, and the lack of dedication within the KMT made it difficult to develop the strong central administration needed to modernize China from above and led Chiang Kai-shek to his first brief resignation in 1931. In his efforts to revive the spirit of the party's earlier days and more effectively unite the people around a set of common goals, the model provided by fascism in Italy and Germany proved attractive to Chiang, as it did to leaders in other nations, many of them otherwise democratic. Chiang naturally saw himself as the supreme leader and focus for the nation. He was an impressive figure, capable of creating awe in urbane and sophisticated Chinese. The élite corps was to be the Blue Shirts, formed after 1932 around the nucleus of the Officers' Moral Endeavour Corps, rather than the unwieldly mass party itself. Secret police and intelligence functions were performed by Tai Li and his dreaded Special Services group, and the ideological content was to be provided by the New Life Movement, a highly nationalistic blend of old Confucian precepts with a modern twist and a puritanical code of personal conduct.

Chiang Kai-shek's attempt to provide China with a new dedication and a new culture failed but it took place against a background which, while it did not necessarily bring about this failure, nevertheless made success much more difficult. First, there was mounting Japanese pressure on China and the occupation of the rich Manchuria. Secondly, the CCP had managed to survive and struck new roots in the mountainous countryside of the Kiangsi border regions. There, Chu Te and Mao Tse-tung evolved techniques of peasant mobilization and built the Red Army from the disaffected, landless, and semi-bandit groups of the hill areas. Chiang's own analysis of the situation saw both as diseases affecting the body of China, but he maintained that the Japanese constituted merely a disease of the skin which could be dealt with fairly easily. The CCP forces, on the other hand, were seen as an internal complaint which must be eradicated before the skin disease could be treated. The diagnosis had little relevance to those people of China who suffered gravely from the 'skin disease' and to whom the 'internal complaint' offered a welcome alternative, not simply from Japanese attack and expropriation but from the harsh and exploitative conditions of landlordism under KMT rule as well.

For the great masses of the Chinese people it was land rather than a new ideology and culture that was of paramount importance (see chapter 5). Primogeniture, an inheritance practice whereby the family property passed intact to the eldest son on the death of the father, was not generally followed in China. Instead, the family was seen as a single group, with all sons having a more or less equal right to ancestral property. Thus many of the holdings were reduced in size as time went on until they were not economical and could no longer support a farmer and his family. Although the average size of holdings and the pattern of ownership varied greatly from one region of China to another, one can still generalize and state that during the early part of this century land was becoming scarcer throughout China and more farmers were being forced to sell their land and either rent land from landlords or seek employment as full-time agricultural workers. Inflationary pressures, high rates of interest on seasonal borrowings, and high taxes, often payable years in advance, tended to increase the concentration of land ownership in fewer and fewer hands. As Mao Tse-tung observed to Edgar Snow in 1936, 'Whoever solves the land question will win the peasants'. Winning the peasants, of course, was the necessary condition for holding China, but on this most important of issues the KMT was unable to act decisively. Politically the KMT was too closely linked with landlord interests to advocate thorough-going land reform and ideologically the existing system of land tenure was justified as having evolved slowly in answer to China's historical needs, whatever they were, and therefore inviolate. This did not prevent the KMT from carrying out surveys and passing resolutions and even laws to reduce rents, provide loans at low interest, and extend irrigation works. In the event, war and the operation of bureaucratic institutions and corruption prevented much from being achieved until it was too late.

The CCP, on the other hand, had accumulated considerable experience in questions of land policy and administration by 1936. The Maoist leadership recognized that the existing system of land tenure, landlordism, and high rents were not simply social evils in themselves but could also be used to mobilize the peasantry of China for political action. The fighting bands under Chu Te and Mao managed to expand their area of control and by 1931 were able to establish the Chinese Soviet Republic embracing a large part of Kiangsi Province, independent not only of the government of Chiang Kai-shek but also of their own Central Committee in Shanghai. Chiang's early 'bandit extermination campaigns' against them had little success in the inaccessible soviet areas and a fairly tough agrarian policy was pursued with little interference. Many local landlords were driven away or killed and their land was redistributed among the poorer peasants, thus winning these elements over to the Communist cause not simply because they were grateful but because they also realized that, having been implicated in the deaths of landlords and seizure of land, unless they defended the soviet and supported the CCP, they would certainly be executed should the KMT restore control in the district.

In 1934 Chiang Kai-shek mounted his Fifth Bandit Extermination Campaign against the Kiangsi Soviet Republic, which by this stage formed the main centre of Communist power and had come under the command of the Central Committee. The KMT forces, led by the German von Seekt, employed an expensive strategy of slowly surrounding the soviet areas with a ring of fixed emplacements against which the guerrilla tactics evolved by Chu and Mao were less effective. The blockade threatened to strangle the soviet areas and it was decided that an armed force of about 130 000 should break out, abandon Kiangsi, and establish another base area somewhere to the north and west where KMT control was not so strong. The Communist forces therefore set out on what has become famous as the 'Long March'. For more than a year they marched and fought their way across Hunan, Kweichow, Szechwan, and Kansu until they eventually met up again in northern Shensi. There they were later to experiment with other agrarian policies and organizational forms during the second attempt to co-operate with the KMT.

The Long March was, by most standards, a major defeat. When it was over the CCP had lost not only its large Kiangsi base but over 100 000 fighting men besides. But it was a defeat marked by such bravery and feats of endurance that it bred a heroic tradition which has continued to provide inspiration for later generations and forms an important part of modern China's political culture. To have survived those 10 000 kilometres on foot and those hundred-odd major engagements with the enemy along the route was to bind one to the cause and to one's comrades in a special fashion and probably explains the remarkable unity the group displayed after 1938, when the divisive influence of Chang Kuo-t'ao, leader of the Fourth Front Army, was removed. However, with barely 10 000 of its troops intact, Chiang Kai-shek might have been excused in 1936 for thinking that he had all but cured the 'internal disease' of his country.

The political history of the CCP after the defeats of 1927 is a

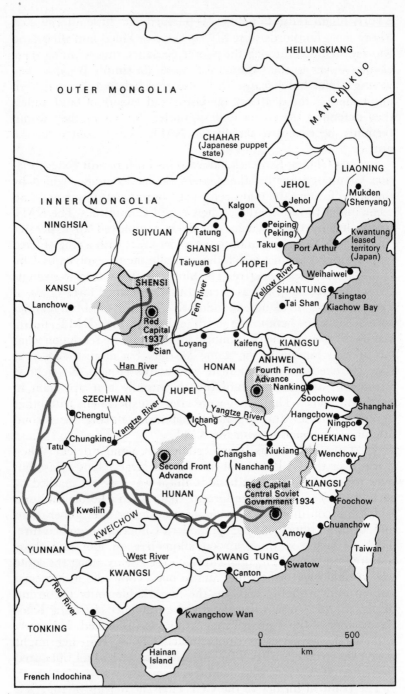

The main route of the Long March

confused one but the leadership passed through a number of hands, all of them strongly influenced or even controlled by the Russians through the Comintern. The directives from Moscow were often vague and contradictory but generally favoured the strategy of urban insurrection long after the prospects for Communist organization and mobilization of the Chinese workers had passed. The first major leader, Li Li-san, may have misinterpreted some of these directives but his failures led to the appointment in 1931 of a new leadership group, all of them young and recently back from study courses in Moscow. The Russian influence at the Central Committee level was considerable and was exercised through a succession of agents sent to China and through training courses for young leaders such as those who made up the 'Returned Student' faction in 1931. The Sixth Congress of the CCP was even held in Moscow. The fruitless urban activities and high-sounding manifestos on Comintern orders with which the Central Committee busied itself must have hade an air of unreality for Mao Tse-tung, who was engaged in the more concrete and rewarding task of organizing a soviet republic of over 1 000 000 peasants in Kiangsi at the time. He remained alienated from the leadership of his own party until the Tsunyi Conference, called during a halt in the epic Long March from Kiangsi to Shensi, at which he managed to remove some of the Russian-trained leaders and assert his own control. From January 1936 until at least 1942 Mao Tse-tung worked to eliminate the influence of this group and no doubt developed serious misgivings not only about the wisdom of sending young men to Moscow for training but about the value of the training they received there at the hands of the Comintern officials, all by this stage under the command of Stalin himself.

At the same time as Mao was completing his Long March and beginning to consolidate his leadership, the Japanese forces were making fresh advances in Manchuria, meeting little resistance from Chiang Kai-shek's armies but having much more trouble with the local forces under the Young Marshal, Chang Hsüeh-liang. Chiang, seeking to enlist these troops in a final assault against the CCP stronghold in Yenan, instead found himself kidnapped by the Young Marshal, who was resentful that the central authorities had not done more to prevent him from being driven from his own territory by foreign troops. The CCP, while in no position to do either, had declared war on Japan from Kiangsi in 1932 and passed a death sentence on Chiang Kai-shek for failing to oppose the foreign invasion. The Young Marshal, although anti-Communist, was therefore well disposed towards

The former Communist Party headquarters in Yenan. Note the cave dwellings behind. These are a common feature of the town and Party leaders lived in such dwellings while Yenan was their capital, between 1936 and 1947

Mao Tse-tung, and Chou En-lai was sent to Sian where Chiang was held prisoner. A promise was extracted that he would henceforth concentrate his energies against the Japanese instead of against Mao and his patriotic forces. The CCP thus won a brief respite and Chiang retained power, for Mao Tse-tung at least agreed with Stalin on the point that in 1936 Chiang was the most likely leader able to unite China against Japanese fascism. In the event, the Sian Incident resulted in the Second United Front between the KMT and CCP while the one loser was Chang Hsüeh-liang, who was soon arrested by the KMT and spent most of the rest of his life a prisoner.

The War against Japan and its Aftermath

The fortunes of the CCP began to improve from this point, so much so that some authorities claim that it was the appeal of their strongly anti-Japanese stance alone that brought the Chinese peasantry behind the Party and lifted its membership from about 50 000 in 1937 to close to 1 000 000 by late 1940. This is to over-simplify a complex development but it is true that the CCP achieved an acceptance amongst hitherto hostile sections of the population when they were seen to be actively opposing the foreign invasion during the war against Japan (1937–45). But Mao Tse-tung did not totally submerge his programme for social and economic change in China when confronted with the immediate danger from Japan. Partly because he was in formal alliance with the KMT and partly because he saw the need to unite all sympathetic sections of the society against Japan, this Second United Front period placed serious constraints on the tough policies based on class struggle which had been followed during the Kiangsi period. Yet even the mild policies to reduce rents and reduce the rate of interest charged on loans, when effectively implemented, brought about a great improvement in the welfare of the peasants and were therefore popular although they involved no drastic change in the system of land tenure. Later, after the New Fourth Army Incident in 1941 in which KMT forces attacked the Communist army while it was crossing the Yangtze, the virtual breakdown of the united front and the worsening of the war against Japan put the Yenan base area under great pressure. In response to these circumstances yet another set of policies was evolved, many of which were to prove very useful when the CCP's responsibilities stretched far beyond the remote loess hills of northern Shensi.

The Yenan period (1936–47) was built on the spirit of the Long March and saw the development of techniques of mass mobilization which have since characterized Mao Tse-tung's approach to government. As a guerrilla leader he had long before learnt the importance of maintaining good relations with the people amongst whom he had to fight, on whom he must depend for both food and intelligence about the enemy, and from whom he had to gain recruits. To 'serve the people' provided, then, the basic orientation. Mao had also learnt on the Long March the feats of which ordinary, underequipped peasant soldiers are capable, given the proper motivation. Political work subsequently became the basis for mobilizing the people for defence, attack, and production and political officers attached to the army were seen as at least as important as the line commanders and in some situations more so. The Long March and the blockade of the Yenan base showed that, when forced to be self-reliant, the results are sometimes quite spectacular and the Production Movement brought the CCP forces to virtual self-sufficiency in food, clothing, and weapons in 1943 once they could no longer depend on the KMT for these supplies. In Mao's experience, as he puts it, 'it is a good thing and not a bad thing to be opposed by the enemy', simply because it forces one to be self-reliant and therefore more confident. Moreover, when not being opposed by the enemy, there is a tendency to slacken one's efforts and slip into selfish or bureaucratic habits. Rectification campaigns, really periods of concentrated political study to improve the general approach to work, were evolved during the Yenan period to cope with this problem. The practice of sending senior officials down to work for set periods amongst the peasants was also developed to avoid the problems of relative peace and to develop closer links with the people. This has become an important part of the axiomatic 'mass line' which is said to have guided the party throughout its history, although it must have fallen into disuse on some occasions, such as before the Cultural Revolution.

Eventually the Japanese forces were defeated but by June 1946 the uneasy truce with the KMT broke down and China was torn by civil war. The CCP had emerged from the war with control of almost one quarter of China and over 100 000 000 people living in its several 'liberated areas'. The KMT could not tolerate this for long and there was no real prospect of coalition government succeeding, despite the intermediary efforts of the Americans. US support swung behind Chiang Kai-shek but was not sufficient to back up a regime which was by now demoralized, rent by rivalry and opposed vested interests, and in general corrupt. In September of 1949 the main body of KMT leaders fled to Taiwan, Chiang Kai-shek having temporarily resigned yet again, and on 1 October 1949 Mao Tse-tung proclaimed the Chinese People's Republic and announced, 'China has stood up. Never again shall China be a humiliated nation.' He had probably proved another of his paradoxical maxims, 'It is men and not weapons that decide wars', in the process.

Note

1 Wuchang, Hankow, and Hanyang are three neighbouring cities. Their collective name is Wuhan, which is currently the capital of Hupei Province, central China.

Select Bibliography

Ch'ien Tuan-sheng *The Government and Politics of China, 1912–1949*, Harvard University Press, Cambridge Mass., 1950, Stanford paperback, 1970. A comprehensive and penetrating study of the Kuomintang regime.

Houn, F.W. *A Short History of Chinese Communism*, Prentice-Hall, Englewood Cliffs, 1967. A good, short account, tracing the Chinese Communist Party's evolution from a small, Soviet-directed movement to its independent triumph and the establishment of the People's Republic.

Pye, L.W. *China: An Introduction*, Little, Brown and Company, Boston, 1972. An interpretative account of twentieth-century China.

Schram, Stuart *Mao Tse-tung*, a Pelican book, Harmondsworth, 1966. A scholarly biography that describes the long story of Mao's struggle to free the greatness of China.

Schurmann, F. and Schell O. (eds) *China Readings 2, Republican China*, a Pelican book, Harmondsworth, 1967. This is a collection, with introductions, of passages from numerous English-language sources. It describes the tumultuous period between 1911 and 1949 in an informative as well as analytical manner.

Chapter 3
Nationalism in China before 1949

Wang Gungwu

It is not very easy to deal with the topic of nationalism in China. The Chinese have looked upon China as a single entity for some twenty centuries and it can be argued that this must constitute the basis of some form of nationalism. At the same time it must be recognized that the Chinese do not seem to have evolved the concept of nationhood. Normally you will find that the history books refer only to the Chinese empire. Sometimes you will find references to the Chinese world order or the Chinese Confucian state. This raises the question as to what this political unit was which we call China and how we are to equate it with what we understand to be nations or nation-states, and with those countries which claim to be nationalistic. There are many terms involved here and one of the difficulties in explaining many historical problems arises from our understanding of what these words mean.

Nationalism and Traditional China

Normally a nation must require a people which has a common distinctive culture, a desire to live together after having shared a common history, a common language and literature, sometimes a common religion but not necessarily, and an area which is more or less clearly demarcated. But one of the key concepts in the idea of nationhood has also been the concept of a state, which is why you have the modern term, 'a nation-state'. A group of people not only feel that they belong to the same nation but also that they are capable of organizing themselves politically as a state. This makes nationalism something more than merely an abstract idea of identity or just the sense of belonging to a nation but also an organization with a political system, with a political goal, with political values, and ideas about where that particular group of people is heading. The nation-states really evolved in Western Europe. It was there that the concept of a state was most clearly defined and was given a legal framework which made it necessary, for instance, to establish laws about the relations between states, the concept of many nations and international relations. The idea arose that a state had a distinct political and legal right to exist. It had sovereignty, the right to defend itself and the right to assert itself as a single integrated political unit.

Once we have looked at what a nation and a nation-state are and are expected to be, we begin to realize that the Chinese people's concept of themselves throughout history does not really fit such definitions. On the contrary, while they had the makings of a nation, while they had a common culture, a common history, and a geographical territory more or less clearly demarcated, they did not subscribe to the idea of nationhood or of being a nation-state. Instead they had a rather abstract idea about the moral oneness of human beings and the embracing nature of Chinese civilization. This was embodied largely in a modified form of Confucianism which took the view that all men were brothers and that the world consisted of different kinds of men but who were all subject to the same kinds of natural, universal, social, and moral laws.

The Chinese were not terribly clear about how large the world was but they had the idea, fostered from time to time by their political power or the strength of the imperial armies and by the quality of their civilization, that theirs was the central civilization and that theirs was the most superior civilization on earth. This view was thought justified by the Chinese for many centuries and it was not until the nineteenth century that it was seriously challenged.

Because of this view, the Chinese in the past could not accept that they were merely a nation and that other peoples belonged to separate and equal nations, equal to the Chinese. Because of their assumptions about their superior civilization and a world order in which the central kingdom or central area would be China, it was difficult for them to see themselves merely as equal to other nations. They were more than equal in their own eyes and, largely because of this, the concept of nations in which there was implied the concept of equal nations—nations with equal rights to exist—did not find its way into Chinese political thinking until recent times.

You can see now why it was so difficult for the Chinese to change their ideas about nations. But their ideas did change and the story of how they became nationalistic is a fascinating and important subject. What started them on the road to nationalism was the nineteenth century experience of Western powers seeking independent equal relations with China, an experience which forced the Chinese to think again about their political ideals and institutions.

Initially it seemed so simple to the Chinese. All they had to face were a few European traders wanting to trade off the coast of China. Eventually, however, it became clear that the problem was not quite so simple. Different European powers came to the coast of China. They began to compete with one another for certain rights, certain concessions in China, and in the competition they began to make greater and greater demands upon what was then still the Ch'ing or Manchu empire, and these demands upon the Chinese became more and more difficult for the Chinese to accept without a sense of humiliation. The resistance the Chinese put up turned out to be very feeble and the Western powers found it fairly easy to impose their will upon them. In 1840 British warships attacked China imposing upon her the humiliating Treaty of Nanking (1842); while from 1856 to 1860 China suffered invasion from the forces of several foreign countries, being forced to sign four unequal treaties. There followed other humiliations arising from the murder of missionaries in different parts of the interior of China. Then, in 1884–85, the French made further gains in the south of China; and in 1895 the Japanese, to the surprise of everybody, particularly the Chinese themselves, defeated the Chinese and imposed on them demands similar to those of the Western powers. Finally in 1900 the Chinese made frantic, desperate but futile efforts to drive away all foreigners. This last effort was the well known Boxer uprising and was an attempt which was supported partly by the imperial court and by officials but was largely a force derived from the sense of frustration among ordinary Chinese at the sight of China and its civilization being threatened by foreigners.

So the nineteenth century experience of a series of humiliating defeats, of constantly having to submit to claims and demands made first by the Western powers and eventually by Japan, brought out from the Chinese firstly strong anti-foreign feelings, and then anger at and opposition to the weak and feeble government which was constantly making concessions to these outside powers. By this time the failures of the Chinese empire against foreign encroachment had led the Chinese to put all the blame on the Manchu rulers of the Ch'ing dynasty. This quickly turned into a feeling of anti-Manchu nationalism.

The subject is not a simple one because, although the Manchus were non-Chinese in origin, they had in fact, in terms of their cultural institutions and in terms of the way they governed China, become more or less Chinese. It was therefore really not justified to place the blame solely on the Manchus for the failures of China in the nineteenth century. It was just as much a failure in the political institutions themselves that the Chinese empire had run down as a system. It was not effective enough, not healthy enough, not strong enough to regenerate itself in the face of Western attack and encroachment. This was not due to the failure of the Manchus alone but to the rigidities of the old social and political system and the conservatism of the ruling classes, both Chinese and Manchu.

Nevertheless many Chinese did not look at it that way. As with most people when they are in difficulties, they looked for scapegoats—a very common historical phenomenon—amongst the ruling Manchu aristocracy. They blamed all the failures on them. Of course it was quite easy to arouse Chinese feeling against the Manchus, and to equate this sentiment with something like the resentment of a conquered people against its conquerors, although it was hundreds of years since the Manchus had become part of a greater Chinese world order.

We must not forget, of course, that the sense of frustration had first developed against the West. Anti-foreign feeling had already manifested itself largely in the murder of missionaries in the interior of China. Catholic and Protestant missionaries were seen to be the agents of Western powers, paving the way for Western advances into China. And there was some justification for this because every time a missionary ran into trouble, some Western power stepped in to demand compensations and it was thus easy to see the missionaries as being the advance guard of Western political and military intervention.

It was in this context of anti-foreignism strengthened by an anti-Manchu feeling because of the government's failures that we see the development of a kind of nationalism. This must seem to be a negative form of nationalism. It did not base itself upon any clear definition of what the national goals were or upon any inspired feeling of what the Chinese nation should be developing into. On the contrary, it was merely a reaction against foreign incursion; against the Manchus for the responsibility of the failure of the Chinese imperial system. Out of this, the Chinese people were aroused by some of the educated Chinese like Sun Yat-sen who had been educated abroad, who came back with Western ideas about the future of China, and who managed, in fact, to explain to the Chinese that their anti-foreignism and their anti-Manchu feelings were really the beginnings of the wider phenomenon of nationalism. It was Sun Yat-sen who first put together Western ideas of the nation-state and nationalism, and brought them to the attention of his supporters within China. He made them feel that nationalism was not just a negative force but that it should also be a force uniting the Chinese for some positive good, integrating them, and giving them a political unity which they had never really had. At the same time Sun Yat-sen and his contemporaries also reminded the Chinese of their own traditional social system, that it had largely been based upon rural agricultural communities without a great deal of communication between one area and another, and that the people involved in those communications were a few officials and a few merchants, so that when one spoke of China one was really talking about a large conglomeration of loosely structured village communities spread over a very extensive area and ruled by a very small élite.

Therefore nationalism, Sun Yat-sen argued, was necessary to make the Chinese feel as one people; to make them come together and realize their common destiny much more consciously than they had ever done before. It was in this context that nationalism gradually came to play a part in arousing the self-consciousness of the Chinese as a people, to take them out of their small rural centred loyalties, and lead them to a greater loyalty towards the country as a whole.

This, very briefly, is how the Chinese became more and more nationalistic from the beginning of the twentieth century. Sun Yat-sen's contribution was to turn a large number of educated Chinese from merely negative anti-foreign and anti-Manchu feelings to a more positive sense of national destiny, so that it can be argued that the 1911 revolution was a nationalist revolution. The revolution overthrew the Manchus and, a step beyond that, did away with the Chinese imperial system and substituted for it a kind of republicanism—a republican government with a president, a cabinet, and a parliamentary assembly. In short, it destroyed not only a foreign dynasty and an imperial system which had lasted two thousand years, but at the same time it also attempted to create a new political system modelled upon Western countries like the United States and France.

Nationalism in the Republican Period

At the next stage, after 1911, China went through terrible agonies, with warlords and different groups of Chinese fighting one another for some twenty-five years. The groups were all more or less nationalistic but they differed in methods and ultimate goals. There were Communists, socialists, anarchists, constitutionalists, fascists, and militarists, and the struggle among them about what the new China was to be like was bitter and often violent. The agonies of the period from 1912 to 1928 raise the question as to whether the nationalist revolution was in any way achieved in 1911. Did Sun Yat-sen only have a superficial understanding of the needs of China? Was the idea of a national destiny for all Chinese simply premature?

There is considerable evidence to suggest that the answer to both questions is yes. The vast majority of Chinese, the peasants of China, were simply not ready to think of this national destiny that Sun Yat-sen had distilled from the experiences of nationalists in Europe and America. This idea simply could not penetrate the traditional ideas of the autonomy of different villages and the primacy of local loyalties which had persisted for so many centuries.

The warlordism, the militarism, the provincialism, the regionalism—all these features of the two decades after 1911 illustrate the great difficulties which met early efforts to make the Chinese nationalistic. Yet among the educated Chinese there existed without doubt a perception of themselves as a nation—a people who could produce, if they could only agree upon the form, a nation-state.

In all the schools, universities, and colleges in the country, the message was being passed on. It probably would only be a matter of time before it would reach the majority of the Chinese people. The question was: how much time did the nationalists have, while at the same time fighting off all kinds of pressures from the Western powers and from Japan, and from the various external interests—trading, military, and political—which were constantly interfering and intervening in the domestic affairs of China? The militarists, for example, were able to fight one another for so long because they were always able to get British, French, Russian, or Japanese help, normally in the form of loans to buy arms. Different political groups, like the Nationalists and the Communists, were later also able to draw on Russian or American help to fight one another. In other words, internal disunion and instability invited constant external pressure, intervention, and interference, so that there was never really much peace in the country for the Chinese to be able to see where they were going. In the midst of all this, it was not surprising that the Chinese moved away from the early nationalism which had fed on anti-foreignism and anti-Manchu feelings. We find that this form of nationalism was not vital enough to deal with the problems that they were facing. Again it was thought necessary to look for scapegoats; to find simple formulas, simple slogans to try to unite the Chinese people in ways that they had never been united before. This the educated Chinese found in the slogan of anti-imperialism; a new stage in the effort to rebuild a new China.

What was this anti-imperialism? What was so different about it? In some respects, of course, anti-imperialism is just one form of nationalism. When a national group or leadership of any country wants to get rid of its colonial rulers or stop any imperial power from interfering in its own affairs, you can call this anti-imperialism a mere extension of nationalist feeling. But what was being offered, this anti-imperialism from about 1922 onwards in China, was much more than that. It was part and parcel of an attempt by radical political thinkers, Communists as well as others, to try to generalize the experience of China, India, and other countries under colonial rule into a universal problem. The argument was that the fate of such countries had been deeply influenced by constant Western pressures and that these Western pressures—the political power and economic strength of the West, the importation of goods and technology from the West—would undermine and destroy the economies and political systems of the colonized peoples. The real danger to the future came from this constant pressure from countries which were richer and more powerful. It followed that the colonized countries could not possibly become strong and powerful as long as they allowed themselves to be constantly meddled with by others more powerful. The need, therefore, was to join forces among all the countries which were being pushed around by the West to get rid of this interference in the belief that then and only then would the colonial peoples be able to regenerate their own strength and their own power.

This was the persuasive element in the argument. In some respects, more narrowly conceived, it was merely put out as the call for internationalism and of communist solidarity against capitalist incursions which were represented by the Western powers. Others would put it in terms of an extension of nationalism, but nationalism joined up with other nationalisms in a joint effort to get rid of all imperialist pressures.

The springboard of this development in China was largely the success of the Russian revolution in 1917. Almost immediately after the Russians succeeded, they contacted the more radical nationalists in China, particularly Sun Yat-sen who although not in power was a considerable force among the educated intellectuals in China, and offered support. Why Sun Yat-sen accepted this offer is open to question. Sun apparently never believed that China would be a communist country, and took very lightly the idea that communism might become the key to China's future strength. To his death, he remained very much the nationalist who was using whatever help he could get to seek the ends he had drawn up for his country.

The main reason which led Sun Yat-sen to turn to the Russians was that he felt betrayed by the Western countries he had hoped would help him in his nationalist efforts. When he first became a nationalist revolutionary, he had gained support from British sympathizers, from Americans, and from several other groups of people in Europe and Japan. He had hoped that his movement would receive support from the governments of these countries which were, he thought, genuinely interested in making China stable and united once again. In the 1910s, in his efforts to try to establish this republic, he was appalled at the number of governments which seemed to have supported the various warlord groups, and to find that the jealousies among the imperialist powers were much more important than the future unity or integration of China.

Sun Yat-sen was probably naive to believe that the Western powers would help *him* to solve China's problems or be interested in Chinese visions of China's own future. Nevertheless he was disappointed by the way the competition for influence and economic gains among the Western powers led them to support regimes which were divisive and obviously weakened China. It is in this context and with this background that we understand why Sun Yat-sen in 1922 thought that the Russian Communists, who had succeeded in 1917, could be a more sincere and genuine ally against the Western powers which were constantly interfering in China's affairs. It was in this context too that we understand why his party considered the idea of allying itself with the very small and weak Communist Party, which had been founded a year before in 1921. The formal alliance of the Nationalist Party (the Kuomintang) and the Communist Party was made in 1923, that is just before Sun Yat-sen's death. It was made with the support of the Russians and the Third International (the international movement for communism sponsored by Soviet Russia), both clearly motivated by the hope of driving Western influence and power out from China. The slogan which united the Nationalists and the Communists was the slogan of anti-imperialism.

In one sense one could argue that anti-imperialism, as the Communists and the most radical thinkers saw it, was a step beyond nationalism. It was in advance of nationalism, even better than nationalism, because it did not worry simply about the destinies of one people and the selfish interests of any one group of people. Instead it was based upon the joint interests of all people who felt themselves oppressed and were prevented from freeing themselves from those who exploited them. It was in this kind of context that anti-imperialism was put to the young Chinese intellectuals in the 1920s.

We need to look at this question closely because it is very important to understand how the Chinese expanded their ideas of nationalism in this way towards a form of anti-imperialism. The next question is how these two were reconciled and why it would appear in 1949 that the Nationalists failed and the Communists won.

Anti-imperialism and Nationalism in the Struggle between Chiang Kai-shek and Mao Tse-tung

One could argue that there were such things as nationalist anti-imperialism and communist anti-imperialism and that these were the main competitors in China after the break between the Nationalist and Communist Parties in 1927. They were both fighting for the leadership of the Chinese people in the name of anti-imperialism but with distinct and possibly even opposite points of view. Superficially, the Nationalists failed and the Communists won in 1949. And yet the picture is not quite as simple as that. What was the basis of this dispute between the Nationalist Party of Chiang Kai-shek and the Communist Party of Mao Tse-tung? The Nationalists, in their attempts to win support for their leadership of China, emphasized the greatness, the glory, the historical continuity, and the oneness of China against the Western powers and especially against Japan which was expanding directly at China's expense rather more quickly than any other country. The only answer to these kinds of incursions into China was to bind the Chinese together to fight as one people under the Nationalist flag. The response in the late 1920s, in the 1930s to the Japanese invasion of Manchuria in 1931, and right up to the Sino-Japanese War of 1937–45 seemed to justify the Nationalist point of view that it was possible to draw the Chinese together simply under a nationalist banner to fight foreign invasion. Why then did the Nationalist Party fail?

Recent studies suggest that it failed because its leadership was poor, its morale weak, and its urban industrial base in great cities like Shanghai, Nanking, and Wuhan was destroyed when the Japanese occupied them during the war of 1937–45. All these factors contributed towards the gradual and steady weakening of the Nationalist armies and made them incapable of standing up for themselves after the war was over in 1945. This is one point of view.

Another point of view suggests that the Communists under Mao Tse-tung, who had been brought into the united national effort to fight Japanese aggression, had used the opportunity to consolidate their power in the rural areas. They had developed a superior strategy of fusing land reform and peasant welfare with guerrilla warfare in the countryside, embarrassing the Japanese and ultimately winning for themselves the respect of the peasants as national heroes in this great struggle against the foreign invader. In the name of nationalism and social revolution, they had gained the hearts and minds of the majority of the Chinese peasantry by 1945. This was what gave them that extra help during the years 1945–49 which made it possible for them to defeat the superficially stronger armed forces of the Nationalist army.

A third point of view would argue that in fact the odds were by no means clear in 1945–46 and that one of the reasons for the failure of the Nationalist forces was foreign intervention. The Japanese interventions from 1937–45, the stripping of the industrial bases of Manchuria in 1945 when the Russians entered Manchuria and took away all the factories and industrial equipment in Manchuria, and the failure of the United States and other allies to give adequate support to the Nationalist Party in 1945 were all factors in their defeat. The Americans had misread the strength of the Communists and had miscalculated the purposes of the Communist Party. American advisers in China had been advising the United States government that Mao Tse-tung and his supporters were merely land reformers, a radical kind no doubt but not aligned to an international Communist movement. They were principally local rebels deriving their strength from a traditional peasants' revolt syndrome within Chinese history itself. They were offering land reform to the Chinese people, giving land to the tiller, a programme that was just, egalitarian, and morally strong. This kind of advice led the American government to withhold support from the Nationalists at a critical moment in the civil war between the Communists and the Nationalists, and this was a major factor weakening the Nationalist Chinese at this crucial stage.

In each of these views there are important points to be noted. Certainly the Nationalists themselves were disorganized, their morale was weak, and their leadership was corrupt. Certainly the Communists had won the hearts of the peasants and re-emerged after the war as national heroes, and certainly there were miscalculations on the part of the Americans. But what is particularly relevant is that ideas of nationalism were introduced to the peasantry together with ideals for a new social order, and this had never happened before. We need to pay extra attention to this because it is part and parcel of the process of extending Chinese nationalism which was described earlier.

The importance of this extended nationalism is that, in contrast to the ideas of nationalism put forth by Sun Yat-sen and his supporters in the Nationalist Party, Mao Tse-tung and the leaders of the Communist Party helped to stimulate nationalism among the ordinary people in the rural areas who constituted more than 80 per cent of the Chinese population. The earlier nationalism of Sun Yat-sen was largely the nationalism of a small number of well-to-do middle class intellectuals in the cities who accepted nationalistic concepts through the books they read about the West and Japan but whose understanding of these concepts remained peripheral to the inner forces of Chinese history. Nationalism as they saw it from the treaty ports, from the coastal areas, from schools and university campuses, from the lofty heights of journals, magazines, and books published in cities like Shanghai and Peking, did not really penetrate very far and could never have penetrated deeply in that form. These intellectuals simply did not have the time they needed to make the peasantry nationalistic, and they were still talking superficially about national goals and nationalist ideals when the vast majority of the people of China had no sympathy for, or understanding of, these ideals at all.

It was the Japanese invasion of China, when large numbers of the peasantry were directly confronted with the enemy because Japanese troops ravaged the countryside in most of north and large sections of south China, that brought the peasant face to face for the first time with the problem of what it meant to talk about the national destiny of the Chinese. Significantly, it was in this wartime context that the Communists did not talk much about communism. They went to the peasants and talked about the meaning of defending the country from foreign invaders, about how they, not as Communists but as loyal and patriotic Chinese, would organize the rural masses and lead them through this war with the foreign invader. They should fight side by side and they would win. This was the message brought to village after village. It was out of this organization of the peasants into a real confrontation with the enemy, because of the day-to-day problem of survival, that the concept of nationalism finally penetrated below the middle class intellectual level on which the Nationalists depended. And it was out of this nationalism from below that the Communists gained the kind of support and respect they needed to make their movement a successful one. Of course Mao Tse-tung and his colleagues also placed emphasis on ideals of social justice and egalitarianism. All these ideals given concrete form in land and other local reforms were appealing to a peasant population which was greatly impressed by Communist leadership and by their heroic efforts to organize the Chinese against the Japanese. In this kind of context the preparation of the peasantry to receive the broader economic implications of anti-imperialism and the ultimate need for social transformation became a relatively easy task.

Select Bibliography

Chow Tse-tsung *The May Fourth Movement: Intellectual Revolution in Modern China*, Harvard University Press, Cambridge Mass., 1960, Stanford paperback, 1967. A balanced, soundly informative account of the intellectual revolution in which nationalism played a crucial part.

FitzGerald, C.P. *The Birth of Communist China*, a Pelican book, Harmondsworth, 1964. A fluent narrative and an interesting interpretation of the collapse of the Kuomintang and the rise to power of the Chinese Communists.

Gray, Jack (ed.) *Modern China's Search for a Political Form*, Oxford University Press, London, 1969. A collection of scholarly essays on twentieth-century China.

Johnson, Chalmers A. *Peasant Nationalism and Communist Power: The Emergence of Revolutionary China, 1937–1945*, Stanford University Press, Stanford, 1962. A provocative thesis on the nature of Chinese nationalism and the ultimate triumph of the Chinese Communist Party during the Sino-Japanese war.

Wright, Mary C. (ed.) *China in Revolution: The First Phase, 1900–1913*, Yale University Press, New Haven, 1968. A scholarly work with an introduction on the growth of Chinese nationalism at the turn of this century.

Chapter 4
Political development since 1949

Ian Wilson

We have seen that when Mao Tse-tung and the Chinese Communist Party (CCP) came to power in China in October 1949 they brought with them considerable experience in the administration of large areas and large bodies of people. Lenin and his Bolsheviks had much less experience of this sort in 1917 when they won power but over the next fifteen years they developed policies and techniques which served as a model for the Chinese in different ways. The Chinese were able to start out with guidelines for the management of a total economy, in which they lacked experience because their wartime economic administration had been highly decentralized. They were also able to avoid some of the mistakes made by the Russians, particularly in agriculture. We can view the period since 1949 in terms of this search for suitable economic and political forms, the first seven or eight years of which were strongly influenced by the Soviet model and the subsequent years by various experiments to develop measures and institutions best suited to the conditions in China. This search goes on today and will continue, for it must be remembered that the process is a dynamic one. China did not merely stand up in 1949 but set out on a second long march to bring the nation out of its underdeveloped state. Other themes run through the period now under examination but the struggle for development influences them all.

The immediate problems facing the new government were not primarily those of development so much as sheer survival. Eighteen years of war and civil war, coupled with maladministration, corruption, and general loss of morale had left China in a sorry state. Her industry had been largely destroyed or stripped by the Russians, economic administration had broken down, and inflation was rampant. The first three years were devoted to curbing inflation, which was finally achieved only by issuing a new currency, and with keeping such sectors of the economy which were healthy operating smoothly. Gradually reconstruction began and controls for the management of the economy were imposed until in 1953 the First Five Year Plan (see chapter 6) could be launched, although the formal announcement had to wait until 1955.

Meanwhile the government took steps to establish its legitimacy at home and abroad. The form of government was a 'people's democratic dictatorship', an extension of the 'new democracy' which Mao had described almost a decade earlier. Leadership and guidance were provided by the CCP, but the actual government and the ministry contained representatives of all classes that had supported the revolution, including the national bourgeoisie. The latter group, composed of those Chinese capitalists who had opposed the Japanese imperialists and the Kuomintang (KMT), held many important portfolios in the early years because as a group they were better educated and more experienced in economic administration on a large scale than the great majority of CCP cadres or officials. No secret was made of the fact that the eventual economic forms would be socialist ones but it was hoped that this could be achieved gradually and peacefully with the support of the same groups and classes that had united against Japan and the KMT. At first control rested with the various field armies of the People's Liberation Army (PLA) which had liberated the country but the largely civilian Chinese People's Political Consultative Conference, in which CCP members were in a minority, adopted a set of minimal, gradualist goals and it was this Common Programme which gave popular legitimacy to the new government until 1954. Internationally the Chinese People's Republic sought recognition from foreign governments and admission to the United Nations as the rightful government of China.

But the CCP was committed to a fundamental transformation of the social structure in China, unlike the revolutionaries of 1911, and it was to this they next turned their attention. In the old Confucian order the family lay at the heart of the Chinese political system. The traditional value system vested great power in the head of the family, for he made the major decisions about marriage, inheritance, education, and land and crop management that so vitally affected the lives of all members of the family. Moreover, through the village, kinship, and clan systems, the family head held considerable political power at the lower level of society and, not unnaturally, wished to preserve the power and privilege his role carried. Although there had been some changes in marriage customs and family structure under Republican rule, the breakdown of authority under conditions of war and civil war had forced people to rely more on the primary structures such as the family, the village, and the clan for authority and as centres for allegiance. The CCP was concerned that the new government and the Party should be seen as the main focus for allegiance.

Land reform did much to break the economic power of the patriarchal family system by depriving the family head of the right to grant or withhold economic and property rewards for the family members. Landless peasant sons were able to apply for parcels of land from the former landlord estates and branch out as independent small farmers in their own right, no longer subject to parental control over this aspect of their lives. But the Marriage Law was at least as revolutionary in its implications. Instead of being an arrangement made by the heads of two families and involving the superstitious role of the local matchmaker, marriage became the concern of only the two persons intending to marry and the state was brought in purely as the registering authority. Mao had been the victim of an arranged marriage early in life and felt strongly that this aspect of traditional society cried out for reform. Just as land reform met the needs of the land-hungry peasantry, marriage reform gave younger people the power to decide personal issues for themselves and in the same way drew them closer to the China the Party was building; and as the new system was popularized and implemented over the next few years, it was accepted as a sign that the old order had indeed been changed. The social implications of marriage reform are considered in greater detail in chapter 9.

Political Developments in the Countryside during the 1950s

Land reform was not, however, seen by the CCP as the final answer to the land problem in China. It brought to the Party the political support of the poorer peasants and represented a move towards greater social justice in the countryside but it made little difference to the basic problem of increasing agricultural output. Many of the plots distributed were too small to support a man and his family because the actual supply of land had not been increased and on the slightly larger plots there was very little left over for saving and investment after the needs of the family had been met. Free title had been granted with the land in order to provide the richer peasants with some sense of security. This was most important because only the larger farms produced a significant surplus for sale to feed the urban population and to provide raw materials for light industry. In Russia this rich peasant group, the kulaks, had been alienated by the harsh land policies of the Communists and had retaliated by joining the counter-revolutionaries in civil war, killing their livestock and burning their crops. China managed to avoid similar disasters and the consequent famine, but the system of free title allowed trading in land, and the holders of the smaller, uneconomic plots began selling their land to the more prosperous farmers and reverting to landless labourer status once more. A situation in which the rich got richer and the poor got poorer seemingly defeated the objects of land reform but already another step had been taken to transform Chinese agriculture from small peasant proprietorship based on private property in land to a collective system based on social ownership.

This second step in China's agricultural revolution was the formation of mutual-aid teams, based partly on the co-operative experiments developed in Yenan and other liberated areas during the war years but also bearing some similarity to forms of village co-operation which had much deeper historical roots in Chinese rural life. The able-bodied workers from each household were encouraged to group together in teams of about fifty or so to carry out various production and construction tasks once their work on their own farms had been completed. They were urged to think of themselves as members of a labour team rather than as single workers in a particular household and the objective was not simply to speed rural reconstruction but to prepare the peasants for subsequent changes in the organization of agriculture by getting them accustomed to working and thinking of themselves in a collective manner.

Voluntariness became the rule guiding these great changes in China's rural society, partly because the sheer size of the rural population made any other techniques such as force or monetary incentives quite impractical. But Mao Tse-tung's approach to questions of social change had always stressed the importance of first changing men's minds to accept change. He stressed this even before he became a Marxist when he saw China's salvation in terms of the physical education of its people. However it was not a simple matter to convince several hundred million Chinese peasants to change their traditional way of life, even though that life had been so difficult and oppressive over the previous three decades. Large numbers of Party members, activists, and Communist Youth League workers were required to go out into the countryside in a massive education drive, but at the time of its victory the membership of the CCP stood at only 4 500 000, many of them uneducated peasant soldiers with only rudimentary political training. Consequently it was not until 1954, by which time a further 2 000 000 Party members had been recruited and trained, that the next stage of the plan to transform Chinese agriculture could be put into operation. This was the drive for collectivization and again was based on techniques and experiences of the Yenan period.

Collectivization, although it was carefully prepared and introduced only gradually, marked a major break with the past. Land, livestock, and tools passed from private ownership and became the property of the collective, at first a grouping of as few as forty farming households. The size of these Agricultural Producers' Co-operatives (APCs) was later greatly increased and the speed with which they were formed accelerated until by the end of 1956 virtually the entire rural population of China had been organized into collectives. The land was worked collectively and no longer needed to be broken up into small fields; an elected committee took the major decisions on what crop and quantity should be grown; the economy of the APC could be fitted into the state economic plan, making tax collection relatively easy; and the APC members received their main income in the form of work points assessed on their labour contribution to the collective economy. Although there was some peasant resistance to the APCs and some reorganization had to be made, it was a remarkable change, particularly when one bears in mind that the orthodox Soviet case for collectivization did not apply in China. Economists in the Soviet Union and some in the West argue that the greatest advantage of collectivization is that it permits the most rational and economical use of agricultural machinery, and in the Soviet Union the mechanization of agriculture preceded collectivization. In China there was not only very little agricultural machinery but there were no immediate plans to produce it in large numbers. Instead Mao argued that the habits and conditions of collective work and life on the APCs would bring about changes in the thoughts and attitudes of the peasants, making possible an earlier transition to real socialism than Lenin, Stalin, and even many of his own colleagues in the Party leadership had believed possible.

In 1958 the APCs gave way to rural people's communes which are much larger organizations, and constitute self-contained and self-sufficient societies in themselves. Not only is the commune an economic unit with its own industry and agriculture, but it is also a local government unit with its own educational system and its own defence responsibilities through the local militia. Again great hopes were placed on the effects which communal life would have upon the peasants' outlook and during the enthusiastic period of late 1958 the Chinese believed that the foundation of the people's communes would lead quickly to the establishment of a communist society which would replace the existing socialist one. It was claimed that the communes would become the basic units of a new communist society in which the socialist system of distribution, 'from each according to his ability, to each according to his work', would be replaced by one in which distribution would be based on the principle 'from each according to his ability, to each according to his need'. This expectation was not realized.

The reorganization of agriculture was motivated by the need to establish political control in the countryside as much as it was by the need to raise output and was more successful politically than economically. But the techniques employed were largely developed in China in response to the aims of the Party and the very considerable experience of rural conditions and people built up during the early revolutionary period.

Moscow, the Cold War, and the Chinese Political Economy

When it came to the management of the total economy, however, the CCP had no relevant experience and was forced to rely on the model provided by the Soviet Union, being the leading socialist country. Stalin was also anxious that all socialist countries follow the Soviet model as closely as possible and, although he was unable to exercise the same sort of control in China that he could in Eastern Europe, China's First Five Year Plan was similar in many respects to the Soviet plans. The provision of Soviet economic aid and technical assistance, even with the plan itself, assured this. Moreover some members of the leadership were particularly influenced by Soviet methods in economic matters, including the head of the State Planning Commission, Kao Kang. The basic strategy of the plan involved massive investment in heavy industry to the neglect of light industry and agriculture, but this approach was not to come under criticism until 1956 by which time it had only one year to run. Despite the claims made ten years later that there had always been an oppositionist group within the leadership blocking Mao Tse-tung's policies, most of the evidence indicates that the CCP was united on most issues during these early years. An exception was the powerful Kao Kang who was removed suspiciously soon after the fall of his mentor, Soviet police chief Beria.

China was unable to move steadily towards building a socialist state by employing a mixture of Soviet and domestic methods because of the influence of a third factor—the international environment in which China had to exist. The effect of international politics, particularly their Cold War aspects, was important in determining the direction of China's political development during the first decade of the Chinese People's Republic (CPR). The leadership agreed that China should, in Mao's phrase, 'lean to one side' and this meant support for the Soviet Union and the socialist bloc rather than the West or even the emerging non-aligned nations. However the outbreak of the Korean War in 1950 probably forced China closer to Moscow than had been intended at first. China's entry into the war, the denial of her representation in the United Nations, and the economic blockade imposed by the United States all served to push her lines of economic and diplomatic contact towards Russia and Eastern Europe. Because the trade embargo made it difficult to obtain certain types of equipment needed for economic development, China was also forced quite early to be more self-reliant and develop the manufacture of this equipment herself, rather in the same way that the dangers and uncertainties of trade during the Second World War forced Australia into areas of manufacturing she had not before attempted.

The pressures of the Cold War and the conflict in Korea brought about changes in China's domestic politics also. Those Chinese businessmen who had chosen to stay on rather than flee their country had been able to continue to operate their enterprises after 1949. The new government had no wish to disrupt the private sector of industry and was busy enough reconstructing the large and foreign-owned industries which had fallen into their hands. Furthermore, as was the case with many of the intellectuals, the administrative skills of these non-Party elements were desperately needed and some found high places in the ministries and other organs of government. But with the danger of attack from the

KMT and the United States and with the construction of a ring of bases and military alliances aimed against China from Japan south through the Philippines and Taiwan to Thailand and East Pakistan (now Bangladesh), the Chinese authorities became alarmed about the political reliability of the non-Party people. Harsh compaigns against corruption and 'counter-revolutionary sympathies' were conducted within the ranks of the bureaucracy and the national bourgeoisie. Inevitably the net was sometimes cast too wide, much as happened in Senator Joseph McCarthy's search for 'un-American activities' in a somewhat similar period of hysteria and imagined threat. The Cold War thus increased the pressures towards political conformity in both societies.

With the end of the Korean War and China's diplomatic initiatives at Geneva in 1954, the CPR seemed to be adopting a less militant stand at home and abroad. In September revolutionary control through regional joint military and civilian councils gave way to regular civil government under a constitution which ennumerated certain rights for the people. Elections for the supreme popular body, the National People's Congress (NPC), were held and the Congress went on to approve a cabinet-like executive body, the State Council under Premier Chou En-lai, and a standing committee of the NPC which would operate between congress sessions. Popular councils to carry out the work of government at provincial, county, and district levels were also elected. In September 1956 the CCP held its own full congress, the first to be convened since 1945 and only the eighth in the whole history of the Party. Again the main theme was the orderly progress towards socialism through a system of central planning and controlled change under the leadership of the Central Committee. Internal opposition was no longer a serious problem, the First Five Year Plan seemed to be meeting its targets, and the collectivization of agriculture was almost completed. Most of the leading speakers felt that class struggle was no longer the central feature of Chinese politics and that within a short time a code of laws could be introduced for the orderly management of a society that was united behind the CCP and in which class differences would shortly disappear. With only a few reservations, the model for development was still the Soviet Union.

Mao Tse-tung began to have doubts about the Soviet Union on several counts during the mid-1950s. Firstly he doubted the capacity of Stalin's successors to lead Russia and the rest of the bloc, and secondly he doubted that Soviet experiences, approaches, and models were altogether relevant to the markedly different conditions of China. Mao's dispute with N.S. Khrushchev covered a wide area, much of it more to do with foreign policy and bloc leadership, but he took strong exception to the way in which Stalin's memory had been attacked at the Twentieth Congress of the Communist Party of the Soviet Union (CPSU) in early 1956. He pointed out that China was all too aware of some of Stalin's mistakes and had suffered for them, but in the longer historical view Stalin had performed a useful role in holding the nation together and doing the basic work of constructing socialism. Too sudden a relaxation of Stalinist controls might be unwise and by the end of the year this view appeared to him justified by the outbreak in Hungary of a major revolt against Communist rule which had to be put down by the Red Army. Mao also worried about what he thought were capitalist tendencies in Soviet society and again blamed the leadership. This was not the sort of society he wished to see created in China.

Russia, while backward by European standards at the time of the 1917 revolution, was nevertheless much more advanced than China in the 1950s. The level of industrialization was much higher, communications were relatively easy, and the population size was still just amenable to central control and direction. It was also possible to assemble quickly a trained statistical service upon which the central planning machinery could rely. China was at a very different stage of development and was faced with a population of about 600 000 000, the majority of them peasants to whom the concepts of change and development were foreign, let alone the means of achieving them.

In April 1956 Mao made his speech 'On the Ten Great Relationships', which are listed below.

1 Promote agriculture in preference to heavy industry.
2 Develop coastal industry rather than inland.
3 Promote economic construction faster than defence spending.
4 Production units are more significant than state organs.
5 Decentralize the planning system.
6 Promote nationalities and minorities.
7 Cut Party bureaucracy by two-thirds.
8 Send counter-revolutionaries to agricultural co-operatives for re-education.
9 Allow the people to make revolution: it is right to rebel.
10 Increase the confidence of the Chinese people; despise the lordly.

Mao criticized some features of the orthodox Soviet approach to development in the Chinese context and showed that he was searching for a more appropriate set of guidelines. He discussed the economy in terms of a set of conflicting factors or 'contradictions' and, just as during the anti-Japanese war when the classic contradiction between the national bourgeoisie and the working class was resolved in the face of Japanese invasion, he suggested that the apparent contradictions within the economy could be resolved. Instead of seeing heavy industry, light industry, and agriculture as rival claimants for scarce investment capital, his starting point was the generation of capital. Light industry, which was dependent on agriculture for its raw materials, was the fastest generator of capital so more should be invested in that sector in order to be able to develop heavy industry better. He also argued for a greater degree of local rather than central control and for the encouragement of individual and small unit initiative. These ideas were to form the basis of the economic strategy of the Great Leap Forward in 1958 although they received little publicity at the time and were not referred to at the Eighth Party Congress only six months after the speech was delivered.

By 1957, the end of the first planning period, the choice was whether or not China should be content to maintain a moderate but unspectacular rate of growth using the current approach. Most of the leadership seem to have opted to continue as before and a second plan was drafted employing broadly the same economic strategy but with somewhat higher allocations to agriculture, a sector which had performed poorly to date but upon which China had to depend for food, raw materials, a surplus for capital investment, and even for some of the foreign exchange needed to purchase goods from abroad. The issue was largely decided, however, outside China by the Soviet Union. Soviet economic aid with large industrial projects had been a vital part of the first plan and it was assumed that this aid would continue and it was on this assumption that the 1958–62 plan had been drawn up. But under Khrushchev international solidarity with the other socialist countries, particularly if they seemed in no immediate danger of collapse or invasion, assumed a less important place in his diplomacy than did the winning of new friends within the United Nations. Egypt, India, and Indonesia found themselves in receipt of aid, while China's share sank so low that by 1958 she was repaying more in terms of earlier loan repayments than was coming in. Clearly the necessary capital for investment could not be raised at home, so a new economic strategy had to be found. Little more was heard of the Second Five Year Plan.

From the Great Leap Forward to the Cultural Revolution

A new strategy, known as the Great Leap Forward, was proposed and was based on making the fullest use of the one resource that China had in abundance—labour. Mao remembered what feats his men had performed under pressure during the revolutionary period and hoped that if the population could be properly motivated through intensive mass political campaigns, then China's rate of economic growth could be boosted to the point where she could overtake Britain in fifteen years. The Great Leap Forward, although based on ideological and political considerations, was most important for its economic aspects, and is discussed in greater detail in chapter 6.

The dreams for the Great Leap were not realized but it was not the complete failure it is sometimes painted. Three very bad seasons of drought and floods, coupled with administrative dislocations associated with the hasty creation of the communes, meant that the years 1959–61 are still referred to in China as the 'three lean years' in agriculture. Domestic iron and steel production was not a success in terms of sheer output, but the initiative demanded from the peasants provided them with their first contact and experience with modern though simple technology and the groundwork was laid for a more appropriate and better prepared programme of rural industrialization a decade later. In heavy and light industry and some branches of extractive industry the more realistic targets were met. But the subsequent food shortage did place strains on China's political and social system at least as severe as those of the Korean War period, and the 1960s opened with popular morale low and large sections of both the Party and the People's Liberation Army (PLA) seriously disaffected. Unrealistic targets had been set for the lower level Party cadres by the Great Leap and in attempting to meet them they often alienated the people amongst whom they had to live and work, only to find that they were then blamed by the central authorities for the agricultural failures. Many simply drifted out of the CCP, the communes were partly dismantled, and a few even returned to individual farming. The PLA, being a peasant recruited force, deeply felt the hardships experienced in the countryside and blamed the leadership. At a Central Committee meeting held in August 1959 the Minister of Defence, P'eng Te-huai, attacked Mao personally for his advocacy of the communes, the Leap, and the acerbation of the dispute with the

Soviet Union. P'eng Te-huai was replaced as PLA chief by Lin Piao but Mao had stepped down from his post as Head of State earlier in the year and was much less prominent as Chairman of the CCP after these criticisms.

Chinese society was obviously far less united than the leadership had imagined at the end of 1956. Early in 1957 Mao had delivered an important speech, 'On the Correct Handling of Contradictions among the People', in which he did not say that class struggle was dead, but he did assume that in the future most of the conflicts or contradictions would be 'non-antagonistic' ones which could be settled peacefully. He sought to break down some of the divisions separating the Party from the people with the 'Hundred Flowers Campaign' in which non-members were invited to criticize the performance of the Party. Hitherto such Party rectifications had been strictly internal affairs. The virulence of some of the criticisms, particularly from the intellectuals, revealed cleavages in society and led to an Anti-Rightist Campaign designed to purge the CCP of disloyal elements, strengthen the hand of the more doctrinaire wing, and pave the way for the Great Leap. But, as we have seen, the CCP was unable to push through this programme for accelerated social and economic change without resorting to coercion and the strategic retreat from the policies of the Great Leap was accompanied by a certain political relaxation. The intellectuals once again resumed their criticism, this time through allegorical plays and stories, and in the countryside a partial return to a free market economy was permitted in order to maintain production and peasant co-operation. Economic incentives, which had largely given way to moral exhortations after 1958, were restored and China seemed to be in the hands of pragmatic bureaucrats again rather than the ideologues of the Leap period. Then, at a Central Committee meeting in September 1962, Chairman Mao instructed the party never to forget class struggle and launched a Socialist Education Campaign in the countryside to counter what he saw as a return to capitalism along Soviet lines.

The Communist Party itself reflected these rifts in society and has never restored the unity of its first decade in power. Institutional pressures widened the rifts caused by the policies of the Great Leap Forward, for those concerned with the day-to-day repair work of administration after 1961 found it hard to accept a return to such a strategy of economic development, however strongly they might have believed in the experiment in 1958. Mao, on the other hand, from his vantage point out of the front line of administrative work, retained his faith in the approach and preferred to blame insufficient preparations on the part of the bureaucrats for its shortcomings. The Leap had been preceded in 1957 by considerable decentralization of decision-making to the regional and provincial levels of administration and this also had repercussions when it was not accompanied by the regular transfer of top provincial officials to other posts every three or so years. By the mid-1960s many of the first Party secretaries had been running the same province for up to ten years, had developed great political power, and had also adopted a new set of loyalties which often put the interests of the province, on the performance of which they were judged, above the interests of the centre. As Li Ching-ch'üan, Party chief of the populous grain-surplus province of Szechwan, remarked when Peking ordered him to launch a political campaign, it was better to launch a campaign to collect fertilizer because fertilizer grew crops and politics did not. Chairman Mao had good reason to believe that his Party was no longer the responsive instrument he had once built. No longer so forceful in its top councils, Mao turned to the PLA as an alternative or countervailing force which might later be used against the Party bureaucracy. In many ways a modest man, he nevertheless appreciated the value of a banner when marching. Lin Piao was rebuilding the morale and the political rectitude of the PLA under the banner of the political thought of Chairman Mao. Mao's thought, which had a prominent place in the Party constitution of 1945, had been removed when the new constitution had been announced in 1956.

The Cultural Revolution and its Aftermath

There were, then, a number of issues on which opinion was divided during late 1964 and early 1965. There was the question of the direction and intensity of the Socialist Education Campaign. There was the question of general education policy. There was the question of whether or not to be satisfied with a moderate growth rate now that recovery from the set-backs of 1959–61 had been achieved. There was the question of the role of the military in political life and whether or not a general shake-up and politicization of both society and the Party itself were needed. All this was taking place against the background of worsening relations with the Soviet Union and an escalation of the US commitment in Vietnam which posed at least a potential threat to China's security. The year 1965 was marked by serious and remarkably

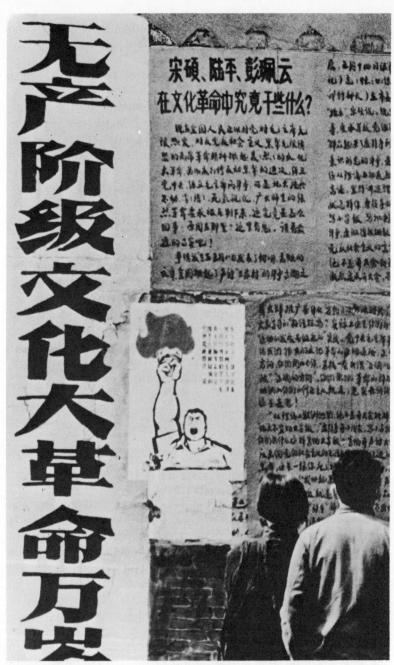

Big character posters which were one of the commonest ways of expressing an opinion during the Cultural Revolution. The slogan on the left says 'Long Live The Great Proletarian Revolution'

public debates on these issues within the top leadership and at one point Lin Piao, Minister of Defence, and Lo Jui-ch'ing, his Chief-of-Staff, took divergent views on both the significance of and the desirable response to the US bombing and troop build-up. Then in November a Shanghai newspaper attacked a Peking literary figure for his criticism of Mao in 1959 and 1961. Lo Jui-ch'ing disappeared and it later emerged that Mao and Lin had discounted the danger of a US attack and with it the need to paper over China's dispute with the Soviet Union. The time had come for a thorough-going revolution in the cultural and political spheres of the CPR before she 'changed colour' and took the 'capitalist road' as had the Soviet Union.

Mao was not calling for just another 'rectification campaign' of the type which the Party periodically conducted to smarten its performance and perhaps replace a few officials who had become slack, yet this was the spirit in which the Party bureaucracy approached the Great Proletarian Cultural Revolution. This was proof that the CCP was no longer responsive to his will and that he would need to call upon other forces if China's political consciousness was to be set firmly in the direction of socialism once more. He was unwilling and possibly unable to use the PLA against the Party bureaucrats and so he turned to the urban youth of China, particularly the under-privileged high school students who were finding it increasingly difficult to gain entry to universities and were quick to blame the system for favouring the children of China's 'new bourgeoisie'—that is, the higher officials of the Party and government bureaucracies. The Red Guards were called into existence and although they were given no strong or permanent organizational structure they nevertheless managed over the next two years to exert enormous political influence. Loosely guided by Mao's wife, Chiang Ch'ing, and a small group close to her in Peking, the Red Guards launched verbal attacks on leading officials who were then removed from office. There was naturally resistance to these activities, sometimes violent in nature, and in January 1967 it became necessary to give the Red Guards some army backing. Whole provincial Party administrations were toppled and many branches of the government were unable to function. The PLA stepped in to fill the resultant vacuum, often through new and simplified organs called 'three-way alliances' on which some representatives of Red Guard and other mass revolutionary groups and a few former Party officials loyal to Mao also served. What had begun as a drive to correct the nation's ideological outlook had assumed the character of a major struggle for political power in which Mao, Lin Piao, and a few associates, together with many of the military, had largely seized control from the CCP bureaucrats by early 1968.

At this point the more revolutionary and anarchistic slogans which had been employed to rouse the masses were slowly replaced by others that laid more stress on the themes of unity, order, and the need to keep production going. The Red Guards, lacking any real structure, were easily disbanded and many of their members were sent out into the countryside. Meanwhile a few more Party leaders of the upper and middle ranks began to reappear, it being announced that they had been reformed, although Liu Shao-ch'i, the former Head of State, and Teng Hsiao-p'ing, the former Secretary-General of the Party, remained in disgrace. Premier Chou En-lai had been the object of some mild attacks but retained his post throughout and demonstrated his indispensability to Mao and Lin by keeping the essential work of government operating despite the upheavals. By late 1968 it was obvious that the CCP was in the process of being rebuilt and in April 1969 its Ninth Congress was held at which a new Central Committee was formed. The Great Proletarian Cultural Revolution was over.

The PLA retained much of its political power and was heavily represented in both the new CCP organs and the government bureaucracy, but it was not completely united. Some of the regional commanders who held power in the provinces were far from loyal to Lin Piao and it has since been revealed that Mao was growing increasingly uneasy about Lin's own loyalty, even though he was still described as Mao's 'closest comrade in arms' and his appointed successor to lead the Party. In September 1971, according to later reports, Lin was killed in a plane crash after having failed in a plot to remove Mao and seize power. This marked the end of the ascendency of the PLA and in August 1973 the CCP held its Tenth Congress at which PLA representation was greatly reduced. Since Lin and some of the military had much earlier stripped Chiang Ch'ing and her radical group of their former authority, these developments left Mao and Chou En-lai in a strong position of command with some of the military commanders from the provinces and a Shanghai-based younger group still associated with Chiang Ch'ing as the other power groupings. Chou En-lai had brought back more of the former Party leaders dismissed during the cultural revolution, including Teng Hsiao-p'ing and Li Ching-ch'üan, but old age had at last begun to take its toll of that outstanding generation of leaders that had formed the CCP, led the Long March, and eventually won power and built a socialist China.

Just before the Tenth Party Congress there began a new political movement which showed that the Chinese leaders' determination to maintain their people's revolutionary will had in no way slackened. This was the Campaign to Criticize Lin Piao and Confucius, and its aim was to prevent 'restorationism', in other words any kind of slipping back towards the social and political attitudes which had prevailed before the Cultural Revolution or before 1949.

In the view of the proponents of this movement, the two archetype representatives of restorationism were Confucius and Lin Piao. Confucius (551–479 BC) had traditionally been regarded as a great sage, but was now seen as a reactionary who attempted to restore the declining slave-owning classes of his own time and to obstruct the consolidation in the power of the rising land-owning classes. He was thus trying to turn back the wheel of history. Lin Piao was similarly accused of being the 'disciple of Confucius' because he attempted to prevent the completion of the process whereby power passed from the bourgeoisie to the proletariat.

The appeal to Confucius as the symbol of conservatism makes sense in the Chinese context because of the *attitudes* embodied in the traditional Confucian ethics. These include especially the idea that models of virtue and good government must be sought in the past rather than the present, that the peasantry should accept a lowly place in society, and that women should not question the authority of men. Such attitudes were still very strong in the Chinese mentality before the Communist revolution and have survived to some extent to the present day. They are undoubtedly contrary to the revolutionary ideals of Mao and his followers, and it is not farfetched to suggest that they would re-emerge with increasing strength if not checked.

The Campaign to Criticize Lin Piao and Confucius appears to be aimed principally at reminding provincial and grass-roots cadres of the dangers of backsliding. So far the highest levels of the central leadership have been very much less affected than was the case during the Cultural Revolution. Speculation towards the end of 1973 that Chou En-lai was under attack has proved groundless, while Teng Hsiao-p'ing continues his upward rise. The only high-level leaders apparently threatened are a small number of regional military commanders, and this suggests that the civilians have no intention of allowing the PLA to regain the ground it lost at the Tenth Party Congress.

75

This brief political survey shows that the years since 1949 have been marked by many swings and changes of pace and direction. The struggles and the search for appropriate policies and organizational forms will go on and the problem of political succession may well introduce new instabilities in the years to come. But Mao has shown that stability is not necessarily a virtue in itself and that progress comes only through struggle. Having done so much to form the political culture of China and the context within which these struggles will take place, Mao Tse-tung has ensured that, whatever the outcome of the struggles, China will continue to move forward and continue to set her own goals. This is the real significance of the Chinese revolution.

Select Bibliography

Adams, Ruth (ed.) *Contemporary China*, Peter Owen, London, 1969. A collection of essays on China's foreign policy and internal politics, social transformation, economy, agriculture, population, science, and education.

Baum, Richard (ed.) *China in Ferment: Perspectives on the Cultural Revolution*, Prentice-Hall, Englwood Cliffs, 1971. A collection of scholarly articles, abridged from the original, on the origins and nature of the Cultural Revolution.

Hinton, Harold C. *An Introduction to Chinese Politics*, Praeger, New York, 1973. A political analysis of the events and factors that have shaped the Chinese political system since 1949.

Schurmann, F. and Schell O. (eds) *China Reading 3, Communist China*, a Pelican book, Harmondsworth, 1967. This volume describes the nature of the Communist government and the social, political, and economic changes culminating in the Cultural Revolution.

Townsend, James R. *Politics in China*, Little, Brown and Company, Boston, 1974. Part of a series on comparative politics of various countries, this book analyzes the concrete processes whereby China is governed.

Part 3
Economic development
Chapter 5
The Chinese economy 1900-49

Bruce McFarlane

China may be unique among the nations which, not having developed a native capitalist and industrial economy of their own, were penetrated by the industrialism spreading from Europe at the beginning of the nineteenth century. Unlike India, China was not portioned into provinces under direct Western administration and native states which were ruled indirectly through their princes. Like India, however, China had reached a *pre-industrial* level as high as that of Europe, not only in philosophy and the arts, but in productive techniques ranging from textiles to metallurgy.

There has been much debate about the reasons for China's failure to go from high pre-industrial achievement to a process of industrialization between 1850 and 1920. There is some agreement that what was lacking was the combination of a suitable social structure and market incentives favouring the emergency of a native capitalist class interested in the promotion of mass production through labour-saving devices. For by the mid-nineteenth century such a path of development was already too late. China was defeated in a series of wars and had to submit to dictated treaties, the purpose of which was the promotion of trade rather than industrialization.

Sources of Economic Growth and Barriers to Development

Even by the end of the Second World War, China remained a predominantly agrarian society and not an industrial one. True, a wide variety of industrial projects had been started by 1900. In the main these were promoted by Chinese *compradors*—Chinese merchants accumulating funds from foreign trade and its related services. Others were the result of the activities of foreign interests in the treaty ports. Yet, as pointed out in greater detail in chapter 7, economic development had been slow, uneven, and concentrated in only a few regions.

One reason for the difference was that in 1900 industrial development outside the treaty ports was still carried out on a family basis. Joint stock companies, in which capital is held by a number of shareholders, were rare; craft guilds controlled industry, and the only important entrepreneurs were the viceroys of a few coastal ports. The widespread use of power-driven machinery, methods of flotation of companies, and the concentration and centralization of capital which sustained classical industrialization were underdeveloped.

Yet we should be careful how we explain this slow Chinese start towards economic takeoff and subsequent economic development. Much of what has been written has assumed theories of economic growth which have been developed for other countries in situations quite different from China's. Consequently these theories are quite irrelevant when explaining Chinese economic growth. One example is Ginsberg's *The Pattern of Asia*, which was published in 1960 and reflects the author's view, almost universal in the West in the 1950s, that Western modes of 'development' were greatly superior to any other. The study argues that scientific attitudes failed to develop as a result of the philosophy of Chinese society, that 'China's civilization is the main reason for its laggard industrial development'. Yet this whole argument has been exploded by the Cambridge team headed by Dr Joseph Needham in its *Science and Civilisation in China*, which mentions not only the highly developed hydraulic technology, road building, and public works which were promoted by the rulers of China hundreds of years ago, but a long list of China's 'firsts' in science and technology. These included printing, gunpowder, the magnet, mechanical water clocks, the kite, and weaving looms. In fact there was little to choose between China and Europe (the former was at least a century ahead in applied hydraulics) until about 1730–90, when the combination of the steam engine and the automatic loom launched the industrial revolution and aggressive mercantilism in England.

More important is the way that Western intervention is seen as restricting itself to extending Chinese government income and launching industrialization, that is most Westerners regard Western intervention as benevolent. I shall argue that this misconceives the role of foreign capital in China. Here it is important to note Ginsberg's account of the economic difficulties of pre-

Communist development. He argues that the chief bottleneck was the lack of capital to finance new enterprises under a free enter-prise system. This is attributed to poverty, giving rise to a shortage of savings for investment, to the distrust of 'impersonal Western-style stock companies', and the traditional feeling that farmland provided the safest and most valuable form of investment.

Ginsberg's approach reflects the assumption that the experience of Japan and Britain is universally valid, and that China should be examined through the prism of this experience. By doing this we miss certain features which are special to China, such as its unique social structure and its 'key economic areas' or regionalism. These two factors are discussed below.

Ginsberg's attitude also reflects the notion that the main factors hampering economic growth in most agrarian countries are *the lack of a pre-existing amount of total savings*, the external balance of payments, and the underdeveloped state of 'entrepreneurship' and capital markets. Such an approach pays too little attention to the fact that rapid rises in total output may outweigh any smallness of the savings fund: investable sources can be found not only by reducing consumption in order to increase savings but by rapid increases in real product per man hour. Modern research attaches as much importance to investment in education and public health (in 'learning by doing'), to what happens during boom periods of the business cycle, and to monetary disturbances, as it does to the kind of issues that were stressed by growth theorists in the 1950s. Let us look at the influence of social structure and regionalism, and see what difference their intrusion makes, as compared to the earlier treatment. In fact let us argue that the social structure and regional differences were the key background elements in the Chinese economic system of 1900, and were at work in shaping its subsequent development.

Social Structure

While some writers (notably Wittfogel) have suggested that China was governed by oriental despotism under a fantastic concentra-tion of total power, this had ceased to be the case by the twentieth century. The truth appears to be rather that the government of China was a landlord's dream.

By 1925 land in China had become almost entirely private property. The state held only about 7 per cent. Of the remainder, about three-quarters was owned by the farmer himself and one quarter rented. But there were big differences in tenancy relations between regions. In the wheat growing regions of the north, private ownership predominated, accounting for seven-eighths of the land. Such tenancy as existed was in the form of share-renting. However in certain other areas of the northeast—later the most powerful areas of Communist support—landlordism was rampant and deeply rooted in the social structure. In the rice-growing areas of the south, the landlord was an even more important figure than in the northeast. Over several provinces, the area of rented land came to 40 per cent and more. Near the big cities, owner-occupied land was rare indeed; the absentee landlord, collecting rents chiefly in cash, had become the characteristic figure by the late 1920s.

As Barrington Moore points out in his *Social Origins of Dictatorship and Democracy*, the political map of 1925 tells a familiar story; that of a society in which commerce, far from destroying pre-capitalist forms of agrarian ownership as a prerequisite to modern private enterprise economic development, was eating away at peasant proprietorship but also concentrating wealth in the hands of a new social formation.

It was this group which formed the main social basis of the Kuomintang. While issuing decrees, and paying lip service to land reform, its agrarian policy in practice was one of trying to maintain and restore the *status quo*. In addition, the presence of the Communist rival tended to polarize the situation and make Kuomintang policy more reactionary and oppressive. As Linebarger, an American scholar sympathetic to the Kuomintang, wrote in his *China of Chiang Kai-shek* in 1942, 'the Communists act as the inheritors to temporarily fanatical peasant rebellions: the National Government and the Kuomintang to ascendant mandarinates'.

The Kuomintang, of course, inherited the power structure of the Manchu dynasty of 1911, in which real power had passed into the hands of local warlords, where it remained for a decade and a half. During this period sections of the gentry clung to power either by turning into warlords or by allying themselves with local militarists. Their successors were to be landlords pure and simple, or gangsters, or a combination of the two, something that lay just below the surface in imperial times. It remained for the Communists to forge a new link between the village and the national government.

Attached as a foreign body on the fabric of Chinese economic society were Western economic imperialism and its implications: control of revenues, concessions, encouragement of the *comprador* class. It cannot be said too often, that the aim of Western and Japanese imperialism was *not* to 'modernize' or 'develop' China. Quite the contrary, the various 'treaties' were designed and imposed in order to prevent the emergence of a strong local capitalist class with its own interests and desire for independent opportunities for profit making. Even the railways, ports, power lines, and so on were designed mainly as adjuncts to foreign business affairs and as clearing houses for merchant finance. On the question of whether imperialism develops a 'traditional society', S.H. Frankel wrote in his *Economic Impact on Underdeveloped Societies* that 'the history of investments in Asia and Africa affords many examples of railway lines, roads, ports, irrigation works etc. in the wrong places which not only failed to lead to income-generating development, but actually inhibited more economic developments which might have taken place'. This comment certainly has some validity for China. In 1930 industrial enterprises were still concentrated around four or five cities as a result of Western controls, not because of entrenched attitudes about investment in land. Foreign control of mineral resources (56 per cent of coal, 82 per cent of iron) and of heavy industry generally, confined industrial China to certain limited areas. In 1930 six provinces—Kiangsu, Liaoning, Hopei, Kwangtung, Shantung, and Hupei—accounted for 92 per cent of foreign trade, 63 per cent of railways, 64 per cent of coal and iron ore output, 93 per cent of cotton yarn spun, 92 per cent of silk reeled, 86 per cent of oil pressed, and 87 per cent of electric power capacity. Of 1975 larger factories (measured by employment levels) in 1930, 42 per cent were in Shanghai. A native capitalism, even by then, was only just beginning.

In Chinese history, two separate cultural traditions had developed. Standing in opposition to the entrenched Chinese social structure and foreign interference were the egalitarian and utopian traditions of China. Sun Yat-sen spoke of the continuity that links modern socialism to Taoism and Confucianism. Sun insisted on the specifically Chinese sources of socialism which he proposed in his 'Three Principles of the People' and argued that 'when the people have communalized everything that concerns the State we shall have realized the *ta-t'ung* or world of great harmony wished for by Confucius'. Similarly Mao Tse-tung, in his 'On the People's Democratic Dictatorship', stressed that the historical mission of Chinese communism was to achieve the aims of the native radical traditions. Mao said that 'the power of the State and political parties will disappear quite naturally and thus allow mankind to enter the era of *ta-t'ung*'. The ideal of a fraternal society was also expressed by the idea of *ching-t'ien*, a system whereby a square piece of land is divided into nine equal but smaller square plots, of which eight are cultivated by one household each while the ninth, in the centre, is public and worked collectively by all the eight families. This utopian myth of agrarian communism was extremely vital in China before the twentieth century though it remained forever an ideal. Not only did Chinese communism in the thirties, and again during the period of the communes, develop against the background of peasant egalitarianism, but revolutionary Kwangtung in the 1920s adopted a flag with the characters for *ching-t'ien*, while Yen Hsi-shan, a warlord of Shansi Province, sought to introduce a *ching-t'ien* system under a ten year agrarian reform plan in the 1920s. The importance of this 'other trend', then, is that it helps to explain the support for Maoist agrarian communism in the 1930s. It is vital not to see only the despotic strand in old China and in the feudalism of nineteenth century China, but to be aware of the radical tradition as well. This can prevent the outside student from developing a patronizing attitude to the development of science and technology in the old China, and help him to understand clearly the force of radical peasant ideology in shaking the China of Chiang Kai-shek.

For the repressive social structure described above was almost intact as late as 1932. In this *Land and Labour in China* (1932) R.H. Tawney wrote:

> The rural population suffers horribly through the insecurity of life and property. It is taxed by one ruffian who calls himself a general, by another, by a third, and, when it has bought them off, still owes taxes to the Government; in some places actually more than twenty years' taxation has been paid in advance. It is squeezed by dishonest officials. It must cut its crops at the point of a bayonet, and hand them over without payment to the local garrison, though it will starve without them.

Tawney showed remarkable insight when he drew the following conclusion from his survey of social conditions in China in 1932. 'The revolution of 1911 was a bourgeois affair. The revolution of the peasants has still to come. If their rulers continue to exploit them, or permit them to be exploited, as remorselessly as hitherto, it is unlikely to be pleasant.'

The importance of looking at the social structure may now be seen. It was warlord and landlord control which inhibited development. Capital moved from rural districts where it was really needed, to be buried in the concession ports. Expenditure on war at regional levels absorbed resources which could have been used for primary education and health—the foundations of self-sustained development. Internal trade and communications were paralyzed—partly by soldiers, partly by the Manchu *likin* tax (internal transit fee) which extended to set points within provinces, as well as to provincial borders. This tax was not abolished until 1930. Savings could not be mobilized because all surplus incomes were devoted to paying off moneylenders and dealers, while the wealthier classes dissipated their revenues in ostentatious living and war. Merchants owned factories, so a labyrinth of small undertakings developed rather than the larger modern factories.

All of this underlines an important fact for interpretation: more important than lack of joint stock companies or banks or savings are the social relations in the rural sector and in the individual regions.

Regionalism

Looking at the structure of the Chinese economy in the eighty years before the Chiang Kai-shek regime, one notes the importance of regionalism. The first social and economic development actually took place in the south. Canton was the traditional location of intercourse with foreigners. The leaders of the Taiping revolution were southerners who had experience with the West in Canton. The tradition of rebellion and advanced ideas and of the secret societies was in the south, far from Peking and imperial power. Sun Yat-sen's government was centred in Canton. It was from here that the expedition to fight the northern warlords was launched. In 1928 Sokolsky, writing in the *China Yearbook*, noted that 'the financial policy of the Nanking Government is based upon the supposition that what is good enough for the people of Canton is good enough for the whole of China. The Ministry of Finance has sought to extend to Kiangsu and Chekiang, and more particularly to the Shanghai area, taxes peculiar to Canton.'

While it is true that regional warlords between 1911 and 1949 fought each other, betrayed each other, and increased their economic pressure on the ordinary peasants, the system was not entirely different from that which was followed in the late years of the Manchu dynasty. For up to 1910 many provinces were contributing half of their revenues to the central government as well as subsidizing adjoining provinces which were paying the 'Boxer indemnity' to foreigners. In Szechwan Province, for example, the pattern of government expenditure indicates that in 1909 the system was not one of governors interested only in themselves but one approaching centralism as part of a two-tier system in which revenues flowed to the centre and were also used for domestic economic growth. In that year Szechwan spent 10 000 000 of about 18 000 000 *taels* on itself, sent some 5 200 000 *taels* to the central government and nearly 500 000 to other provinces.[1]

Between 1911 and 1920 these arrangements began to break down, as warlords took control of regions; defying the centre, they became remote independent 'kingdoms'.

Landlords backed the compartmental structure of the country and its high proportion of local self-sufficiency. For the landlord got the maximum revenue out of his land when there was a surplus of competing peasants. The landlord was instinctively alarmed by any development which tended to draw peasants away from the region.

After 1920 the basic regional difference was between the commerce-dominated north (not including Manchuria in the northeast) and the landlord-dominated south and southwest. The eastern states were the prominent units in earlier times. The concentration of people in the east was enhanced by a strong emphasis on irrigation, resulting in high production per acre and high population density; but the eastern areas declined as the first decades of the twentieth century unfolded. Thus the aggregate population of the four Yangtze provinces—Chekiang, Anhwei, Kiangsi, and Hupei—declined by 36 000 000 between 1850 and 1953. In part this reflected the saturation of the rice economy, the expansion of which had supported the rise of population in these areas. In part also, these provinces were the ones most devastated during the Taiping revolution.

It was the retreat of the Nationalists after 1937 from these regions to the landlord-dominated groupings of Kwangtung-Kwangsi and Szechwan-Yunnan that extinguished the last embers of any Nationalist reforming zeal, and convinced educated Chinese that no effective reform, or effective economic government, was possible from the right-wing forces. Economic development then moved decisively to the north.

Looking now at regional shifts from the viewpoint of the unfolding of the Communist revolution, we will notice that the Communists also were originally strongest in Kwangtung and Hunan. Later, with the Long March, the situation reversed itself. Looking at a political map of China one sees that during the civil war (and during the Cultural Revolution) the 'red power' was established unevenly, but quickest in Heilungkiang Province and in Shensi. It was consolidated with difficulty, and more slowly, in Kwangtung, Szechwan, and Yunnan. This underlines the *itinerant character* of the developing Chinese Communist revolution—there are dynamic shifts from centre to centre with uneven levels of political consciousness. It follows that geopolitics must be of prime concern to an understanding of Chinese economic and social development before 1949.

Industry and Transport

Although a few economic historians have dated the beginnings of China's industrialization as far back as 1862, heavy industry, apart from the state arsenals, hardly existed in China before 1890. In that year an iron and steel works and a modern coal mine were built in Shanghai, while the first cotton mills were established. Even in 1910, despite a certain stimulus to the growth of the manufacturing industry in the treaty ports after the Treaty of Shimonoseki (1895) permitted foreigners to establish industrial plants, there were only twenty-six cotton mills, thirty-one modern flour mills, and about 7200 kilometres of railway in the whole country. This rail network was less than that of Britain at the same time, even though the area disparity between the two countries is immense.

The First World War, by cutting off foreign supplies, presented Chinese producers with a monopoly of the home market and the opportunity to promote industrial expansion. Between 1918 and 1930 rapid growth took place in the face of regional disorder, high taxation, and forced loans. Thus the output of coal in 1929 was 79 per cent above that of 1913 and railway mileage was 76 per cent higher. A sharp increase in imports of machinery and raw cotton pointed to a growing number of cotton mills and factories.

A process of economic development had begun to get under way by 1930 and this continued as a moderate growth until the fall of the Nationalists in 1949. According to estimates by John K. Chang, the output of industry, defined as manufacturing, mining, metallurgy, fuel, and power, grew over the whole period 1912–49 at an average annual rate of 5·6 per cent per annum (see reference in bibliography).

Between 1880 and 1894 a few railway lines were constructed, but not on a substantial scale till after the Sino-Japanese War of 1894–95. By 1930 about 15 300 kilometres of railway had been laid, three-quarters of which was built between 1900 and 1915. In fact transport has continued to be a major bottleneck holding back faster economic growth right through to the present time.

Certainly internal trade between 1900 and 1949 could not expand to its potential. Coal could not be easily moved and the cost of raw materials at industrial sites was high. In agriculture, by 1930, only 47 per cent of the crop was consumed by the farmers themselves, while the other 53 per cent was disposed of by sale, forming an important *net agricultural surplus* which had to be transported. Railway traffic was insignificant for this task— waterways, carts, and manual labour were the main methods of transport. The costs were extremely high. A report by a US Trade Commission for the American Department of Commerce in December 1929 estimated the road mileage at a mere 56 000 kilometres, with 8 000 kilometres under construction. Although this represented a 76 per cent growth between 1913 and 1929, the greater part of the motor road system had been built after 1920. (In the province of Kweichow there were no roads at all in 1925.)

As the railway and motor road mileage slowly increased in the twenty years from 1929 to 1949, rural isolation was gradually broken down. To grasp the *economic* significance of this development, consider that an estimate in 1930 for the cost of transporting 1378 tonnes of wheat (for the purpose of famine relief) a distance of 375 kilometres in Shansi Province was 50 silver cents per tonne per kilometre by cart, 8 cents by tractor and trailer, and (if a railway had existed) by train an estimated 1·25 cents. It became obvious that the technologies of mass production which were so bound up with foreign-owned industry could not be marketed until communications improved: industrial development was highly correlated with the improvement of transport. It was in the foreign interest to open up the hinterland. This was the basic reason for the building of railways; it explains why the first railways did not follow the lines that might have been adopted by an independent country planning its own development. By breaking down the old geographical compartmentalization of eastern China, railways developed a market, but one which was really an international market rather than the national market of a sovereign state. This observation relates to the wider issue of the social and political consequences of the treaty ports. Through them the industrial impact was concentrated on a tight geographical pattern of targets. Local businessmen who wished to develop an industrial system found that in order to do so, they had to capture the foreign positions of economic privilege. Many who failed to do this later linked with the intelligentsia in a general shift to the left.

Labour Conditions

By the 1920s the handicraft system coexisted with the modern factory system (Chinese and foreign). In the former, guilds (in practice the managers) controlled labour conditions. In the latter, the owners themselves, often through the Chamber of Commerce and local police, dictated labour contracts. The Provisional Factory Regulations, which were suggested by the central Chinese government in 1923, were not in force outside Shanghai, Nanking, Tientsin, and Harbin. Even trade unionism itself was rare beyond these areas. The result was that labour conditions were universally poor; they were possibly better in non-Japanese foreign factories, but even in these they were often unnecessarily bad.

In 1924 Mr Ramsay MacDonald as British Secretary for State instituted an enquiry into labour conditions in extraterritorial districts in China under British control 'to support the request of the Chinese government that the International Labour Conventions should be applied to territories under non-Chinese sovereignty'. The subsequent report[2] gives a graphic account of general conditions of adult and child labour in British, Japanese, and Chinese mills in Shanghai and in various workshops of Wuhan, Chefoo, and Foochow. Requests for information were also sent to the consuls all over China, including Harbin and faraway Chungking and Chengtu (Szechwan Province). The acting consul in Chengtu, in his reply, noted that:

the Chinese Provisional Factory Regulations are unknown in this district... regulations regarding wages in any particular trade are issued from time to time by the City Council or the Chamber of Commerce (through the police); it is doubtful whether anything so foreign to popular ideas as much as the draft convention would find a ready acceptance.

The consul also made a comment of interest, however:

the nearest approach to trades unionism is the system of guilds which regulate wages and other conditions of labour and provisions for apprentices. There is also a so-called Labourers Self-Government Society, started some four years ago by self-seekers with a political object; its strength lies in championing foreigners' servants against their masters, and it also endeavours to win a little notoriety by violent speeches on such occasions as Labour Day.

The overall impression given in the British government's report (and in the report of the Child Labour Commission appointed by the Municipal Council of Shanghai of 9 July 1924 which was attached to it) is quite clear. Where no 'workingman's societies' existed, there were no limits on hours of work, no precautions against disease, few holidays, low wages, and frightening conditions for child workers. In the words of the Acting Consul in Chungking:

> in native enterprises of all kinds nothing is known of limitation of hours of labour, provision for unemployment, regulations for dealing with the employment of women and children, health services, or any other of the points dealt with in the draft conventions and recommendations of the International Labour Conference; it would almost be safe to say that no single person amongst the population of Szechwan estimated at 60 000 000 to 70 000 000 has even heard of such ideas.

All of the advice coming in from cities outside Shanghai, Tientsin, Nanking, Harbin, and Canton indicated similar arbitrariness of employers towards workers. Clearly trade unionism was by no means entrenched in any part of China: guilds and/or foreign factory managers determined the conditions of labour, even against the wishes of the central government itself.

On the other hand, it is now recognized that between 1919 and 1927 urban working class organization—often semi-secret in character—experienced a rapid growth, culminating in the militant working class uprisings of Shanghai in 1926–27, which were bloodily repressed by Chiang Kai-shek. Without this working class movement, the Communist Party would not have become significant as quickly as it did. For the main seat of working class strength was in the cities, especially in those most affected by the West, like Shanghai and Wuhan. The presence of the foreign power was decisive in tipping the balance between the bourgeoisie and the proletariat in favour of the former. In Shanghai, not only were there foreign banks and other vested interests, but in spring 1927 there were 22 000 foreign troops to aid the local military. After the massacre of 1927 the militant labour movement was almost non-existent. Chinese Communism shifted to the countryside—but this was a strategy dictated by circumstances rather than (as often thought) because the 'town' is missing in Mao's writings or because Mao's followers saw a special messianic role for the peasantry as a force uncorrupted by industrial society. In 1968 Mao wrote that 'the proletariat is the greatest class in the history of mankind. It is the most powerful revolutionary class ideologically, politically and in strength.'

Agricultural Development

If working class ideology was important in Chinese Communism, it was the peasantry which ultimately carried out successful revolution. Their dissatisfaction stemmed from high rents, military conscription, and inflation. Thus in the early part of the twentieth century, Szechwan Province produced about 15 000 000 tonnes of grain: the landlords received some 5 000 000 tonnes or 50 000 000 *shih*[3] of husked grain, a figure about the same as that of the land-tax revenue of the central government. (One could arrive at similar figures by combining Kwangtung and Kwangsi or Chekiang and Fukien Provinces.)

By the nineteenth century China had begun to run out of readily cultivable land, and per capita output was declining between 1800 and 1900. The 20 000 000 casualties of the Taiping revolution 'alleviated' the population pressure, without which the rising population of 1880 to 1920 would have outstripped the ability of Chinese agriculture to provide adequate food supplies.

As it was, according to Perkins in his *Agricultural Development in China*, 'the first half of the twentieth century may have witnessed a more or less equal match between rising population and increased output'. But the dramatic rise of China's northern cities, made possible by railway construction, and the new requirements of industrialization resulted in difficulties for the grain market in the first few decades of the twentieth century. Because people moved from farms to cities, those remaining had to increase their marketing of grain. This burden fell unevenly on different provinces, being particularly heavy in Hunan, Hupei, Kiangsi, and Szechwan. Within each province the burden was also uneven, falling most seriously on landless labourers and small tenant farmers. Landlords, making up less than 4 per cent of the population in these areas, directly controlled (according to Perkins) about 20 per cent of the output. Moreover price fluctuations made dependence on the market for food a risky business: a farmer who planted all his land with cash crops (beans and other vegetables) might physically survive a 50 per cent decrease in the price of rice, but his losses might be sufficient to deprive him of his market or his land.

Periodic droughts and floods continued to take their toll (see also chapter 1). Moreover there were severe limitations on the resources that governments or warlords were willing to commit to famine relief. These instabilities, on top of the man-made ones, gave the peasantry a considerable thirst for reform.

Monetary Factors and the Collapse of the Nationalist Economy

Finally, let us glance briefly at some monetary factors in the economy. Money-lending had reduced peasant initiative to a low ebb by 1900. High repayments took away much of extra output. The growth of modern banking, although much slower than in Japan and the West, helped to reduce the burdens and to supply investable funds to the growing industrial sector. By 1935 there were, in addition to 43 foreign and 20 Chinese-foreign banks, about 140 Chinese banks, of which 93 had been established after 1929.

Later, the existence of a sophisticated banking system helped for a time to stave off Chiang Kai-shek's economic collapse, by selling bonds in foreign exchange markets, mobilizing foreign exchange earnings and remittances, and the like. But when, from the end of 1945 to May 1947, the Central Bank lost nearly two-thirds of its foreign exchange and gold reserve without substantially slowing down the tempo of internal currency inflation, the writing was on the wall for the Nationalists.

In 1936 foreign capital accounted for 10 per cent of total output and a higher proportion of non-agricultural activity. But domestic failures in the control of money, budgets, and public works eventually led to economic collapse. The story of how this came about is essentially the story of the Chinese inflation 1937–49.

The prime mover of the Chinese inflation was in the government sector which made two kinds of expenditure; that in local and that in foreign currency. As the anti-Japanese and civil wars intensified, local taxes could not be collected, so the government spent its foreign currencies—it sold bonds abroad or ran down reserves. This eventually brought about inflationary consequences, as did the fiscal or budgetary policies pursued by the government sector: instead of reducing budget deficits or cutting down non-government spending to offset its deficits, the government merely transferred the pressure to the international sector by expanding its outlays in foreign currencies. Moreover, after 1945, foreign remittances from overseas Chinese, which had once bridged the gap in China's trade balances, were sharply curtailed while the growing government expenditure in foreign currencies, the speculative investments by merchant bankers and government officials in gold and foreign assets, and the purchase of food and supplies from abroad increased the balance of payments deficit. This weakening of the international sector meant that it was unable to relieve pressures arising from phenomenal expansion of money supply—both bank credit and printed notes.

This out-of-control 'financing by the printing press' caused hyperinflation. In all, the price increase in the early war years was 160 per cent each year, climbing to 300 per cent annually in the whole period 1941–45 and to more than 1000 per cent during 1945–49. Such trends could only cause many inequitable effects which would bring important changes in the social system.

Inflation, then, was a chief factor in weakening the Nationalist regime and strengthening support for the Communists. Labourers, teachers, soldiers, and civil servants were its chief casualties.

The Communists were never to forget the lesson of the dangers of inflation. Price stability has, ever since, been almost an obsession with them. Once in power they managed to halt the inflation, and by mid-1950 to clear the road for economic reconstruction and development, so consolidating support behind Mao's 'new democracy'.

*　　*　　*

This survey of the Chinese economy in the first half of this century has one obvious implication: it is not surprising that the Chinese responded well to the revolution. Foreign economic imperialism was a real and not an imaginary factor which bred deep resentment of the *status quo*. Labour conditions were such that the workers had nothing to lose and everything to gain by throwing in their lot with the Communists. Above all, the peasantry could not help but desire change and the overthrow of a system which exploited them so savagely. Only the rich classes, whose numbers were comparatively few, stood to gain by the continuation of the old order. Given the able leadership and determination of their revolutionary opponents, they could not hope to hold down the masses of the poor for ever.

Notes

1 See S.A.M. Adshead 'Viceregal Government in Szechwan in the Kuang-hsü period (1875–1909)' in *Papers on Far Eastern History*, **4**, September 1971, p. 43. In 1930 1 *tael* was equal to 1·5 *yüan*, and 1 *yüan* to US $0.26.

2 House of Commons Papers; Accounts and Papers, **30**, 1924–25, *China No. 1*, Cnd 2442.

3 1 *shih* = 100 litres

Select Bibliography

Chang, John K. *Industrial Development in Pre-Communist China*, Edinburgh University Press, Edinburgh, 1969. A straightforward modern economic history of China with a rather academic interpretation. He argues that there was steady, indeed impressive, industrial development under the Nationalists after 1930.

Moore, Barrington *Social Origins of Dictatorship and Democracy*, Beacon Press, Boston, 1966, Chapter VI. A comparative study of the English, Russian, and Chinese revolutions. Moore says that all present societies which are stable have had violent revolution in the past. Such upheavals are natural and not abnormal in human history.

Myers, Ramon H. *The Chinese Peasant Economy, 1890–1949*, Oxford University Press, London, 1971. Another very scholarly book by a Nationalist sympathizer. It re-works a lot of valuable data originally compiled by J.L. Buck on the land-holdings and rent burdens in specific areas of China.

Perkins, Dwight H. *Agricultural Development in China, 1368–1968*, Edinburgh University Press, Edinburgh, 1970. Looks at the broad sweep of trends in agricultural output and population. Good section on the 'Malthusian spectres' as they operated in China: famine, rebellion, war.

Tawney, R.H. *Land and Labour in China*, Allen and Unwin, London, 1937. A justly famous classic by a leading English Fabian socialist. A brilliant account of China in the 1930s. Tawney is interested in the exploitation of the peasants, corruption of the landlord class, and the cruel position of the urban masses.

Chapter 6
The economy of the Chinese people's republic
Bruce McFarlane

While it would be possible to evaluate the Chinese Communist economic performance by reference to rates of growth of production, investment, and per capita income levels, this would leave out what is perhaps the most unique feature of what has been happening in modern Chinese economic life. This is the substantial improvement in the quality of China's human resources: levels of education, health, cultural activities, and *participation in decision-making processes*.

For while it is undoubtedly useful to estimate the rate of change of important indices of material progress, we must not lose sight of the fact that *qualitative* economic planning has been as important in the People's Republic of China as efforts to improve quantities of resources. We cannot look only at the revolutionary changes that have occurred in *institutions* such as those of nationalization, planning, and collectivization, but must take account of the *operational significance of revolutionary ideology*. For in China an attempt is being made, on a scale which has no precedent, to imbue peasants and workers with a revolutionary outlook. In factories, fields, and schools a vast socialist education movement has been carried out. There have been rectification movements, anti-rightist campaigns, a cultural revolution. The continuing aim of these movements is to make the ideas and energies of masses of people a material force, by encouraging the idea of serving the people' rather than oneself; of placing human relations above 'profit' and 'productivity'; of being concerned not only with one's local area, but also with the whole nation and, beyond that, with the conditions of the world's poor.

Economic Development in the 1950s

At the time of the revolution in 1949 the Chinese economy was a shambles, with industrial and agricultural output well below their previous peak levels. China was one of the poorest countries in the world. Yet, by 1960, China had shown the world a rate of economic growth greater than that achieved by most other countries. The gross national product between 1950 and 1959 grew by more than 10 per cent per annum in real terms (that is allowing for price rises). These substantial gains were based on a heavy investment programme in machinery, averaging about 25 per cent of total output. This ratio of investment to production was truly amazing for an underdeveloped country with China's low level of per capita income. One result was that industrial production rose during the decade at an average annual rate of 20 per cent. On the other hand, agriculture is thought to have increased by 4 per cent yearly over the 1950s.

The gains of the decade were also, however, based on very great improvements in transport, education, medicine, public health, and scientific research. Those in transport and education are considered elsewhere and require no further detail here. In the medical field there was also a crash programme. In 1949 1313 people were taking a degree in medicine. By 1960 there were 20 000. Moreover there was a very big breakthrough on large-scale public health projects. Typhoid, smallpox, cholera, and venereal disease were all eliminated by a combination of modern and traditional medicine.

A continuing battle was also fought against the strong inflationary pressures that were inherent in the heavy investment programme. Since relatively little investment was allocated to agriculture, the state attempted to increase output by social and political reorganizations that were intended to raise incentives and efficiency. Land reforms, mutual aid teams, agricultural co-operatives, and communes were the principal innovations along these lines. These attempts to improve the supply side of production were supplemented by restraints on the demand for goods— relatively low wages, stimulation of private saving, restraints on government consumption, and increases in taxes and other budget revenue sources.

In the first Five Year Plan period (1953–57), the Chinese government had a number of goals: to raise output per head, to reduce the gap between urban and rural living standards, to improve communications, and to develop 'human capital'. However it is probably fair to say that priority at this time was given to industrialization and to maximizing the rate of economic growth over a fairly short time period. There was, for example, a great deal of talk about reaching the levels of industrial production prevailing in Great Britain.

The development strategy adopted in the mid-1950s was heavily influenced by the USSR 'model'. This involved the following elements: (i) high rates of saving and investment; (ii) priority for heavy industry, particularly machinery (see chapter 7), as the leading sector; (iii) a bias in favour of capital intensive technologies in key industries, together with labour-intensive techniques in agriculture; (iv) the utilization of under-employed agricultural labour to build public works, irrigation, and flood control projects etc; (v) in international trade, a policy of exporting agricultural products and importing industrial goods.

In general technology in the modern sector was borrowed from the Soviet Union, while there was a general policy of learning from Soviet experience in industrial design, planning techniques, and economic institutions. This overall strategy was followed successfully until about 1958 although there were temporary deviations from it.

In the *implementation* of the strategy there were a number of notable features. While allowing for a good deal of regional self-sufficiency, a centralized planning system was set up for major industries. Again, while permitting a good deal of scope for ideological or 'moral' incentives to motivate workers and peasants, the emphasis was predominantly on material incentives (such as financial rewards, bonus wages, and prizes). Skill and expertise were promoted. Education policy tended to be élitist, being designed to build a pyramid from a large mass base. Political criteria for selection of students to enter tertiary education certainly existed, but were of less significance than performance. In the bureaucracy, and in the army, there was an explicitly hierarchial system.

The elements mentioned so far add up to a 'bureaucratic-rational' model, that is one which emphasizes orderly planning from the top; a hierarchy of duties and rewards; the importance of cost, productivity, the rate of return on state investments etc. In short, it was very similar to that which has long prevailed in the Soviet Union. However there were two additional elements which do not fit this pattern, and which have come to be associated as specially 'Maoist' in orientation. The first of these was the emphasis on an egalitarian system of income distribution. Equalization of investments between regions, the 'squeezing' of the wealthy, the rationing of basic foods and cloth at lower than market prices—all these were characteristics of the 1950s. (Later, they were to be revived in the Cultural Revolution.) The second element was manpower policy, which set the pattern for later periods and continues today: the seeking of full employment via technological dualism or 'walking on two legs'[1]. And, of course, there was the continuing concern expressed about revolution and the inculcation of the Maoist moral values which emerged from the Communist experience in Yenan in the 1930s: hard work, frugality, a serious attitude to solving problems, working selflessly for the common good, etc.

Towards the end of the first Five Year Plan period many Communist leaders were, nevertheless, becoming disillusioned with the usefulness of the Soviet model for Chinese conditions. At the Eighth Party Congress in 1956, a new plan was drafted which indicated some rethinking about the development pattern that had hitherto been pursued. Primarily there was a sense of frustration about being dependent on Soviet aid, about the failure to achieve full employment, and about the minor role given to agricultural investment. It was decided to pay much more attention to achieving higher agricultural supplies, and to pursuing more labour-intensive technology in order to solve problems of manpower absorption.

New ideas gradually evolved. One of the first results of the rethinking process was Mao's 1956 speech, 'On the Ten Great Relationships', described in chapter 4. As the reader will recall, this document downgraded the priority given to heavy industry and modified the 'bureaucratic-rational' model of economic planning; it also looked forward to great decentralization of decision-making and to fuller mobilization of the masses through emphasis on moral incentives.

It was in 1956, too, that Mao proposed his 'National Programme of Agricultural Development for 1956–67', which recommended tactics that were to become familiar later: more self-reliance in the matter of fertilizer and agricultural machinery, and rapid expansion of irrigation works through mobilization of local labour power.

All of these new ideas crystallized in the new strategy adopted in 1958–59. This has come to be known as the Great Leap Forward, the first big exercise (the Cultural Revolution was the second) in developing a leftist revolt against the imperatives of classical industrialization and against the bureaucratization of the revolution.

The objectives of the Great Leap were to raise output rapidly, but to do it by a heavy infusion of ideology as a motivating force,

Scenes from two rural people's communes. *Above*—a peasant dwelling on a commune in Shensi Province. *Below*—members of a commune in Szechwan tend a vegetable garden, killing pests and applying fertilizer

and through a decentralized command system involving the setting up of communes with a high degree of self-reliance. In practice, output maximization was sought at the same time as employment maximization. Such a twin objective required labour mobilization, promotion of 'walking on two legs' in technological policy, and mobilization of savings within agricultural co-operatives and communes.

One of the most important aspects of the Great Leap Forward was the setting up of the people's communes. Most of the land had earlier been collectivized, but communes differed from the previous co-operatives in that they were seen as all-round organs catering for all fields of social and economic life, not merely for agriculture (see chapter 4). Moreover they were very much larger than co-operatives, more than 240 000 of which merged into 24 000 communes. However one should add that the earliest were found to be too large and the number of communes later rose to 74 000, and today there are about 50 000.

In order to make the efforts of the Great Leap Forward workable, it was also necessary to step up the policy of egalitarianism (equal sacrifice) and to upgrade the importance given to investment in agriculture. It was also necessary to promote 'redness' as against the 'expertness' so favoured in the First Five Year Plan period.

The positive aspects of the strategy of the Great Leap Forward need to be noted, since most Western comment has tended to assume, without qualification, that the Great Leap Forward was a disaster.

The period from October 1957 to September 1958 alone saw irrigation and flood prevention works dug equal to that of three hundred Panama Canals. It saw an additional 16 500 000 mou^2 of land irrigated and brought into cultivation. The establishment of communes proved to be successful from a number of viewpoints. The agricultural unemployed (and the formerly tied-down women) could be mobilized at little cost to the state, and used on construction work in local areas. The communes also allowed a *complementary* relationship to develop between agriculture and small-scale industrial plants in which the latter supplied tools, machinery, fertilizers, and insecticides for agriculture, while farming supplied not only food, but raw materials to be processed in local small-scale chemical and concrete factories.

Where raw materials (iron ore and coal) were located close by the communes a wider distribution of plants became possible, thereby facilitating regional self-sufficiency. This not only kept

The cultural centre of a production brigade on Hainan Island. People's communes are many-sided in their functions and are not merely agricultural bodies. The cultural life of the members is catered for in rural clubs or cultural centres which provide reading material, organize amateur dramatic or other performances, and look after sporting activities down required transport investments, it also achieved a continuing objective of Chinese economic policy which was to keep people in the rural areas. This policy aimed to 'freeze' the population level of cities by bringing carefully rationed samples of the fruits of industrial society to the peasants in their local areas.

It was also found that the small-scale enterprises promoted during the Leap were less demanding on the quality of construction, thereby reducing investment costs, and that they brought high *gross output* results, as well as quicker returns on investment.

Once these achievements have been outlined, it is also necessary to point to the many errors of economic policy, which resulted from unrealistic planning, excessive mobilization of labour, and a 'subjective' attitude to objective economic bottlenecks. One of the main sources of waste was that an excessive number of irrigation canals were constructed in relation to the necessary drainage canals. Not enough care was taken to complete detailed studies of topography, silt content, river flow, and weather patterns.

While steel and coal production certainly soared in 1958, the lurch forward had come to a halt by the end of 1959. There was a slowdown in economic growth, at first in the consumer goods sector and agriculture during 1959, and in capital goods by 1960. Bad weather in 1960 and 1961 created a collapse in agricultural supplies. Slowly the economic crisis became a crisis of the system as a whole. It created a political conflict between Mao and those, like the Defence Minister Marshal P'eng Te-huai, who favoured a return to the earlier model which owed more to Soviet influence. More important, to the extent that it was quickly halted, the Leap was a failure as an exercise in purely Maoist strategies on the economic front. It forced a retreat from leftist ideas; in fact, between 1957 and 1962, Mao's ideas were pushed into the background as a political shift developed within the Party leadership in favour of more reliance on market forces and orderly planning and less on mobilization and ideological fervour. The ideas of the 'Ten Great Relationships' were in full retreat. The Great Leap Forward ended in economic difficulties on a wide scale; it was a watershed which led to a sharp reversal of economic policy.

The 'New Economic Policy', 1961–65

After the Great Leap Forward, the economy was brought under the influence of a stabilization policy which emphasized agriculture as the first priority, and restored wage incentives and profitability criteria in industrial planning. The objectives of the new policy were economic recovery and increased self-reliance. All of this took place against the strains induced by the withdrawal of Soviet aid in 1960, successive droughts, and lack of investible funds brought on by stagnating production.

The immediate results of the new policy were an increase in fertilizer and other 'modern' inputs for the agricultural sector, the development of the oil and petroleum industries to full self-sufficiency, and an attempt at balanced industrial growth generally.

By 1963 agricultural output had recovered to 1957 levels, while the gross national product in 1965 is thought to have attained the previous peak level of 1958. In achieving this, the policy of 'walking on two legs' was modified as more modern technologies were brought into play. The industrial structure was substantially modified, less emphasis was given to iron and steel and more to light industry and chemical fertilizer production.

While recovery was achieved, it was also brought about at the cost of a considerable ideological break with the left. In industry, President Liu Shao-ch'i was associated with the implementation of a seventy-point industrial charter which gave more power to the managers, raised profitability to the forefront as a key 'success indicator' of factory performance, and encouraged a wider spread in wage rewards through piece-work rates, bonus payments, prizes, and so forth. In agriculture too, material incentives were stepped up. More private plots were encouraged on the communes, while agricultural fairs and other kinds of market forces increasingly influenced the level and composition of agricultural output. This policy was pursued in the face of much opposition both at the local and highest leadership level. The primacy of moral incentives was temporarily pushed aside.

By 1964 political disagreements about this aspect of the new line were apparent. In 1962, at a Central Committee meeting, Mao Tse-tung had issued the call, 'never forget class struggle'. Two years later, in an obvious tilt at Liu Shao-ch'i's policy, Mao extolled the virtues of the peasants of Tachai brigade[3] who had achieved brilliant production feats while downgrading financial incentives. Mao also launched the Socialist Education Movement in the countryside. Another call by Mao was to 'learn from Taching', a reference to a northeast China oilfield where advanced industrial workers had echoed the efforts and ideas of their peasant counterparts in Tachai by stimulating production through moral and ideological pressure on their fellow workers.

It seems to follow from consideration of these points that the all-important question of the scope to be given to ideology as against management technique was not definitely solved in the years 1960–65: the struggle over these two criteria continued throughout the period. Many planners and political figures in China rejected the overemphasis on material incentives. They were determined that China, once its temporary economic setbacks had been overcome, should seek an economic system in which man, while seeking a better life, would not pursue this aim *only* through personal consumption and by handing over the creation of an industrial society to technocrats, academics, and planners. The 'New Economic Policy' of 1960–65 ended, then, in a transitional stage and not as the beginning of a new socialist economy. The trend away from ideology was nipped in the bud by the Cultural Revolution launched by Mao Tse-tung in 1965, with its emphasis on the 'human factor' in economic development and the priority to be given to 'moral' rather than 'material' incentives in motivating economic activity.

Economic Policy in the Cultural Revolution, 1966–69

Essentially the Cultural Revolution reversed the principles of the 'New Economic Policy' and restated the basic Maoist ideas on the relationship between making revolution and improving productivity. Cultural Revolution supporters argued that Liu Shao-ch'i's policies and the seventy-point industrial charter would, if unchecked, endanger the development of a new socialist man, and might even influence the political superstructure in the direction of capitalism. A threat was seen to be emerging to the whole value system of Chinese society and to the continuation of revolutionary *élan*.

More specifically, the Cultural Revolution was a response to the character of the education system with its emphasis on technical expertise and professionalism rather than political outlook, and to the danger of growing class differentiation or 'kulakization'[4] in the countryside. The major emphasis in production units swung towards egalitarian wage policies. Bonuses and graduated wage scales were drastically modified, while mobilization around ideological slogans reached a new height.

In the short term, the Cultural Revolution produced some disruption of transport and foreign trade. However 1967 and 1968 were also years of good agricultural results, while the economy as a whole was again booming by 1968. By that time, too, the social and political goals had been largely achieved: the education system was thoroughly transformed to emphasize a more practical and selfless spirit, while scientists and graduates appeared to become more committed to Mao's ideas on the desirable shape of a future Communist society.

The Period of Consolidation, 1969–71

Mao speaks of Chinese policy (and the populace generally) as going through cycles of struggle-criticism-transformation. If this is so, the years 1969–71 are probably best described as a period of transformation, in which the best aspects of the old system were selected to be combined with new approaches thrown up by the Cultural Revolution.

A distinct effort to mechanize agriculture got under way in 1969, with big increases in the tractors available reported from different rural areas. The phenomenon of the 'barefoot doctors', that is young peasants with a few years education and a short course of a few months in basic medical practices, appeared strongly in the rural areas as part of a determined effort to improve public health and hence labour quality.

In some areas a considerable change of emphasis occurred, by comparison with the peak of the Cultural Revolution. There was, for instance, increased resort to foreign technology imports after 1968, as the Chinese sought increasingly to import whole factories. Perusal of the press also indicates a more relaxed attitude to profit criteria within industry, while reports of innovations extolled not only those of the lowly, but also those of people in managerial positions. Besides this, a number of scientists and top administrators who had lost their posts during the Cultural Revolution re-emerged in their old jobs. Even in the new phase, however, it was quite clear that China would continue to follow the doctrines of Mao. It would continue to consider as a 'fetish' the pursuit of maximum economic growth.

Looking at the whole evolution of Chinese economics since 1949, it would be possible to categorize the 1950s as a period of rapid development without full employment; the 1960s as a period of industrial adjustment, regional autonomy, and full employment; and the 1970s as the renewal of industrialization and the achievement of a sophisticated economic structure.

Future Economic Prospects

The most detailed estimates of future Chinese economic development have been compiled by the Nomura Research Institute
in Japan. They predict a 6 per cent annual growth for the
Chinese economy in the 1970s, with industry growing annually
by 8·2 per cent, agriculture by 3 per cent, and other sectors by
6 per cent.

Any acceleration of the growth rate above 8 per cent would
require placing undue burdens on the peasants who are still
regarded as the bulwark of the Communist system. It would also
call for maintaining gross investment at the extremely high rate
of 38 per cent, which would be politically difficult. The survey
points out that an extra 1 per cent growth annually would be
achievable by increasing Chinese trade with the non-Communist
world, and making full use of China's present idle capacity.
Agriculture might remain a big bottleneck. With most arable land
already under cultivation, China is approaching the limit in its
use of chemical fertilizer. It may therefore be necessary, before
the turn of the century, to irrigate the North China Plain—a huge
project requiring many dams and heavy diversion of capital and
manpower resources.

The Chinese Economic Model Summarized

For some people 'development' means increasing the rate of
growth of production at the greatest possible speed through the
use of the most modern methods of science and technology. In
China a wholly different approach prevails although, as we saw,
some Chinese leaders once fought for such a 'maximization' and
'modernization' approach.

The main features of China's development model today,
however, are as follows:

The classical Western pattern of industrialization is avoided. The basic
idea of Chinese communes, first introduced as the main cell in
social life in 1958, has been to halt the flow of peasants to urban
areas. Rather the aim is to bring to the peasants carefully rationed
samples of the fruits of industrial society. Hence Chinese economic
development must be seen in the context of developing an agrarian
socialism, avoiding large-scale labour transfers to the cities. A
decision was taken in 1963 to stabilize the urban population at
110 000 000 and to send graduates and others back to settle in the
countryside as agronomists, as 'peasant doctors', teachers, and so

on. This also means that agriculture has to be given priority, that most new jobs are created in rural areas, so that the terms of trade are being turned in favour of agriculture and against industry.

An egalitarian policy is pursued. Not only is a narrow wage-spread encouraged within the industrial enterprises, but regional disparities are avoided where feasible. The Chinese refer continually to the need to introduce into economic planning, at all levels, the aim of 'overcoming the three differentials'. This refers to the breaking down of sharp distinctions between town and rural living standards, between industry and agriculture, between manual and mental labour. Many development projects are judged on how well they fit in with these criteria, so that Chinese economic planning becomes increasingly 'qualitative' and not one-sidely quantitative. Instead of making a fetish out of maximizing the rate of increase of gross national product, problems are handled as they appear in the regions, and planners develop a qualitative breakdown of economic goals into sectors and priorities.

Choice of technique is designed to create employment. The Chinese strategy allows for more labour-intensive technologies to be chosen than is usual in the course of industrialization.

The human factor and motivation are promoted. An essential element in Chinese practice is the mobilization of moral incentives. Examples of this are commune members working on irrigation projects without any pay in their spare time. Another is the 'worker innovation' movement whereby workers, utilizing scrap metal and material, will sleep at the factory, working overtime together as a team, in order to improve the quality of machinery and raise productivity. Workers who make innovations are often sent around the country with their bedding on their backs to spread such knowledge. Other factories often receive visits from such 'barefoot engineers'. In the rural areas peasants do part-time medical training so that they can undertake treatment of minor ailments, give advice on birth control, organize eradication of pests, etc. Such 'barefoot doctors' now number more than 1 000 000 in China. However Chinese policy also seeks to avoid placing an excessive emphasis upon moral incentives: some material incentives are used, and the system offers solid benefits to all in improvements in the standard of consumption, social services, and economic security.

It is noticeable that there have been five continuous elements of concern: economic growth, income distribution, manpower stabilization, professional expertise, and regional balance/imbalance. At times there have been very sharp clashes on how these issues ought to be handled. Behind all the ideological sound and fury, however, there has been considerable continuity, since about 1955, in building up rural administration and rural 'infrastructure'—public health, water control, agricultural planning, and so on. The Chinese Communist Party has played an ever widening role in agricultural life. The reason is that it has a fraternal life for its members and is not just an administrative structure, while the local officials that it has supported have generally been sensitive to the demands of the local people.

This survey concludes by drawing attention once again to the unique feature of the way that the Chinese Communists have tackled the problem of industrialization within the context of a relatively underdeveloped economy. This is the movement of people from the city to the countryside instead of the reverse pattern, which is universally familiar in India and Latin America. The success of this rustification movement is being closely watched by development economists who will want to know how successful it is, at what economic cost it has been carried out, and what lessons it implies for social development generally.

Notes

1 'Walking on two legs' is a term used in China to denote the use of labour-intensive and capital-intensive technology simultaneously, and the simultaneous use of small-scale and large-scale plants and of Chinese and foreign methods.

2 10 *mou* = $\frac{2}{3}$ hectare

3 A brigade is a subdivision of a people's commune.

4 Kulakization is a reference to the rapid growth of wealthier farmers in the Soviet Union between 1922 and 1928. The kulaks flourished in the relaxed atmosphere towards private agriculture that followed Lenin's New Economic Policy.

Select Bibliography

Buchanan, Keith *The Transformation of the Chinese Earth*, G. Bell and Sons, London, 1970. Marxist geographers are rare, and Keith Buchanan is not only New Zealand's outstanding geographer, but one of the world's best. In this book he stresses the geographical diversity of China and the consequent significance of the province as a centre of social life in modern China. Chapter 5 contrasts Chinese development strategy with the Soviet model and the industrialization path that has been pursued in the West.

Chao Kuo-chun *Agrarian Policy of the Chinese Communist Party 1921–1959*, Asia Publishing House, London, 1960. This book begins with the Yenan period and shows how China's agrarian blueprints took shape in embattled rebel outposts. Excellent section on the land reform 1948–52 and the collectivization drive 1953–56, concluding with an evaluation of the commune movement which swept China in 1958.

Li Choh-ming (ed.) *Industrial Development in Communist China*, Praeger, New York, 1964. A valuable collection of essays on economic policy and economic growth in China before the Cultural Revolution. Particularly noteworthy is the chapter by Franz Schurmann on the right wing 'New Economic Policy' adopted between 1960 and 1964.

Wheelwright, E.L. and **McFarlane, Bruce** *The Chinese Road to Socialism: Economics of the Cultural Revolution*, Monthly Review Press, New York, 1970. This book has been written as a non-technical study of Chinese economic policy. Its main theme is the important role played by ideology and the promotion of the human factor in economic development.

Wu Yuan-li *The Economy of Communist China: An Introduction*, Praeger, New York, 1965. Very clear and concise, covering all sectors of the economy. The author tends to concentrate on showing gaps between proclaimed government objectives and actual results. Very good sections on regional policy.

Chapter 7
Economic geography

Ian Davies

This chapter will endeavour to cover some of the more important aspects of China's economic geography, and will focus on the changes that have taken place since 1949 in the regional distribution of agricultural and industrial activity.[1]

The Rural Sector

About 85 per cent of the Chinese population is rural—or more than 700 000 000 people. These 130 000 000 or so peasant families must not only produce sufficient food for themselves and for the urban population, but also provide raw materials (such as cotton, silk, and oilseeds) for at least half of China's industrial production. In addition, they must produce a small surplus for state taxation (6 per cent), and for export (4 per cent), the latter currently providing half of China's foreign exchange. Agriculture is thus the basis on which the whole economy rests, in spite of the rapid industrialization experienced over the past two decades. Being the pivotal sector of the economy, future economic development will ultimately depend on its rate of progress.

The Distribution of Agricultural Land
Almost all cultivated land—112 000 000 hectares or 11·5 per cent of China's land area—is located in the eastern half of the country. Nearly 80 per cent of China is unsuitable for agriculture because of climatic and topographical limitations, while a further 100 000 000 hectares of pasture, forest, or marshland has only been partially (4 per cent) reclaimed. In view of the large population and the relative shortage of farmland (0·15 hectares per rural inhabitant), arable land must be used in a way that ensures the greatest possible yield.

Thus agriculture in China has been characterized by intensive cultivation with relatively high yields per unit area, but low output per man. This unfavourable balance between land and rural population can be expressed another way—China, with less than 8 per cent of the world's cultivated area, has to support almost 25 per cent of the world's population. This degree of imbalance has often been regarded as inhibiting economic growth, although the Chinese have pointed out that the rational mobilization of their large labour force is an enormous source of capital accumulation, from which further wealth could be created if used properly and wisely.

Being large, and being the world's most populous country (with a population of nearly 900 000 000), it is not surprising that China is also the world's largest producer of many important food crops —rice, sorghum *(kaoliang)*, soybeans, millet, barley, peanuts, tea, and sweet potatoes—and a producer of a wide variety of foods and industrial crops. Rice, wheat, potatoes, maize, and beans, in that order of importance, have been its food staples, with wheat predominating in the north and rice in the south, and an even combination of both along the Yangtze River Valley.

Of China's industrial crops, cotton is by far the most important, followed by other fibres and oilseeds, many of which are exported. Pigs, poultry, and fish provide the bulk of animal protein, while a wide variety of vegetables and fruits are becoming large and increasingly important elements in the Chinese diet. But the diet and calorie intake of the average Chinese is tied very closely to each season's harvest; there is very little surplus to fall back on in the event of a poor crop. However hunger and mass starvation, which characterized China in the first half of this century, have now been eliminated through increased food output combined with relatively effective government control over the distribution system.

Furthermore, state reserves of grain have now been built up to a level equivalent to over two months of grain supply for every inhabitant (four times as large as in 1957–58), guaranteeing protection to the Chinese against even the worst harvests. In the future the Chinese hope to raise the per capita food intake largely through greater per hectare yields and the expansion of double cropping. This is now expected to be achieved through the adoption of more scientific farming methods, the greater use of chemical fertilizers and mechanization, and the expansion of irrigation and drainage facilities, rather than through bringing new land into cultivation, as was the policy during the 1950s.

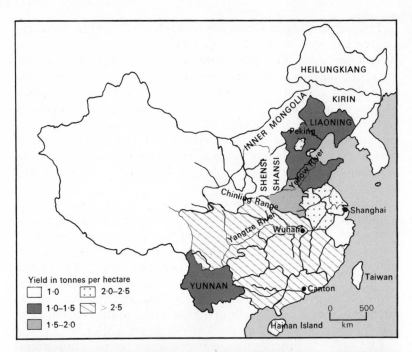

Yield in tonnes per hectare

- □ 1·0
- ■ 1·0–1·5
- ▨ 1·5–2·0
- ⋯ 2·0–2·5
- ▧ > 2·5

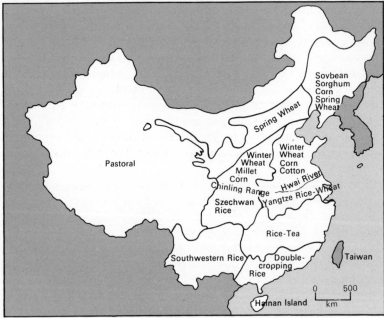

Above—Grain yields in eastern China, 1957

Below—Agricultural areas of China

Foodgrains

The top map opposite shows clearly the wide variation in grain output per unit area in China. The Chinling Range-Hwai River boundary clearly divides the high yielding predominantly rice areas of the south from the lower yielding wheat and coarse grain areas of the north. As a result, the diet in the south and east is based largely on rice, while that in the north is more varied being based on wheat, sorghum, millet, barley, corn, and beans. However a considerable amount of rice is consumed in the north. The bulk of this rice has to be transported to the north from surplus areas in the south, such as Szechwan, Kwangtung, and Hunan. The accelerated growth of northern cities during the industrialization drive of the 1950s increased the level of interregional shipments of grain. In addition to the rice shipments, considerable quantities of wheat were railed from Heilungkiang and Inner Mongolia to supply these cities and such traditional grain deficit provinces as Liaoning, Hopei, Shensi, and Shantung. During the 1960s and 1970s imports of wheat from Australia, Canada, and Argentina into the coastal cities considerably reduced the long interregional shipments of wheat, thereby relieving the overburdened railway system. However of greater significance was the achievement of self-sufficiency in grain in Hopei and Shantung Provinces in 1970 and in Honan Province in 1972. This was largely the result of the expansion of irrigation facilities associated with the Hai, Hwai, Han, and Yellow River water control schemes.

Rice accounts for roughly 45 per cent of China's total grain output and is the highest yielding grain in China. Current production is in the vicinity of 115 000 000 tonnes. Rice has traditionally grown south of the Yangtze and in the valley itself. Over the last fifteen years, however, rice cultivation has been extended northward through the expansion of irrigation. Greater use of fertilizer, better water control, and improved seeds have also contributed to a rise in rice yields, particularly in the traditional areas of the south. It is now common practice for two rice crops to be grown in the south and for rice and wheat to be double cropped in the Yangtze-Hwai regions.

Second to rice in terms of area under cultivation and total production is wheat, which has long been the staple grain product for over 30 per cent of the population—those living in northern China. It is cultivated mainly in the sorghum and winter wheat regions of Honan, Shantung, Hopei, Shansi, Shensi, and southern Kansu. The Yangtze Valley is also an important wheat producer where it is grown with rice and cotton. The lower yielding spring wheat (sown in spring) accounts for 10 per cent of total wheat production, and is generally grown north and west of the Great Wall—in Heilungkiang, Inner Mongolia, western Kansu, and Sinkiang—where colder winters and shorter growing seasons do not favour winter wheat (sown in autumn and harvested in summer). The level of mechanization in wheat sowing and harvesting is higher than other crops, and particularly in Northeast China, Sinkiang, Hopei, and Shantung Provinces (where up to 50 per cent of the farmland is now tractor-ploughed). Total production of wheat in China is currently estimated at 40 000 000 tonnes.

Foodgrains other than rice and wheat belong to the category of the 'coarse grains' and include corn, millet, sorghum, and barley. These grains account for about 30 per cent of total grain output. Corn is the most important crop in this category, with production currently around 30 000 000 tonnes. It is grown mainly in hilly areas, or where rice or wheat cannot be grown, and in southwest China it is double cropped with rice. It is found widely throughout China, from Yunnan through to Northeast China.

Oil-bearing and Fibre Crops

Oil-bearing crops account for over 10 per cent of the total sown acreage in China, and are extremely important in a country where there is a traditional shortage of animal protein and fats. Soybeans are by far the most important of these. Production of soybeans is around 10 000 000 tonnes, of which nearly 40 per cent is grown in Northeast China, and over 35 per cent in north China and Shantung Province. Soybeans are often grown in rotation with sorghum, millet, or corn. While principally for human consumption, in the form of oil and bean curd, it is also an important raw material in the manufacture of soap, paint, lubricants, and fertilizer. Other oil-bearing crops include peanuts (grown mainly in Shantung, Hopei, and Honan), cottonseed, rapeseed, and sesame seed. Rape is cultivated along the Yangtze while sesame is grown largely in central China. Tung oil, used for varnishes and enamels, is produced from the tung tree and is harvested mainly in Hunan and Szechwan Provinces.

Among fibre crops, cotton is the most important, followed by jute, ramie, hemp, and flax. Cotton grows principally in north China and the loesslands of Shensi and Kansu. However the Yangtze Valley and Szechwan are also important producers, and since 1957 there have been attempts to introduce the crop in areas further south. Per hectare yields have been rising in recent years (being highest in the Yangtze Delta), with the result that production of ginned cotton has increased from around 1 600 000 tonnes in 1957 to about 2 500 000 tonnes today (production of cotton during the 1930s averaged only 1 000 000 tonnes).

Cotton is largely grown in rotation with wheat or sorghum in north China and double cropped with rice along the lower Yangtze Valley. In recent years China has had to import 10 per cent of her cotton requirements from the United States and the Middle East to enable her to meet her rising textile export commitments and provide more clothing for the domestic market.

The Cropping Pattern in China

The pattern of agriculture which has developed over the centuries has been mainly determined by climatic conditions, although water utilization and the availability of transport and marketing facilities have also exerted considerable influence on land utilization. This pattern is quite complex, but it is possible to divide the country into simplified agricultural zones. Three classifications are given below.

The first zonal classification is that of J.L. Buck, who carried out his research between 1929 and 1933 (see the bottom map, page 114). These basic zones depict clearly the Chinling Range-Hwai River dividing line between the predominantly southern rice region and the northern wheat and coarse grain region of China Proper. A second method of classification, used by Chinese and Russian geographers, divides the country into four zones, based largely on temperature and the length of the growing season. These zones, and some of the factors relevant to them, are shown in the table on page 118 which refers specifically to 1957 (the only year for which detailed statistics are available).

A third zonal classification of Chinese agriculture is of Chinese origin and is rather more detailed than the previous two. It brings into sharper focus the diversity of the Chinese countryside. The map on page 120 indicates the major crop assemblages in China; many of the previously mentioned zones and major divides are recognizable in the map. In addition other land uses, such as tree crops and fruits, sugarcane, sericulture, and livestock grazing, are shown.

From these three regional classifications, it can be seen that it is in the heavily populated delta and plain regions of eastern, central, and southern China that agriculture is most intensive and

Type of zone	Regions applicable	Type of produce	Rural population (millions)	Agricultural population (millions)	Cultivated area (per cent)	Agricultural production (per cent)	Cultivated land per rural inhabitant (hectares)
one crop per year	north of Great Wall	spring wheat, spring-planted coarse grain crops	51·3	10·2	22·8	16·7	0·5
three crops in two years	south of Great Wall, north of Chinling Range	wheat, sorghum, millet, corn, soybeans, cotton	163·0	32·4	37·9	28·1	0·26
two crops per year	Hwai-Yangtze Valley, Hunan, Kiangsi, coastal Chekiang, Fukien, Szechwan	cotton, rice, tea, sweet potatoes, tobacco	239·5	47·6	31·1	45·7	0·15
three crops per year	south of Nanling Range, southern Fukien, Kwangtung, Kwangsi	rice, sweet potatoes, maize	49·3	9·8	6·2	9·5	0·14

highly productive. These two and three crop per year regions accounted for only 40 per cent of the cultivated area in the late 1950s, but contributed to 55 per cent of crop production, indicating the higher yields obtainable from paddy rice.

The availability of irrigated land and a longer growing season in these areas, together with adequate labour and animal power (derived from greater population density), have been the key to the higher productive nature of these regions. Conversely, a higher yield has been necessary to support the higher population densities of the east and south. Compared with the average area of farmland per rural inhabitant in China (0·2 hectares in 1957), the colder coarse grain region of Northeast China can only support a rural population density of 0·5 hectares, whereas the more fertile and productive Yangtze Delta could support a density of 0·07 hectares per rural inhabitant, while that of the Chengtu Plain in Szechwan could support a density of 0·10 hectares.

Because of the substitution of higher yielding rice on acreage formerly sown to lower yielding coarse grain or wheat, overall yields have risen considerably since 1949—between 1950 and 1957 the average per cultivated hectare yield in China increased by 33 per cent, and between 1957 and 1971 by 35 per cent. The expansion in irrigation and drainage has been the key to the overall increase in output of grain in China over the last two decades, as the area under paddy rice can only be extended further by means of irrigation, while high and stable yields of wheat, cotton, and coarse grain in northern China can only be guaranteed by various water conservancy and drainage measures. In the past inadequate and unreliable rainfall has been the major deterrent in the northward extension of rice cultivation, while inadequate labour, animal power, and fertilizer have been barriers to an extension of double cropping acreage.

In the 1930s the practice of double cropping was largely confined to the provinces of Kwangtung, Kwangsi, and Fukien. Double cropping was unknown in Szechwan. By 1957, however, double cropping of rice had doubled, and spread to Szechwan and the Yangtze Valley. As a result the three original southern provinces accounted for only 45 per cent of double cropping rice acreage in 1957, while central and southwestern China accounted for 42 per cent, compared with 11 per cent in the early 1930s.

Following a re-examination of agricultural policies in 1960–61 as a result of very poor harvests in 1959–61, the rural communes were reorganized into smaller units (now there are more than 50 000 communes, each with an average population between

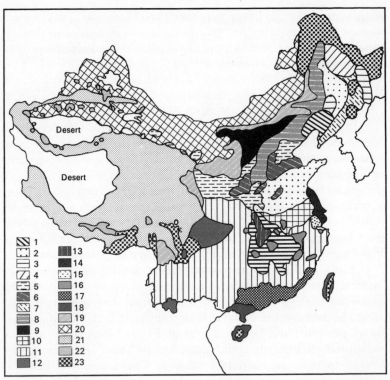

Major crop assemblages (from K. Buchanan *The Transformation of the Chinese Earth*, G. Bell and Sons, 1970)

Key 1 cotton/sorghum, 2 soybean/sorghum, 3 sorghum, 4 wheat/oil seeds,
    5 wheat/miscellaneous grains, 6 cotton/wheat, 7 maize, 8 maize/millet,
    9 potatoes/grain, 10 rice/wheat, 11 rice/maize/timber, 12 rice, 13 cotton/rice,
    14 cotton, 15 rice/wheat/silk, 16 tea, 17 rice/sugar/tropical fruits,
    18 rubber/tropical crops, 19 semi-farming/livestock, 20 desert grazing,
    21 mountain grazing, 22 oases (including agricultural area of Tibet),
    23 forest

Cultivated, sown, and irrigated land in China (million hectares)

Year	Cultivated land	Sown land	Irrigated land	Per cent of irrigated land serviced by mechanical pumps
1933	98·07	131·4	26·53	–
1952	107·92	141·26	25·85	negligible
1957	111·83	157·24	34·67	0·4
1964	112·00	160·00	37·00	3·2
1974	112·00	175·00	over 40	14·4

10 000 and 15 000) and state investment in agriculture was increased. Investment was channelled into rural electrification, the greater mechanization of irrigation and farmwork, the expansion of chemical fertilizer and insecticide production, and the adoption of improved seeds and farming methods.

Attention was also given to drainage in the north (to overcome the adverse effects of salinity and alkalization caused by various ill-considered irrigation schemes built during the Great Leap), the expansion of smaller irrigation works (in contrast to the earlier concentration on the large Hwai, Yellow, and Yangtze Valley projects, which were more related to flood control than irrigation), and to efforts to boost production in areas which produce large agricultural surpluses (in the Yangtze and Pearl River Deltas, the Hsiang River Valley, and the Chengtu Plains of Szechwan). These developments resulted in the total irrigated land reaching 37 000 000 hectares in 1964, or one-third of the total cultivated acreage in China.

Rural electrification jumped twenty-five-fold between 1957 and 1964, extending the area serviced by mechanical irrigation and drainage pumps and, as a result, the area capable of sustaining high yields. This, together with a five-fold expansion in the number of tractors and the spread of mechanized threshers, have enabled the double cropping of rice and other crops to expand much further.

Developments in the late 1960s and into the 1970s have reflected the continued high priority enjoyed by the agricultural sector. Although mechanization is still on a small scale, the level has recently accelerated, particularly as a result of the widespread use of small hand tractors in southern paddy fields, mechanized transplanters, and the expansion of rural electrification. By 1974, rural mechanical pumping capacity had increased by five times compared with that of 1964, and was over forty times as great as in 1957. Irrigation is estimated to have expanded to over 40 000 000 hectares by 1974, of which nearly 15 per cent, concentrated in the North China Plain and the Yangtze-Hwai River Valleys, is mechanized.

The use of chemical fertilizers has also increased rapidly (in the past decade it rose six times), although it remains considerably below the level current in Japan and Taiwan. Chinese farm practices, however, include the use of large amounts of pig manure, human nightsoil, and green manure (nitrogen rich weeds and crops which are ploughed back into the soil). These recent improvements undoubtedly played an important role in the steady increase in grain output during the late 1960s. In 1974 grain production exceeded 260 000 000 tonnes, up 40 per cent on the 185 000 000 tonne harvest of 1957, or comfortably ahead of the rate of population increase.

As a result of this recent 'modern' revolution in Chinese agriculture, two rice crops a year are now common between the Yangtze and the Hwai Rivers in Anhwei and Kiangsu Provinces. In addition, the Hwai River no longer acts as a clear demarcation point between the three crops in two years zone and the two crops a year region, since the latter practice has now spread northwards with the completion of the major irrigation projects associated with the Hwai and the Hai Rivers. Even the countryside around Peking is currently changing over to two crops a year: rice and wheat—excluding the vegetable growing sector. Elsewhere rice yields are rising and many regions south of the Hwai, such as Chekiang and Kwangtung, are now producing six tonnes per hectare.

Animal Husbandry and Fisheries
The raising of livestock has always been a sideline endeavour in China Proper, but is the principle occupation among many of the non-Chinese groups of western China and Inner Mongolia, where large pasturelands are located. Because of the dense population of eastern China, little land can be spared for grazing. In addition, traditional Chinese agriculture has always depended heavily on draft animals for ploughing and transportation and on pigs for manure. Consequently the per capita consumption of meat (excluding poultry and fish) is very small, and averages only 4 kilograms per annum or 2 per cent of the Chinese diet (the Australian consumption level is one of the world's highest—at 95 kilograms per head).

The most numerous domestic animals are pigs, which live on farm refuse. The pig population has increased steadily since 1949, except for the poor harvest years of 1959–62, and is currently estimated to number over 200 000 000. They are raised throughout China, the majority being privately owned, and are particularly numerous in provinces with dense rural populations such as Szechwan and in the Yangtze and Canton Deltas. They are valued for the abundant fertilizer (manure) which they produce, for their bristles (for export), and for pork, which accounts for the bulk of meat consumed in China.

Oxen and water buffalo are found throughout southern China, while horses, donkeys, and mules are common in areas north of the Yangtze. They are used as draft animals and producers of fertilizer and are rarely slaughtered for their meat. Moreover the dairy industry is fairly small because of the Chinese dislike for milk. Sheep and goats are also found throughout China Proper, but are more numerous in Inner Mongolia and western China where they are found in large flocks. They are kept primarily for their wool, manure, and milk, but in Inner Mongolia and in areas inhabited by Moslems mutton is the staple food for the local herdsmen. In contrast, mutton is regarded with distaste by the Chinese.

Fish is one of the major items of animal protein in the average Chinese diet, especially in coastal areas. More than half of the total catch, averaging 7 000 000 tonnes per annum, comes from the sea and, in particular, in shallow water off the coastal provinces of Chekiang, Fukien, and Kwangtung. One-third of the fish consumed in China is of the fresh-water variety.

Forest Resources

In 1949 forests in China covered about 85 000 000 hectares, or 9 per cent of China's total area. Only Szechwan and Northeast China had plentiful timber resources. Areas north of the Yangtze were treeless; to the south, forested areas were more widespread. In the past deforestation had caused a serious shortage of construction timber and fuel, and led to severe soil erosion, particularly in north China.

To overcome these handicaps, a vigorous campaign of tree planting started after 1949. During the First Five Year Plan over 11 000 000 hectares of land were afforested, but during the Great Leap Forward a further 40 000 000 hectares were planted, an area almost equivalent to the size of France. This campaign has continued throughout the 1960s, with the result that by the early

1970s the forested areas of China are estimated to have doubled to become 20 per cent of China's total area.

Commercial reafforestation, largely pine, has been concentrated in areas south of the Yangtze. Much has also been done in Inner Mongolia, the Loess Plateau, and northern Kansu, largely to halt the advance of sand dunes. Fruit trees, poplar, willow, bamboo, and pine now cover most of the hilly terrain of southern China and line almost every canal, road, and railway throughout the rest of China. China's finest timber grows in the Great and Little Khingan Ranges and the Changpei Mountains of Northeast China, and includes Korean pine, spruce, larch, oak, Japanese birch, and pine trees. This area accounts for 40 per cent of China's timber production.

China is still short of timber and imports logs and sawn timber from North Korea, Africa, and Southeast Asia. Vast areas of north China still remain treeless, although farm and village woodlots are much larger and more numerous than two decades ago. Thus an enormous amount of effective afforestation will still be required in the future to keep pace with lumbering operations, and to maintain a higher level of desert control and a higher pace in soil erosion control.

Population and Land Pressure

A question commonly asked by Westerners is 'can the Chinese living space accommodate the growing multitude of Chinese—or will the future bring a gigantic overspilling into Southeast Asia or elsewhere in the Pacific area?' The writer believes the answer to the first part of the question is 'yes', while there is little evidence to support the latter suggestion.

China's population density is comparatively high (1·1 hectares per head), but as large areas of China are inhospitable because of climate and topography, two-thirds of the Chinese people are concentrated in one-seventh of China's surface, resulting in very congested rural areas in eastern China, where the average area of cultivated land per rural inhabitant is only 0·15 hectares. This in turn leads to a situation where five hundred people may derive their living from an area equal to that of an American or an Australian farm supporting a family of five.

Despite this relatively low level of agricultural productivity, the Chinese have been able to maintain a rate of agricultural expansion above that of population growth over the past two decades, thereby allowing a gradual improvement in the standard of living. Higher crop yields and the introduction of a widespread family planning programme since 1968 (see chapter 9) have proved very effective in relieving China's land pressure problems, but the potential to develop high-yield farmland and to reduce population growth is far from exhausted. For instance, the purchase of urea fertilizer plants from the West in 1973–74 and China's own construction programme will, if supplemented by proper water control facilities, give the potential for a rise in grain production between 1973 and 1980 of 30 per cent, or double the expected rate of population increase. Furthermore, the wider use of high-yield seeds, the expansion of double cropping and mechanized irrigation and drainage facilities, the leveling and terracing of farmland, and the expansion in cultivated land should enable the Chinese to tackle their population/land problem in the foreseeable future. Migration from the congested eastern regions into the sparsely populated areas of the northeast, northwest, and Inner Mongolia has also relieved land pressure in the high density regions. The intensification of these programmes will be necessary in the future to absorb the growing population, but on the basis of China's past performance and in view of China's grand plans over the remainder of this decade to boost agricultural-support industries, there is no reason to believe that population absorption cannot be maintained in the future. If 'overspilling' is to eventually take place, it will be in the underdeveloped areas of western and northern China, rather than in the Southeast Asian region.

The Industrial Pattern

The new Communist government in 1949 inherited a relatively backward and partially destroyed industrial base from the Nationalists. In addition, the new regime had to cope with raging inflation, a disrupted railway network, a disorganized agricultural system, and severe shortages of fuel, food, and investment funds. On coming to power, the Chinese Communists made it quite clear that following rehabilitation, their aim of industrializing the economy on a socialist basis was paramount, with priority to be given to heavy industry and a wider transport network. They were conscious of the fact that what modern industry existed in China was heavily localized along the coast and in Manchuria, while potentially rich inland areas of north, central, and southwest China had long been neglected.

Accordingly their prime task, apart from rehabilitating the Manchurian industrial base with Soviet aid, was to promote the industrialization of the inland. The inland, therefore, has been given priority attention in Chinese industrial investment programmes since 1950, but initially (1950–55) this was done at the expense of coastal industry. Following a review of industrial location policy in 1955–56, coastal plants were no longer neglected, as it was found that considerable excess capacity existed in Shanghai, Tientsin, and other port cities which could be effectively utilized without large outlays in investment.

During the Great Leap Forward (1958–60) inland industry was expanded more rapidly, but instead of concentrating investment in a few inland centres as in the First Five Year Plan (at Wuhan, Sian, Lanchow, Chengtu, Chengchow, Loyang, Paotow, Peking, Changchun, and Harbin), a more decentralized (in management) and dispersed (in location) industrial pattern arose, largely in the smaller and medium cities. Although many of the small plants which emerged during this period were closed down during the following economic crisis and rationalization programme (1961–63), the basic pattern as established in 1958–59 continued throughout the 1960s and 1970s, with the small and medium plants being emphasized once again after 1969.

As a result, total industrial capacity today (1975) is not only seven times as large as the level in 1952 (representing an industrial growth rate of 9 per cent per annum), but through the dispersal of industry, it has now achieved a high degree of regional balance, in which China's seven major economic regions and most of her provinces have developed independent and in many cases self-sufficient industrial zones. The re-emergence of the small industry sector after 1969 on a more economically rational basis has created the basis for what appears to be a successful rural industrialization programme, which will in turn create a denser industrial pattern and a more complicated industrial structure. During the current Fourth Five Year Plan (1971–75), it appears that inland centres will continue to receive priority treatment, with particular attention being given to southwest China (following the completion of important railway trunk routes in the southwest in 1970 and between the southwest and central China in 1973–74), with coastal industries in Shanghai, Tientsin, Canton, Shantung, and Liaoning providing most of the funds for this inland development drive.

Currently it is estimated that China's coastal industries still produce 50–60 per cent of total industrial output, but this is a great change from the situation in 1949 and 1952 when coastal centres accounted for 77 and 73 per cent of the nation's industrial production respectively. No longer is China burdened by a situation which existed in 1952—in which 50 per cent of the nation's industrial enterprises and workers were located in the single city of Shanghai, while inland areas had only very few modern industrial enterprises, but 86 per cent of the land and 58 per cent of the population. Today the inland is estimated to produce around 40 per cent of steel output, one-third of cotton cloth, 50 per cent of machinery, paper, and electric power, and 65 per cent of coal output.

Northeast China remains the country's foremost centre of heavy industry, and is the largest producer of electricity, iron and steel, coal, petroleum, timber, paper, trucks, and heavy machinery. East China leads in the manufacture of textiles and other light industrial goods, but has also become an important heavy industry and machinery region since 1957. The bulk of this region's industrial capacity is centred in Shanghai city. North China ranks third in industrial production, and is a major producer of coal, steel, chemicals, electricity, textiles, and machinery. The two major industrial centres are the Tientsin-Tangshan-Peking zone and Taiyuan city.

Central China is the nation's largest producer of tractors, and a major producer of textiles, steel, heavy machinery, and non-ferrous metals. South China is a major light industry region, specializing in foodstuffs, sugar, paper, silk, and ordinary consumer goods, although it also has a well developed non-ferrous mining industry. Southwest China's industrial development began during the Second World War, but since then the steel, electrical machinery, chemicals, textiles, and non-ferrous metal industries have expanded many times, creating a diversified industrial and self-sufficient region. Northwest China has very little industrial capacity, but since 1949 the petroleum, coal, and textiles industries have experienced a modest build-up. The lack of markets in the northwest, and its remoteness, will inhibit the large-scale development of this region for many decades.

The Iron and Steel Industry
China's iron and steel industry in 1974 was the fifth largest in the world, producing 27 000 000 tonnes of steel and over 35 000 000 tonnes of pig iron, or approximately 5·0 and 5·9 times the level of output in 1957 respectively. Currently the industry is 85 per cent self-sufficient, importing 4 000 000 tonnes of steel products, mainly from Japan. Although total steel consumption is higher than that of France and Britain, it is very small in per

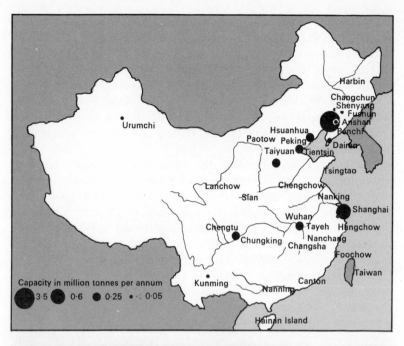

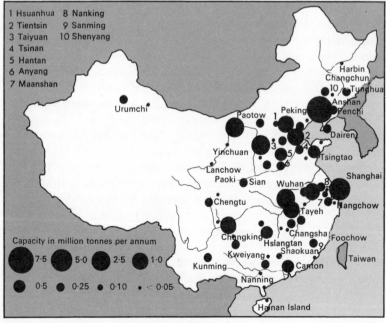

Above—The distribution of steel plants in China, 1957

Below—The distribution of steel plants in China, 1974

capita terms—only 38 kilograms which is 5 per cent of the Japanese and North American level and 6 per cent of the Australian level.

The modern steel industry in China dates back to the 1880s with the construction of the first steel works at Hanyang in central China. During the First World War the now famous Anshan steel centre in Manchuria was established, along with smaller iron plants at Penchi and Peking. Further expansion took place under Japanese control during the Second World War but the entire industry was very lop-sided, as the steel-smelting and rolling industries were neglected while the iron-mining sector was comparatively well developed for the export of iron ore to Japan.

Between 1949 and 1952 the industry quickly recovered and by 1957 had produced 5 350 000 tonnes of steel, of which Anshan accounted for 54 per cent, Shanghai 10 per cent, and Chungking 7 per cent. It was during this period that the Chinese moved to reduce the nation's dependence on Anshan by constructing two large integrated Soviet-assisted steel plants at Wuhan (central China) and at Paotow (Inner Mongolia). These two centres went into operation during the Great Leap Forward (1958–60), when the entire industry was undergoing expansion at an unprecedented rate. This was a period when over a dozen new medium-scale plants were constructed in provinces which formerly had no steel industry, and when thousands of small-scale units using both modern and indigenous methods of production were installed. The small units were soon abandoned because of the poor quality of their products and their high cost.

Very little expansion took place in the 1960s as the withdrawal of Soviet aid in 1960 delayed the completion of the Wuhan and Paotow steel plants, and existing capacity was capable of meeting almost all of China's steel requirements. However the regional distribution of steel production was more in balance with consumption compared with the situation in the 1950s, each major region having striven to attain a relatively high degree of self-sufficiency. Further expansion took place after 1969, with the construction of a new plant at Chiayukuan in Kansu Province, and the building of new facilities at most established large and medium-scale plants. New techniques were adopted and large scale steel-rolling mills were purchased from Japan and West Germany. Currently Anshan produces 30 per cent of the nation's steel output of 27 000 000 tonnes, followed by Shanghai, Wuhan, Paotow, Taiyuan, and Peking. Medium and small-scale plants are estimated to produce 20 per cent of China's steel output.

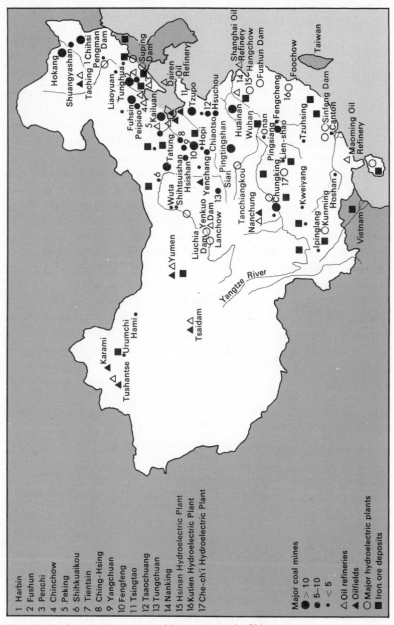

The distribution of fuel, power, and iron resources in China

1 Harbin
2 Fushun
3 Penchi
4 Chinchow
5 Peking
6 Shihkuaikou
7 Tientsin
8 Ching-Hsing
9 Yangchuan
10 Fengfeng
11 Tsingtao
12 Tsaochuang
13 Tungchuan
14 Nanking
15 Hsinan Hydroelectric Plant
16 Kutien Hydroelectric Plant
17 Che-ch'i Hydroelectric Plant

Major coal mines
● > 10
● 5–10
• < 5

△ Oil refineries
▲ Oilfields
○ Major hydroelectric plants
■ Iron ore deposits

China's policy of regional self-sufficiency has also resulted in the relative reduction in the interregional flow of steel products, iron ore, and coking coal, which in turn has resulted in the lowering of transport costs and thereby overall production costs. However many problems still exist, such as the low grade of ore at many mining sites, the inability to produce certain special steel products, and the existence of two high cost unintegrated steel-making centres at Shanghai and Tientsin.

Fuel and Power Industries

The coal industry in China is the third largest in the world, and is by far the most important fuel in the Chinese economy, accounting for over 75 per cent of all primary energy consumed. Production is currently around 400 000 000 tonnes, compared with 130 000 000 in 1957 and a peak wartime level of 62 000 000 (1942). It is estimated that small-scale mines account for 30 per cent of total production today.

Coal production is concentrated in the north and northeast. These two regions accounted for 52 per cent of coal output in 1959, but as other mining centres have been developed in central, east, and northwest China since then, this share is now likely to have declined. They contain fourteen of China's twenty-three coal-mining centres capable of producing more than 5 000 000 tonnes annually. Currently it is estimated that central China produces 12 per cent of coal production, east China 13 per cent, and southwest China 15 per cent. Coal from northwest and south China is mainly mined by small and medium-scale mines.

We turn now to petroleum, in which China was regarded as being deficient before 1960. Her petroleum industry had long been neglected and was largely supplemented by imports and by shale-oil and synthetic oil produced at the Fushun and Fuhsin mines in the northeast. The oilfields of importance before 1960 were in the northwest. All were long distances from the major petroleum markets of eastern and northern China.

In 1960 the Chinese discovered enormous oil reserves at Taching, northwest of Harbin in Northeast China. As a result of the development of the Taching field, the Chinese were able to phase out imports of petroleum to the extent that by 1965 they had achieved self-sufficiency. National production rapidly increased throughout the 1960s, and by 1974 was in the vicinity of 65 000 000 tonnes (or over seventeen times the level in 1959). It is estimated that Taching accounted for 45 per cent of total output in the early 1970s. During the 1970s it is expected that

China will intensify production of oil from the newer fields along the Pohai Gulf (Shengli and Takang), and that China will become a rapidly growing exporter of crude oil to Japan and Southeast Asia. China's major oil refineries are at Taching, Fushun, Shanghai, Peking, Tzupo, Dairen, Chinchow, Chinsi, Nanking, Anshan, Maoming, and in Sinkiang Province. The growth of the Taching and Shengli fields in the 1960s and the Takang field in the 1970s has completely reorientated the petroleum flow pattern of the 1950s—Taching, Shengli, and Takang now supply the refineries and markets of eastern China, while Lanchow and Yumen continue to be the major centres processing oil from northwest China.

Hydroelectric power facilities in China account for around 20 per cent of total electric power capacity, and prior to 1966 were almost exclusively limited to large-scale schemes, most of which were built or expanded during the 1950s with Soviet assistance. However the withdrawal of Soviet aid in 1960 completely disrupted an ambitious plan to construct many hydroelectric plants throughout China. Although some of the projects were completely or partially finished by the Chinese during the 1960s, many are still only on the drawing boards. Since 1969 emphasis has been placed on the development of small- and medium-scale stations by local authorities (particularly in southwest China where hydroenergy resources are enormous), primarily for the purpose of boosting rural electrification.

China's overall electric power industry is based largely on thermal power plants, most of which are coal fired. It is concentrated in north and Northeast China because of the availability of coal in these areas and the presence of China's largest industrial market. However the degree of localization in these two regions has declined following the establishment of new thermal and hydroelectric plants in east and central China during the Great Leap and in the 1960s and 1970s.

Production of power climbed from 19 300 000 000 kilowatthours in 1957 to around 120 000 000 000 by 1974. Although industry absorbs 75–80 per cent of electric power production in China, the most significant development in the past decade has been the rapid rise in the consumption of electric power in rural areas.

Machinery and Metal Manufacturing
The development of the machine building industry and other

metal manufacturing activities in China has been given high priority throughout the past two decades and, as a result, these have been the fastest growing industrial sectors in China since 1949. Before then metal industries were almost totally foreign-owned and were in a rather backward state of development, producing only a limited variety of products. They were mainly concentrated in Japanese-controlled Manchuria and in the coastal seaports, and were largely associated with foreign shipping companies and the making of armaments.

During the 1950s the metal industry received the largest allocation of capital investment among China's major industry sectors, and the bulk of Soviet economic aid. Over one hundred plants were established during the First Five Year Plan; these included heavy machine tool, truck, tractor, aircraft, mining machinery, electrical, locomotive, power generating, shipbuilding, defence, and textile machinery plants.

In addition to the large modern plants which are the backbone of the metal industry, China has installed (after 1957) thousands of medium- and small-scale enterprises in large and small cities throughout every province. These smaller locally run plants cater for simpler machinery such as agricultural equipment or function as assembly plants using components brought in from the larger machinery centres. For instance, most Chinese provinces have a truck assembly plant, and every county has an agricultural machinery assembly and repair plant, producing finished goods largely from components shipped from Shanghai, Peking, or Northeast China.

The leading manufacturing centres are Shenyang in Northeast China, which specializes in heavy machinery, Shanghai (specializing in precision goods), Tientsin, and Harbin. These four cities accounted for nearly 60 per cent of China's metal industry output in the late 1950s. Since then this proportion has declined as new machinery centres have arisen elsewhere in China.

The quality, variety, and level of sophistication in China's metal industries have now reached the stage where China is 95 per cent self-sufficient in machinery of all kinds compared with only 55 per cent in 1957. China now exports machine tools and other light engineering goods to Southeast Asia and Hong Kong and, although she is a net importer of machinery, China in most cases imports only high quality equipment with a high technological content, much of which is used as prototypes for copying (after adjustments to suit China's conditions), thus saving enormous expenditure on research and development.

Above—A cotton textile mill in Peking

Below—A small steel plant in Shanghai where various odd-shaped seamless tubes are produced

The Chemical Industry

Prior to 1949 China's chemical industry could only supply a small proportion of total requirements, and was closely associated with coke by-product plants and the coal industry at Anshan, Fushun, and Kirin in Manchuria, the sea salt industry of Tientsin and Shanghai, and the salt brine industry at Tsekung in Szechwan. During the First Five Year Plan the industry slowly developed around these old chemical centres, the acid, dye, paint, drug, and fertilizer industries being the fastest growing sectors. The chemical fertilizer industry, however, expanded rapidly around the plants of Nanking, Taiyuan, Kaifeng, and Dairen, resulting in total fertilizer output rising from 190 000 tons in 1952 to 870 000 in 1957.

During the Great Leap, and particularly in the 1960s and early 1970s, the fertilizer industry was considered one of the key factors in the improvement of China's agricultural economy and received priority attention. Its growth has consequently been fast. Recently emphasis has been placed on the establishment of medium and small plants dispersed throughout the countryside. By 1974 fertilizer output had grown to nearly 30 000 000 tonnes, of which half was produced by small and medium plants. Currently every province and most counties have chemical fertilizer plants, most of which rely on local coal and phosphate deposits. The greater availability of fertilizer and the closer proximity of these plants to the agricultural market has been one of the major reasons for the recent boost in grain output.

The Textile Industry

The textile industry is China's leading light industry. Before 1949 it had long been the most important of China's modern industries and symbol of the country's economic development. It is dominated by the manufacture of cotton yarn and cloth, but also includes silk, wool, and recently synthetic fabrics. Currently around 8 500 000 000 square metres of cotton cloth, over 500 000 000 of synthetic fabrics, over 200 000 000 of silk fabrics, and 50 000 000 of woollen fabrics are produced annually, compared with 5 050 000 000 square metres of cotton cloth, 15 000 000 of synthetic fabrics, 145 000 000 of silk fabrics, and 10 200 000 of woollen fabrics in 1957.

Cotton is by far the most important of the various types of textile industry. In 1936 80 per cent of the nation's total cotton spindle capacity was concentrated on the eastern seaboard in the cities of Shanghai, Tientsin, Tsingtao, and in Kiangsu Province;

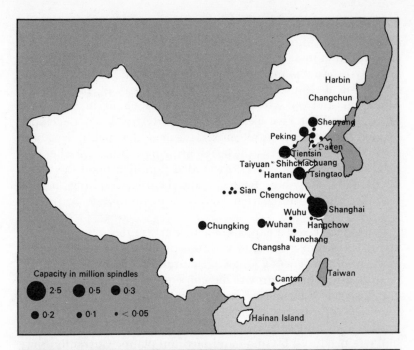

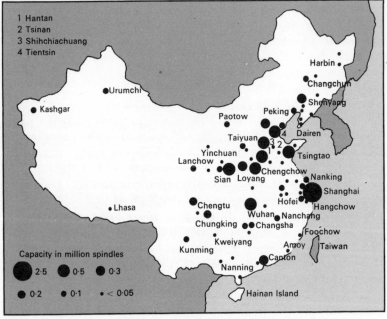

Above—The distribution of cotton textile mills in China, 1946

Below—The distribution of cotton textile mills in China, 1974

Shanghai alone had 53 per cent of the nation's spindles. In contrast, China's cotton crop was grown mainly in the North China Plain, the Wei River Valley of southern Shensi and in central China. Consequently 75 per cent of the cotton crop had to be transported over long distances to the coastal mills for conversion into textiles. In addition, the coastal mills relied extensively on imported American cotton—Shanghai in 1936 imported 48 per cent of all requirements from overseas.

The regional imbalance in 1952 showed no change from the prewar situation. Inland cotton mills accounted for 12 per cent of total textile production but inland cotton regions produced 49 per cent of the total cotton crop. During the First Five Year Plan, in an effort to bring the textile industry closer to the cotton growing areas, the Chinese fostered the construction of forty-four new cotton mills in inland centres, notably at Sian, Chengchow, Shihchiachuang, Hantan, Peking, Hsienyang, Wuhan, and Chengtu. In this period the number of cotton spindles rose by nearly half to 8 100 000 in 1957.

Shanghai remained the main textile centre, but its proportion of the nation's total spindlage declined to 30 per cent in 1957, while its share of total production of cotton cloth was reduced to 22 per cent (compared with over 50 per cent in 1936). However, despite the greater regional balance between cotton production and the output of textiles by 1957, Shanghai still had to ship in two-thirds of its cotton requirements from provinces beyond Kiangsu and, in return, shipped 60 per cent of its cotton textiles to inland markets.

During the Great Leap Forward many new textile centres arose and the total number of spindles had risen to 9 500 000 by 1960. Capital investment in the industry came to a standstill between 1961 and 1964 because of poor cotton harvests and gross under-utilization of capacity, but in 1965–66 an extra 1 400 000 new spindles were added to mills located in the cotton growing areas of north China, Sinkiang, and the middle Yangtze region.

During the 1960s exports of textiles increased rapidly (in 1966 15 per cent of production was exported), as did the variety and quality of the products. China is estimated to be now in the possession of over 11 000 000 spindles, which are now more evenly distributed throughout the nation, and the cotton growing areas in particular, than at any time in the past. However cotton textiles are still in short supply and have long been rationed. The rations vary according to location and are higher in northern regions.

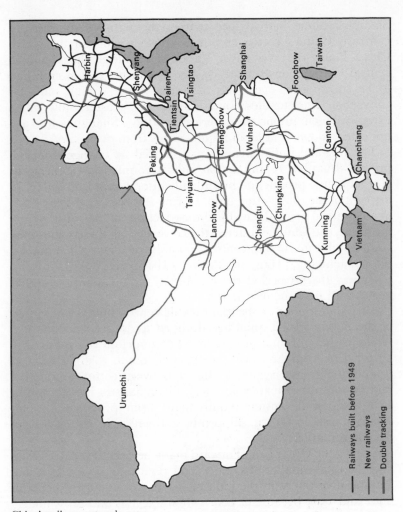

Railways built before 1949

New railways

Double tracking

China's railway network, 1974

Other textile industries, like silk, wool, and synthetic fibres, are very much less significant than cotton. Silk, for which China is traditionally famous, is heavily concentrated in the Yangtze Delta. Synthetic textiles, on the other hand, are a very recent development and are distributed evenly throughout the cities of north and eastern China. This last industry is expected to grow rapidly after 1975.

The Pattern of Transportation

Before 1949 China's lack of an adequate transport system was a major obstacle to the country's economic development. It was also an important factor in creating disunity and warlordism in the past. One of the major problems faced by the new Communist government in 1949 was to construct a transport network large enough to meet the demands of an expanding economy, to ensure the defence of certain vulnerable areas, and to create national unity.

During the past two decades the network has expanded considerably and now links every province and region. However it is still inadequate for China's economic needs; some sectors are primitive while others are overburdened. Railways are by far the most important component of China's transportation system, accounting for two-thirds of the tonnage of freight loadings and three-quarters of the freight traffic. Roads and waterways, both inland and coastal, play a secondary role. In 1949 only 11 000 kilometres of railways were left in operation out of a total length of 22 000 kilometres. Rehabilitation and the construction of new railways in Szechwan, Fukien, south China, Inner Mongolia, and northwest China extended the length of China's railways to 29 800 kilometres by 1957. Further expansion of facilities in northwest, southwest, and central China during the Great Leap, the 1960s, and the 1970s, and the laying of branch lines, narrow forest, and rural railways had boosted railway trackage to about 45 000 kilometres by 1974.

Today all provincial capitals (except that of Tibet) are linked by railway. The construction of the Yangtze River bridges at Wuhan (1957), Chungking (1959), and Nanking (1968) has also considerably improved rail services. However, while other countries have long since converted their railways to diesel, China continued to rely heavily on steam locomotives because of her vast coal resources and shortage of petroleum products. Recently, however, diesel locomotives have been appearing in greater numbers and now account for nearly 20 per cent of China's total locomotive inventory.

China currently has 670 000 kilometres of highways and roads, or nine times the length of 1949. The most significant developments in highway construction in China were the roads built from Szechwan and Chinghai into Tibet and Sinkiang. Very few roads outside the major Chinese cities are macadamized, while China's lorry fleet stands at less than 1 000 000—a small number compared with China's large area and population. Motor transport is significant only in the cities, the Tibetan Highlands, and in Sinkiang. Elsewhere the traditional form of transport—5 000 000 mule and horse carts and 10 000 000 hand carts—plays a vital role.

Inland water traffic (147 000 kilometres in route length) handles three-quarters of the cargo transported by water in China. Almost 70 per cent of this traffic is carried along the Yangtze; the remainder is shared by the West River in south China and the Sungari in the northeast. The principal coastal port is Shanghai, which serves as the basic transhipment centre between the Yangtze River traffic and coastal shipping, and also handles half of China's foreign trade. China's other major ports, in order of importance, are Dairen, Hsinkang (near Tientsin), Tsingtao, Whampoa (near Canton), Chanchiang, and Chinwangtao. China's coastal shipping industry has, until recently, been neglected, because of the shortage of shipping. However the Chinese shipbuilding industry has recently been developing rapidly. As a result, coastal shipping has been put to greater use, especially in the northern shipping zone between Dairen, Tientsin, and Shanghai.

China's domestic airlines total some 50 000 kilometres and connect Peking with most of the large cities of China. The busiest routes are those between Peking and Shanghai, Peking and Canton, Peking and Sian, and Peking to Shenyang and Harbin. International services have long linked China with the Soviet Union (Irkutsk and Moscow), North Korea (Pyongyang), North Vietnam (Hanoi), Burma (Rangoon), Pakistan (Karachi), and France (Paris). In 1973–74 new routes were introduced to Bombay and Addis Ababa (Ethiopia), Tokyo, Laos (Vientiane), Iran (Tehran), and Europe. On domestic flights CAAC, China's airline, long operated relatively old turbo-prop planes of Soviet and British make. However, from 1973, the airline system has been modernized by the introduction of imported Trident and Boeing 707 aircraft. Shanghai and Peking are by far China's busiest domestic and international airports.

Other chapters have explained how social and ideological factors have contributed to the growth of the Chinese economy since liberation. From the point of view of economic geography, however, the most important point is the largely successful attempt to make development not merely centred on a few large cities but to spread it evenly throughout the country. The emphasis on rural industry and regional self-reliance is of special significance in this regard. Undoubtedly the general policy of decentralization has strengthened the Chinese economy to an unprecedented extent and is one factor which allows for considerable optimism over the future.

Note

1 Statistical information in this chapter has come from a wide variety of sources. The majority of figures quoted are from official Chinese sources such as *Ten Great Years*, Foreign Languages Press, Peking, 1960, and various issues of *China Reconstructs* and *Peking Review*. The writer has also relied heavily on figures published in the US Congress Joint Economic Committee, *People's Republic of China: an Economic Assessment*, 18 May 1972, US Government Printing Office, as well as on articles published in *The China Quarterly*.

Select Bibliography

Buchanan, K. *The Transformation of the Chinese Earth*, G. Bell and Sons, London, 1970. A very useful book, with good chapters on key economic sectors; a generally sympathetic approach to the Chinese human experiment.

C.I.A. *The People's Republic of China Atlas*, November 1971. An excellent up-to-date atlas, showing factors such as the distribution of agricultural activity, industrial and mining activity, population, and transport routes.

De Crespigny, R. *China: the Land and its People*, Nelson (Aust.) Ltd, Melbourne, 1971. A useful reference, focusing on the economic and physical features of each major region in China.

Joint Economic Committee of the US Congress *People's Republic of China: An Economic Assessment*, US Government Printing Office, Washington, 1972. Exclusively economic but contains very useful up-to-date statistics.

Shabad, T. *China's Changing Map: National and Regional Developments 1949–71*, Praeger, New York, 1972. This is an excellent up-to-date publication, focusing largely on China regional geography (each province is treated separately).

Tuan Yi-fu *China*, No. 1 in the series 'The World's Landscapes', Longman, London, 1970. An interesting analysis of China's historical and human geography.

Part 4
Society and culture
Chapter 8
Chinese society and culture, 1912-49

Colin Mackerras

During the first half of this century China was subject to stresses as intense as any it had known during the whole of its long history. Revolutions, wars, foreign military occupation, and civil influences from abroad all forced the Chinese people to reassess their traditional values and approach to life. In this chapter, four aspects of this changing society are singled out for particular attention. All are important and reflect the political and military history of the period. They are family life, religion and thought, education, and the arts. In view of the tremendous significance attached to family life in debates on philosophy and in the arts, it will be appropriate to discuss this aspect first.

Family Life

Imperial China was an extremely family-orientated society. In accordance with Confucian precepts, it was based upon 'five relationships': ruler-subject, father-son, elder brother-younger brother, husband-wife, and friend-friend, in that order of importance. Hierarchy was of the utmost significance in this structure and the place given to the father-son relationship, well above the husband-wife, was a sign of the overriding emphasis the Confucians laid upon filial piety. The authority of the father as head of the family was supreme, sometimes even tyrannical. He could beat his children or wives mercilessly, and was allowed to sell the former into slavery.

The position of women was extremely low, probably inferior to that of their sisters in most other countries. Female infanticide was fairly widespread, for although filial piety demanded the carrying on of the family line, only sons were considered really adequate to fulfil this foremost duty, daughters being sometimes regarded as dispensable. One aspect of the low status of women was the custom of concubinage, which was virtually universal among the rich. A concubine usually received poor treatment from the main wife, who was naturally jealous of her, yet she rarely won much comfort from her husband, sometimes hardly ever seeing him except in bed. The main wife had no recourse: divorce was possible for men on a variety of grounds, but women enjoyed no reciprocal rights.

Possibly the worst feature of a woman's life was that her feet were bound. From the age of about five girls, no matter what their class background, had to submit to tight cloth wrappings, which effectively prevented their feet from growing. It appears that the principal rationale behind this custom was to increase the sexual fascination of women, yet naturally this did nothing to reduce the pain. All Chinese of both sexes came to regard large feet as ungainly, and the practice ensured that about half the population was crippled and in constant and severe physical discomfort.

The emphasis on hierarchy and the relatively low position of the husband-wife relationship resulted in a system of arranged marriages whereby the prospective spouses themselves had little or no say in whom they were to marry. Such a choice belonged to the couple's parents, who made all the arrangements themselves with the aid of matchmakers. The bride's consent was unnecessary and she had no chance to refuse. Small wonder that suicide was commoner among unhappy wives than any other section of the population!

The most fortunate members of the community were the old. They enjoyed great respect and all kinds of privileges. Yet, desirable though it was from all points of view, old age was a goal accessible only to the few. The average life expectancy in imperial China was about twenty-five.

It would clearly be unfair to suggest that happiness was all but impossible under the old Chinese family system, or that Chinese women all accepted their lot as submissive objects—examples of the domineering woman, especially the overbearing mother-in-law, are not hard to find. Yet on the whole the system was undoubtedly oppressive and was not something likely to appeal to radicals or other progressive thinkers of our own century. Successive reformers and revolutionaries have wished to uproot the Confucian principles on which old China rested, as well as the roots on which the family was based as an economic unit. Reformers of the late nineteenth and early twentieth centuries, such as K'ang Yu-wei (1858–1927) and Liang Ch'i-ch'ao (1873–1929), already called for changes in the family system. Later on a stronger impetus was added to their appeal by Sun Yat-sen (1866–1925) and men like Ch'en Tu-hsiu (1879–1942) and Hu Shih (1891–1962) who in the second decade of this century led a campaign, known as the New Culture Movement, to promote new literary and social values.

In the intensity and durability of its attack on the Confucian family structure, the New Culture Movement was possibly more important and successful than any which had preceded it. For one thing, this was the first time in Chinese history that the youth had been organized as an effective political grouping. It was largely the young people who set in motion and took part in the demonstrations of the May Fourth Movement which resulted in China's refusal to sign the Treaty of Versailles. Moreover it was largely the influence of the New Culture thinkers that led to the slackening of the hold of the old family structure, as shown in the Kuomintang Family Law of 1931 and Criminal Code of 1935.

The first of these laid down that all people should be allowed to choose their own spouses themselves, and nobody should be forced to enter into a marriage unwillingly. It forbade child marriage and ordained that the wife should be equal in law to the husband. It made divorce possible by mutual consent and abolished the bias against women in obtaining a divorce. The Criminal Code ordered that all marriages should be strictly monogamous. The government had recognized the principle of equality of the sexes in the law of the land.

Seen against the background of the traditional system these were startling advances indeed. Yet they did not break down old prejudices and in practice many people ignored them. Although most urban dwellers declared their disapproval of arranged marriages and concubinage, these institutions continued to be widespread and in the countryside arranged marriages were still the rule, rather than the exception. There, the women's position was in general as lowly as ever. Even the custom of binding their feet was slow to die out completely and could still be found in the thirties. Strong social pressures persisted everywhere against women who obtained a divorce and, despite the law, it remained much easier for a man to dispense with his wife than the reverse.

Yet it should be pointed out that one important feature of the Nationalist period was the existence of a number of women prominent in urban professions. Quite a few doctors, lawyers, and even politicians were women, and so were some of the most highly regarded literary figures of the time, Ting Ling being the best known example. One could characterize the period 1900–49 as one in which the status of women was rising and the old family system breaking down, but the speed of change was much slower than progressive thinkers desired and only the tip of the iceberg was radically affected. The only major aspect of women's oppression totally abolished by 1949 was the binding of girls' feet. By the end of the war the only bound feet still seen in China were those of victims from earlier times.

Despite the gains I have just discussed, progress towards an equitable family system was more spectacular in another part of China: the region under Communist control, more simply and in my view aptly called the 'liberated areas'. In view of the importance of the Communists as the ultimate victors, it will be worthwhile to consider briefly how they fared before they came to power.

Mao Tse-tung and the Communist Party he led from 1935 on have always seen the traditional family system as being based on the economic power of the landlords and the rich. As early as March 1927 Mao observed in his 'Report of an Investigation into the Peasant Movement in Hunan' that there were four 'systems of authority' which bound the Chinese people and of which the political power of the landlords was the backbone. One of them was the domination of husbands over wives, and it followed that only after the destruction of the landlords' power could the status of women improve radically. From the time of the Communist republic in Kiangsi in the early thirties, women were urged to take part in the revolution. Freedom of marriage, the establishment of crèches, etc. were all part of the programme to liberate the female sex.

From 7 to 10 November 1931 the Communists held the First Congress of the Chinese Soviets which promulgated a provisional constitution, Article 11 of which laid down: 'The purpose of the Soviet Government is to guarantee the fundamental liberation of the women. Freedom of marriage is recognized and measures for the protection of women will obtain the material basis to enable them to cast off the bonds of the family by gradual stages, and to participate in economic, political, and cultural life.'[1]

These basic principles were absorbed into the Communist marriage regulations issued on 1 December 1931. In addition to freedom of marriage without any coercion from any third party, these put the minimum age of marriage for men at twenty, and at eighteen for women; forbade concubinage and polygamy; abolished marriage presents and dowries; allowed divorce by mutual consent, but placed responsibility for the upkeep of the children and the divorced wife on the father or husband; and made all children, whether born inside or outside marriage, equal before the law. New regulations issued in 1934 to some extent superseded these laws. For instance, a man was no longer compelled to support his divorced wife unless she was unable to work. Nevertheless the 1931 principles remained the basis of all future Communist marriage law, especially that of 1950. Further changes were made after the Communists left Kiangsi. As a result of the united front principles which governed Mao's policies during the war against Japan, his followers temporarily discontinued the practice of land reform, and this produced effects on female economic independence. Moreover, during that period, the liberation of women had perforce to take second place behind the more urgent task of defeating Japan. Nevertheless the overall thrust of the Communists' policy remained the same and they never abandoned their intention to complete their programme for marriage reform in the future.

Religion and Thought

Just as the Republican period saw both stagnation and advances in the field of marriage and the family and, in a sense, prepared the way for the much more thorough and far-reaching reforms which were to follow liberation, so in the realms of religion and thought some people threw tradition overboard, others clung to it, and China as a whole moved haltingly and unevenly towards the radical secularism of the post-1949 Communist order.

In dynastic times the Chinese state was dominated in most periods by Confucianism. This was a system of ethics, based on certain key concepts like filial piety and the all-importance of humane government, but it included also what one might call 'liturgical' elements such as regular sacrifices to one's ancestors in the ancestral shrine, offerings to heaven by the emperor, and so forth. Educated people espoused Confucianism, or a combination of Confucianism and other faiths; or, if they chose religious life, they might enter a monastery of one of the Taoist or Buddhist sects.

But the religion of the masses was very difficult to categorize. It was an amalgam of Buddhism, Taoism, and other religions, or any number of combinations of Chinese faiths. It is perhaps best called vaguely 'popular' religion and it rested on the belief that if one worshipped and sacrificed to a god or a number of gods or goddesses, he, she, or they would send protection and good fortune. Religion to the Chinese masses was a kind of insurance policy. Christian missionaries who tried to evangelize among the Chinese ran into many cultural and spiritual obstacles. They found it well nigh impossible to persuade the people that there was only one true God. Moreover the fact that the missionaries followed the guns and trade of European imperialists gave them the reputation among many people of being spiritual aggressors, an arm of Western military and financial might.

During the period of the Republic several religious and philosophic trends operated in China. Among urban intellectuals the most important of them was undoubtedly secularism—the belief that all religion was backward and reactionary, a means of keeping the masses in darkness.

In the second and third decades of this century leaders of the New Culture Movement in Peking University—men like Ch'en Tu-hsiu and Hu Shih—not only took an active part in the May Fourth Movement, but also stormed against superstitions of all kinds as bulwarks of tradition, and called for them to be swept away to make room for a new approach based on scientific thought. They established progressive periodicals to propagate their ideas, the main one being *New Youth*, founded in 1915 by Ch'en. Another approach of this movement was to invite progressive thinkers from abroad to lecture in China. The British philosopher Bertrand Russell (1872–1970), for instance, spent about a year in China in 1920 and 1921, and spoke widely there advocating state socialism and the abolition of religion. It was typical of this anti-religious feeling among intellectuals that when the World Student Christian Federation met in Peking in 1922, it provoked a countrywide storm of protest in the universities. Although the worship of science and humanism and opposition to all religion, whether of Chinese or foreign origin, was at its height at about the time of the May Fourth Movement, the influence of secularist ideas remained very strong throughout the following decades, right up to the postwar period and liberation.

In the long term the most important secularists were the Communists. The First World War and May Fourth Movement combined to convince many thinking Chinese that the democratic humanism of Western Europe and the United States had nothing to offer China. The influence of the Socialist October Revolution in Russia spread and in 1921 the Communist Party of China was formed in Shanghai, with Ch'en Tu-hsiu as General Secretary. Unlike the liberals, the Communists organized themselves forcefully not only among intellectuals but also among the workers, and the labour movement made great strides in the twenties. Meanwhile a number of the radicals of the New Culture Movement, in particular Hu Shih, turned increasingly to the right, while after the break with the Kuomintang in 1927 the Communists went underground and transferred their primary attentions to the rural districts. During the thirties and forties they were by far the most influential secularists in the countryside. Mao Tse-tung rightly regarded religion as one of the four 'systems of authority' which kept the landlords in power and took steps to harness its sway in the areas his followers controlled. Generally speaking the Communist policy, especially during the united front period, was to allow religion to die under social pressure by allowing the people to see how much more communism had to offer them than the old-fashioned gods. Nevertheless there was certainly persecution in some places, especially against organized religion, and most adherents to the formal faiths regarded the Communists with implacable enmity.

One of the principal targets of the New Culture radicals, whether Marxist or otherwise, was Confucianism, for so long the ideological basis of traditional China. In the early years of the Republic some scholars, especially political reformers like K'ang Yu-wei, had tried to get Confucianism re-established as a state religion. These men saw Christianity and the West as a threat to Chinese culture and believed that the best hope of a counter-attack lay in a revival of Confucianism. They were doubtless also mindful of their own interests, since they belonged to a social group the influence of which could not survive a turning away from old values. Although their efforts towards official re-establishment failed, Confucian elements did remain quite strong even in government circles. In particular, Chiang Kai-shek's clean-up campaign of the 1930s, the New Life Movement, with its emphasis on orderliness, cleanliness, and morality, harked back to the Confucian restoration of the 1860s.

Another attempt to inject new energy into religion was the so-called 'Buddhist revival', led by certain prominent monks like T'ai-hsü (1890–1947). The movement derived its original motivation from the general lack of spirituality in Buddhist circles and from the destruction and, in their terms, misuse of Buddhist temples in China. It is worth remarking here that all through the Republican period many temples were taken over for secular uses. In 1935 the main Buddhist journal (*Hai-ch'ao yin*) noted bitterly that 'in large cities some 30 per cent of Buddhist properties have been appropriated for barracks and police stations, some 50 per cent for schools'.

T'ai-hsü's specified aims were three-fold; to regenerate the clergy, to rededicate Buddhist properties for the benefit of the people, and to reconstruct Buddhist doctrine. T'ai-hsü was 'modern' enough in his approach to use scientific methods, and under him numerous philosophical study groups began functioning. The Buddhists also tried to organize charitable work on a large scale. They helped with famine relief and established orphanages and schools.

One particularly interesting feature of this movement was the important part played by laymen. In 1912 a strongly anti-clerical group of lay Buddhists led by Ou-yang Ching-wu (1871–1943) even sought Sun Yat-sen's approval to take control of the whole Buddhist church. Moreover there was a plethora of lay societies which carried out such activites as arranging discussion meetings, running vegetarian restaurants, and organizing lectures.

Government reaction to Buddhist efforts was varied. Early Republican authorities were wary of them, and an order of 1915 directed monks to notify the authorities before any public speech, and to inform them of the content. Laws issued in 1929 and 1931 required the Buddhists to submit statements of income and expenditure to local authorities and encouraged the appropriation of temples for education. Yet there were also prominent Buddhist sympathizers in the government, as a result of which monks were exempt from taxation and front-line military service. T'ai-hsü had originally been quite radical, and several eminent monks supported the 1911 revolution. Yet in his later years T'ai-hsü became very conservative and strongly supported Chiang Kai-shek against the Communists. Before liberation the latter made very little attempt to win over the Buddhists.

The 'revival' actually enjoyed very limited success and it is doubtful if Buddhism was really much stronger during the Republic than it had been in the preceding period. There is evidence that Buddhism in the late Ch'ing period was actually not quite so degenerate as biased Christian missionaries made it appear and that the 'revival' was largely a figment of T'ai-hsü's imagination.

By far the strongest of the formal religions numerically was Islam which, before the war against Japan (1937–45), claimed some 50 000 000 adherents. Almost all of these belonged to the national minorities who dwelt in regions like Chinghai or Sinkiang in the west, and were hence outside the mainstream of

Chinese cultural development. Yet there were also eminent Moslems who played a vital part in the Nationalist government, the main one being General Ma Fu-hsiang (1876–1932), who personally subsidized many educational and charitable works in the name of Islam.

The Moslems were well organized, especially by the Union of Islamic Associations centred in Yunnan Province. This body sought to win a political voice for the followers of Mohammed and to some extent succeeded. Moslem leaders also encouraged cultural work. They had the *Koran* translated into Chinese, founded Islamic schools in fairly large numbers, and, even in major eastern cities such as Shanghai and Peking, set up Moslem academies and literary associations.

Another branch of religion which deserves mention is Christianity. In their outward forms both Catholicism and Protestantism reached their heyday in China during the Republican period. The rate of growth in the number of missionaries was larger between 1912 and 1927 than at any other time in Chinese history. But there was a problem here, since many Chinese continued to view the missionaries as a form of foreign aggression. For this reason, both Catholics and Protestants attempted to build up 'national' churches which would be independent of foreign powers. This proved easier for the Protestants than the Catholics, simply because the latter could not abandon the overriding authority of the pope, who was after all a non-Chinese prelate. Yet moves were made in the right direction. By 1930 there were eleven Chinese bishops and by 1949 nearly forty. Meanwhile the number of Christians continued to climb, reaching over 4 000 000 by 1949. However it is likely that many took a traditional Chinese and not a missionary attitude to their Christianity, and there is much truth in the contention that a fair proportion saw it as a source of protection and food—'rice Christians'. Moreover, however many Chinese priests there may have been, the fact remained that money from abroad was vital to Christian strength. In the final analysis, Christianity was most significant for its spread of Western institutional notions and its impact on such social amenities as education.

Whatever the influence of specified religions, it was the 'popular' cults and faiths that remained most important for the masses of Chinese. Only a small minority would have wanted to call themselves Buddhists or Christians, rather than adherents to a combination of various religions. What mattered most to them was the hope that the harvest, kitchen, or other gods would continue (or begin) to send protection. No number of agnostics, Communists, Buddhists, or Christians could convince more than a minority of the average peasants or urban workers that the popular gods had nothing to offer. Such cults survived with relatively little change either in character or extent. No organization was necessary to maintain them, and no counter-organization succeeded in uprooting them.

Education

Generally speaking the changes brought about in the education system during the first half of this century were somewhat deeper and broader than those in either the family structure or religion. There are two main reasons for this. Firstly, the aim of the old education system was to teach students the classics, and thus enable some of them to sit for the official examinations through which successful candidates could enter the bureaucracy. But the examinations were abolished in 1905 and the old educational structure thus became irrelevant. Secondly, what replaced it was based very largely on foreign models and though certain key concepts, like the importance of imbuing students with moral values, remained unchanged, the ideas imparted and the curricula in the new schools were very different from those in the old.

Schools and academies were actually quite widespread before the Western penetration. They flourished not only in the cities but also in the countryside, and were open to the poor as well as the rich. But from the point of view of the educational reformers and 'self-strengtheners' of the nineteenth century, their main shortcoming was the lack of utilitarian and technical subjects in the curricula. To remedy this situation the authorities sent quite a few students abroad to learn practical subjects and techniques.

Meanwhile the missionaries moved in and began establishing schools from the 1880s on. Shortly after, individual Chinese and the government began organizing schools along foreign lines. With the demise of the old educational institutions there were three distinct types of school—missionary, private Chinese, and government-run—and this remained the case until shortly after liberation.

The extent of foreign influence on the education system of the Republic was vast, but the 'foreign' impact was not always uniform. In the first decade Japanese-educated Chinese preponderated in the school personnel, but from 1922 it was those trained in the United States who exerted the greatest weight. The official aim of education changed from a more moral, utilitarian, and military emphasis to the fostering of good character and a 'democratic spirit'. The US system of credits, of undertaking six years of primary, six years of secondary and four years of tertiary education was adopted. The curricula also reflected the particular dominating country's influence. What remained constant was that successive governments saw the education system as a means by which they could instil the people with the official moral and political values.

The pro-foreign bias in the schools declined to some extent in the 1930s, as the Nationalist government attempted to consolidate itself. The missionary schools had been the worst of all in the pro-European bias of their teaching material, and were for this reason the target of strong attack by nationalists. During the 1930s the government insisted on some control over their curricula, so that it was no longer compulsory for students to undergo religious instruction. By the time the war against Japan broke out in 1937 the material taught in missionary schools and universities was fairly similar to that used in those run by Chinese.

Differences between the two types naturally remained, one of them being that the missionary institutions were more élitist and expensive than most Chinese schools or universities. However it is worth noting that few of the educational institutions reached more than a small proportion of the population. Only in isolated places like Tinghsien in north China, where Dr James Yen and his colleagues organized a Mass Education Movement, did education percolate thoroughly to the poorest classes. In 1935, at the height of the Kuomintang era, there were about 260 000 primary schools attended by just over 13 000 000 pupils, accounting for only about 14 per cent of the children in the relevant age group. High schools and universities were much more exclusive and only the children of the rich had any chance to study in them. Although education was in theory open to girls as well as boys, an advance on former times, the balance between the sexes in fact remained extremely lop-sided. In the thirties about one in eight university students was a girl, and about 70 per cent of rural Chinese men and almost all women were illiterate. These proportions had changed only marginally by the time of liberation. Only about one in five tertiary students attended missionary universities and the proportion at secondary level was about one in eight.

The favoured few who got beyond primary school lived adequate but spartan lives. Most lived on the campus away from home. In high schools dormitories had fifteen to twenty beds, in universities much less. Furniture was sparse, and many students took extra work to help them pay their way through their course, but almost never manual work. Most studied very hard and the level of patriotism and idealism was high.

Not surprisingly, this was true to an even greater extent in the liberated areas. Although there were many points of similarity between the education systems of the liberated and Kuomintang regions, a few important points on education under the Communists are worth pointing out. In the first place there was much greater emphasis placed on adult education, with the result that the peasants in the liberated areas were far less apathetic and more interested in the world around them than their brethren under Kuomintang control. Related to this point is the fact that, even though they suffered more acutely from a lack of qualified teachers, the Communists worked harder to wipe out illiteracy. The proportion of children going to school was probably somewhat higher than in the Kuomintang areas, and in the Communist Shansi-Chahar-Hopei border area may have been over 25 per cent.

Like the Nationalists, the Communists saw education frankly as a political weapon, but this did not mean that it was necessarily they who directed curricula everywhere. During the war a system of 'people manage, public help' schools was introduced. Under this system, education authorities would contact cadres in the villages and suggest the founding of a school. A meeting would take place at which the locals decided if they wanted a school and, if they did, elected a committee to invite a teacher and lay down curricula. If the villages wanted the instruction to follow traditional Confucian lines, as sometimes happened, the education authorities intervened but were in general forbidden to be authoritarian. Once founded, the schools themselves decided on the hours of the classes, which had to be arranged carefully so as to allow the children to assist with peasant production.

Universities, medical schools, and secondary schools existed but were not very common. The education system was expressly utilitarian and much better geared towards China's current needs than that which prevailed in the Kuomintang regions. Conditions were extremely simple, since neither the populace nor the government had much in the way of material goods. It was absolutely vital that all should avoid unnecessary luxuries.

The Arts

We now turn to the complicated subject of the arts in which, as in so many other social aspects during the Republican period, the Chinese wrestled to find a suitable mixture between their own traditional heritage, the forms and content introduced from the West, and the progressive culture spawned at about the time of the May Fourth Movement. Some artists insisted on retaining the tradition unscathed, but the majority of the most outstanding talents felt it necessary to use their art as a political weapon, and against what they saw as oppressive, particularly the family system.

For reasons of space, I have selected but three of the many forms of art for discussion: prose fiction, drama, and painting.

The New Culture Movement produced a tremendous impact on Chinese literature because one of its central tenets was that authors should write in the vernacular in order to make themselves comprehensible to the masses. Up to that time the educated man almost always despised works written in colloquial language and used only classical Chinese, which only the highly educated could read. Indeed, to be caught reading 'popular' literature could earn a boy a severe beating from his father or tutor. The Republican period was the first in which respectable literature used the vernacular.

In a survey held among students in the thirties, two modern Chinese authors emerged as the most popular, and consequently the most influential. They were Lu Hsün and Pa Chin. Both were vitally concerned with their own society and its faults. They may be taken as representative of the best and most vital that Chinese fiction writers of this period have to offer.

Lu Hsün was the pen name of Chou Shu-jen (1881–1936) born into a declining official family in Chekiang Province. Throughout his life he was progressive in his political sympathies; Mao Tse-tung described him as 'an unprecedented national hero on the cultural front'. He was in the forefront of several literary societies, the most important being the League of Left Wing Writers, founded in Shanghai in 1930.

Lu Hsün's style shows the influence of China's elegant tradition but is also highly laconic, acid, and witty. He wrote many essays and short stories and is also the author of the excellent *Brief History of Chinese Fiction*. His best known work is *The True Story of Ah Q*, a long short story, or short novel, completed in 1921. It is set in the last days of the Manchu dynasty and early Republic and deals with a typical Chinese coolie. Ah Q wants to join the 1911 revolution but is rejected by its local leaders, who are in fact the same men who bullied him in former days but have joined the republican cause for opportunistic reasons. The author is saying that in fact nothing has really changed in China's power structure. Ah Q is finally executed for a crime of which he is not even aware, let alone guilty, but raises no protest. The point of the story, brilliantly and subtly put forward, is that the Chinese people's greatest enemy is apathy.

A somewhat younger man was the Szechwanese writer Pa Chin, pen name of Li Fei-kan, born in 1904. Though more romantic in approach than Lu Hsün, he was also strongly critical of the traditional order and attacked it in his works. His novel *Family* was one of the favourite books of China's youth in the thirties and deals with the tyranny of the old family structure, especially the authority of the father. In *Family* the young win the struggle against their elders, and the hero leaves the family to take part in political struggle.

Both these writers, especially the former, represent the radical wing of urban literary circles. In the liberated areas, Mao Tse-tung laid down the Communist policy towards art in 1942 in his 'Talks at the Yenan Forum on Literature and Art'. Mao holds that all art is propaganda for some viewpoint or other, whether it sets out to be or not, and that revolutionary writers should consciously propagate the interests of the proletariat. Some people consider his attitude far too dogmatic and conducive to stereotypes in literature, yet much good work was produced in the liberated areas before 1949. One outstanding author was Chao Shu-li, from Shansi, born into a poor peasant family in 1903. His writing is simple, full of colloquialisms and undoubtedly shows great sympathy for and understanding of the peasants. Possibly his best known work is 'Hsiao Erh-hei's Marriage', a charming love story set in a village. Chao is quite frank about the corruption of certain Communist cadres and about the pressures at work from traditional forces even in the liberated zones. The story is witty and exciting, and also a brilliant documentary of the processes whereby Communist power was established firmly in the rural districts.

The characteristics apparent in Chinese prose fiction apply to some extent also to the drama. Yet this latter art survived more strongly in its traditional forms, largely because the greatest actors of the day were exponents of the old theatre and because, with its stylized actions, gorgeous costumes, and rather rigid format, the traditional opera is not as easily adaptable to modern themes as the novel.

The classical opera was a fairly ancient form of Chinese 'people's' art. There were many types, each distinct from the others in its music, dialect, and in the region or regions where it was popular. The most famous of these local kinds is the Peking Opera and the Republican period saw the heyday of such actors as Mei Lan-fang (1894–1961), Yü Shu-yen (1890–1943), and Yang Hsiao-lou (1877–1938). All three were men—most Peking Opera troupes were exclusively male—but Mei Lan-fang almost always played women's roles. Shortly after the 1911 revolution, Mei experimented with performing items on contemporary social themes, but his efforts were not very successful and the Peking Opera remained a conservative art-form. New pieces tended to be based on ancient stories, but even these were much less common than the old-fashioned and traditionally popular dramas inherited from the past.

The same strictures apply to most other regional forms. In fact, their conservatism and lack of innovation was one reason why they tended to decline in popular appeal. They suffered acutely during the war against Japan, and many had come close to dying out by the time the Nationalists fell. One of the major exceptions to this tendency was in the liberated areas, where the Communists placed great emphasis on the local theatre, and were able to adapt it into an effective form of propaganda for their socialist message.

By far the most important new form of drama was the spoken play. This had not existed at all in China before the Western impact—all drama having been sung—and in fact the birth of the play in China is normally dated 1907. Unlike the traditional opera, the spoken play was eminently suitable for political messages. It was an important weapon in support of the 1911 revolution and the May Fourth Movement; it was used against the traditional values in the twenties and thirties, against the Japanese during the war, and by the Communists to further their radical social ideas.

Like the prose writers of the Republican period, the dramatists founded a whole plethora of societies, which patronized the composition and performance of the play. Most of them functioned in the large cities, especially Shanghai, and the most influential tended to be progressive in their outlook. Students and intellectuals played an important part both as performers and spectators.

Among the best known of the dramatists of this period was Ts'ao Yü, born in Hupei in 1910. His most popular play is

'Cock Crowing in the Rain' by Hsü Pei-hung (1895–1953) is an example of traditional Chinese painting

Thunderstorm, first performed in 1935 by the drama club of Shanghai's Futan University. Although it was banned several times for its 'unhealthy' content—one of the themes which can be read into it is incest—it drew record audiences wherever shown. It is a long play, and the influences of Western playwrights like Ibsen and O'Neill are obvious in it. Its theme was typical of its period—the corruption of the wealthy classes and the tyranny of the traditional family system.

The last form of art to come under discussion here was also the slowest to be revolutionized, namely painting. It is true that there were Chinese painters who called for their art to belong to the masses, a sharp break with the theories of dynastic times, and also some who adopted modern Western styles and oil painting techniques, especially Hsü Pei-hung (1895–1953). Nevertheless Chinese artists who had studied in Europe found it difficult to keep in touch with Western trends once they returned home—the foreign community in China was not much use—and most failed to find an effective amalgam with their own heritage.

For this reason it was the traditional type of ink painting that continued to dominate. Even Hsü Pei-hung is best known for his powerful drawings of horses, which are wholly Chinese in conception. Possibly the most successful representative of the old school was Ch'i Pai-shih (1863–1957). Of poor peasant birth, he was originally a carpenter, not achieving renown as a painter until fairly late in life. Even though he followed the old style both in his art and way of living, he was honoured under the Communists and in 1953 succeeded Hsü Pei-hung as chairman of the All China Artists' Union. His paintings are vivid, simple, elegant, and witty, and he is particularly loved for his flowers, gourds, insects, crabs, chickens, and birds. He was extremely prolific, and his output is said to have included more than 10 000 paintings.

* * *

The most striking point about the society and culture of the Republican period is the uneven progress of the Chinese in rejecting what was backward or stereotyped in their own tradition and the equally uneven advances in adopting a new civilization more suited to an age in which industry and technology were so dominant. Intellectuals in the cities abandoned the traditional ways readily, sometimes falling slaves to European habits and institutions which were no better suited to Chinese needs than what they were casting aside. Urban bourgeois culture developed significantly in many ways between 1912 and 1949. At the same time the masses of the peasantry remained static. Out of touch with international developments, it did not occur to them to change old ways they saw as natural. Except in the liberated areas, there was not much change over the decades between the fall of the Manchus and the victory of the Communists.

It is worthwhile noting the magnitude of the problems. Famine was endemic and in bad years took literally millions of lives. Disease was rampant everywhere. The growing urban culture resulted in an ever widening gap between rich and poor in which hopeless squalor existed alongside great opulence. Prostitution, gambling, and vice of all kinds flourished, to the profit of the rich but detriment of the poor. Corruption among officials was near universal. Small wonder that reforms, even though promulgated, proved so difficult to put into effect. Chinese society was so degenerate that only radical measures could offer real hope.

It was the Communists who saw this most clearly and thought out remedial steps most realistically. While the urban intellectuals fumbled and faltered, and most of the peasants felt themselves powerless against oppression, the Communists analyzed the problems and arrived at consistent if flexible policies which could make an effective beginning in correcting China's horrifying backwardness and overwhelming poverty. This was one of the reasons why they succeeded in vanquishing the Kuomintang, and why they have continued to hold the support of the people since they came to power in 1949.

Note

1 Translation taken from M.J. Meijer *Marriage Law and Policy in the Chinese People's Republic*, Hong Kong University Press, Hong Kong, 1971, p. 41.

Select Bibliography

Lang, Olga *Chinese Family and Society*, Yale University Press, New Haven, 1946. An excellent, readable book, based mainly on research carried out in the 1930s, but containing also a section on the dynastic period.

Mackerras, Colin *The Chinese Theatre in Modern Times, from 1840 to the present day*, Thames and Hudson, London, 1975. Intended for the general reader, this book focusses on theatre from a regional point of view and especially on the relationship between theatre and society.

Scott, A.C. *Literature and the Arts in Twentieth Century China*, International Publications Service, New York, 1963. A good, short run-down on the subject, including chapters on literature, theatre and dance, the cinema, painting and the graphic arts, architecture and sculpture, and music.

Ting Yi *A Short History of Modern Chinese Literature*, China Knowledge Series, Foreign Languages Press, Peking, 1959. A good, longer but simple, account written from the Communist (pre-Cultural Revolution) viewpoint.

Welch, Holmes *The Buddhist Revival in China*, Harvard East Asian Series 33, Harvard University Press, Cambridge Mass., 1968. The standard scholarly English-language work on Republican Buddhism.

Yang, C.K. *Religion in Chinese Society, A Study of Contemporary Social Functions of Religion and Some of their Historical Factors*, University of California Press, Berkeley and Los Angeles, 1961, paperback, 1967. Highly scholarly, but readable book with emphasis as indicated in the subtitle.

Chapter 9
Society and the arts, 1949-74

Colin Mackerras

When the Communists came to power in 1949, they were very experienced in the conduct of guerrilla war and administration among peasants, but not so adept in the government of an entire and vast nation. Yet they remained idealistic and, by comparison with the Kuomintang they replaced, extremely incorrupt. Basically their policies in social and cultural matters have followed the patterns worked out in the pre-1949 liberated areas. The Communist success has been mixed and the twenty-five years under discussion here have been far from free of social upheavals. Yet, by comparison with the Republican period, this has been a strikingly stable one and the Communist policies have been very much more effective than those of the Kuomintang.

Thought and Religion

Contemporary China is very much a nation based on a single consistent philosophy—the thought of Mao Tse-tung. This does not mean that all Chinese agree with everything Mao says or that non-Maoist notions are impermissible, but it would be quite unthinkable to denounce his ideas openly. Discussions on philosophy normally take place within the framework of that of Mao Tse-tung.

Maoism is a body of ethics as well as a system of thought. To the Chinese, politics, ethics, and morality are almost synonomous. Politics covers virtually all branches of human behaviour and is in this sense almost a religion, but without the supernatural—a secular faith. For the masses several aspects of this ideology stand out as most relevant, most of them being contained in three of Mao's works; 'Serve the People', 'In Memory of Norman Bethune', and 'The Foolish Old Man Who Removed the Mountains'.

The central doctrine of the first one, and the ethical substance of Maoism as a whole, is the need to sacrifice personal interests to those of the people. One should be unselfish and always willing to help others, whether within one's own family or not. Mao holds, in contrast to many people in the West, that mankind can be trained to be unselfish *en masse* and that it is only bourgeois and feudal social pressure left over from the past which prevents the realization of this ideal. He aims to build a society built not on competition but on co-operation.

Another important point of 'Serve the People' is the need for criticism. This involves constant discussion of personal, social, and administrative shortcomings as a means towards improvement. For instance, a commune or factory member is invited to put forward his views on how affairs should be run within his unit and, especially since the Cultural Revolution, no cadre would ignore his opinion with impunity. The cadre would submit it to the collective for discussion, or run the risk of coming under criticism himself. Although it is true that the overall dominance of Maoism severely limits free expression, the emphasis on criticism and mass participation within the limits set by it leads to a type of freedom of ideas which most peasants and labourers did not enjoy under earlier governments.

'In Memory of Norman Bethune' stresses the need for devotion to one's work, again for the sake of others. The ideal worker takes his inspiration from his usefulness to the masses, not from the thought that he will derive riches, comfort, and prestige. Allied to this point is the desire to persuade professional people like doctors to forsake the cities, which are relatively well provided with the amenities highly skilled technicians can supply, and move around the countryside where the reverse is the case. For the masses of the peasantry, who constitute over four-fifths of the population, the doctor prepared to face the discomfort of the rural areas is of greater use than the one who insists on remaining city-bound, even though he knows much less and is less highly trained. This is what the Chinese mean when they claim that ideological commitment is more important than expertise.

The core idea of 'The Foolish Old Man Who Removed the Mountains' is the necessity for persistence against nature and the difficulties it poses. The article repeats the story of an aged man who, by refusing to give up, succeeds in moving two large mountains which block his way. Though nobody denies his folly in attempting such a task, his spirit is worthy of emulation. No matter how great a problem appears to be, the man who works at it persistently can eventually overcome it.

Communist thought includes not only certain key ethical principles but other aspects as well. Many of them are extremely complicated and outside the scope of this book. It is, however, absolutely necessary to mention the condemnation of élitism and bureaucracy.

Mao and his followers inherited a society in which the rich were very wealthy indeed, the poor extremely poor; a country where the system of government perpetuated the inequalities. Mao held that only violent revolution could overturn this order, for existing channels of protest he believed were designed to alleviate the symptoms but not to cure the disease itself. But once the old society and its functionaries were overthrown, would not the cadres of the new one strive for precisely the same élitism as those they had replaced? To solve this problem Mao has instituted several 'rectification' campaigns, the most intense and largest one being the Cultural Revolution. This movement he saw as nothing less than a new violent upheaval to overthrow the bureaucracy his Party had itself established. Indeed the basic problem persists even now, and further revolutions will be necessary until the social pressures are such that human beings no longer strive to belong to an élite but find it natural to serve only communal interests. The Campaign to Criticize Lin Piao and Confucius, which began in August 1973, is in fact the first of these 'revolutions', albeit on a smaller and less violent scale than the Cultural Revolution. Whereas Confucianism saw hierarchy as desirable, the Communists regard it as the root of all evils, hence the strong denunciation of Confucius seen in China since August 1973.

The establishment of Maoism as a faith embracing virtually everybody has profoundly affected the various religions which existed before 1949. The Communists make no secret of their view that all are backward and will eventually die out, but their attitude towards religion has not been entirely consistent over the twenty-five or so years since 1949.

Mao and his Party base their belief in the ultimate demise of religion on their conviction that socialism can provide the masses with more spiritual and material benefits than any god. Since, as mentioned in chapter 8, most Chinese tend to regard the worship of deities as an insurance policy, the success of communism in 'delivering the goods' would in fact go far towards undermining the strength of religion. The Chinese peasant who takes down the picture of the kitchen or harvest god and replaces it with one of Mao will feel quite satisfied with the new faith if his fortunes actually improve, for the old gods were notoriously unreliable.

This is in fact the process whereby the 'popular' religions are finally weakening in their hold over the masses.

But what of the formal religions, in particular Buddhism, Islam, and Christianity?

The policy of the government towards these branches has been to aim at their long-term elimination through social pressures, but to permit their continued practice provided it is not subversive. Although there have been periods of violent persecution against them, especially during the Cultural Revolution when Red Guards damaged temples, mosques, and churches, and attacked some religious believers physically, it has usually been non-violent pressure which the Communists have used against formal religions. Believers may worship the god or gods of their choice, but not run religious schools or own monastic or church estates; and the only societies which still function are those patronized directly by the state. All societies must register with the government and the government will not allow the establishment of any society of which it disapproves. There are certain religious societies which the state actively encourages, and such societies have some Party members among their leaders. Most temples, mosques, and churches have been taken over for secular purposes.

Christianity has fared worst. Funds no longer flow in from abroad, and the Catholic Church maintains no ties with Rome, for the Communists do not tolerate allegiance to a foreign power. Priests still celebrate Mass publicly in a small number of cities, after a break of nearly six years during the Cultural Revolution, but Christianity, both Catholic and Protestant, is now so weak as to be negligible as a social force. Buddhism is also moribund, although some temples still function. Only Islam has any real vitality left. There are still about 10 000 000 Moslems in China, almost all in the western provinces among the national minorities. However, even though it appears that Islam has resisted the new order more strongly than the other religions, very little news reaches the outside world about what happens in the distant west, and it would be rash to predict the future of Islam in China.

Family Life

The behaviour of the Communists towards the formal religions, especially during the Cultural Revolution, has been subject to criticism abroad, though it is probably not a burning topic in China itself. Their achievements have been much better in other spheres, above all in regard to the family and the position of women.

The most vital respect in which the present family system differs from that of the past is in its basis. Society is no longer built on a hierarchical ideology and the clan is no longer an important economic foundation of the country. The land reform of the early fifties has ensured that no great families can own vast estates, while the introduction of the communes has made it impossible for any clan to wield financial power. The family remains strong as a social phenomenon, but its place as an economic unit has been almost entirely taken over by the 'organization'—the factory, commune, institute, and so on.

One of the first matters to receive the attention of the Communist government was marriage reform. In April 1950 the Marriage Law was promulgated to cover the entire country and has remained in effect ever since. Article 1 reads:

> The feudal marriage system which is based on arbitrary and compulsory arrangements and the superiority of man over woman and ignores the children's interests shall be abolished. The New-Democratic marriage system, which is based on the free choice of partners, on monogamy, on equal rights for both sexes, and on the protection of the lawful interests of women and children, shall be put into effect.

Other articles set the minimum age of marriage at twenty for men and eighteen for women, stipulate the formality for marriage, outlaw concubinage, and allow divorce by mutual consent.

How effective has this law been in practice? The question of arranged marriages is probably the most important and should be considered first.

In the early days of the People's Republic there was a great deal of propaganda on this subject. Resistance from the middle-aged and old was strong, for among them there lingered the feeling that it was immoral for young people to choose their own partners. It is difficult to avoid the suspicion also that they were not too keen to see the young escape the system under which they themselves had suffered. Not surprisingly there was a far readier response among youth to the policy of free marriage. After all they had nothing to lose by it. Nevertheless the old tradition did not break down immediately and even now it would be rash to say that the custom of arranged marriages is totally extinct. In 1965 it was reported in the main Shanghai newspaper that in a certain rural district go-betweens were still active. I recall the case of a friend of mine in China who had been too shy to propose and had enlisted the aid of his parents to arrange his marriage for him. This they did successfully. A remnant of the old system is in evidence here, but with the major difference that the young man chose his spouse himself, and not his parents!

The Communists can probably claim more complete success as far as the age of marriage is concerned. The Shanghai report quoted above complained that some men still married at twenty, and woman at eighteen or nineteen. This would mean that even backward people still observe the law. In fact, however, the Party has encouraged much later marriage. In general it is likely that this goal is much more easily accessible in the cities than in the countryside.

Article 6 of the Law stipulates that 'In order to contract a marriage, both the man and woman shall register in person with the people's government...' Weddings are very simple indeed nowadays, and usually consist of nothing more than the formal registration and a small party. The lavish and expensive celebrations of the past are rare. Although the Law does not go beyond prohibiting 'the exaction of money or gifts in connection with marriages', wedding presents are sparse and cheap, honeymoons and large dowries almost unknown. According to the Communists, money spent on luxurious ceremonies is better used for more essential things, and despite resistance from some, an ever growing proportion of the population seems to agree with this view. Honeymoons were unknown in traditional China and are entirely a Western notion.

Concubinage has either vanished or nearly so. The present law equates bigamy with concubinage, regarding both as criminal offences. While this practice persisted into the fifties and even the sixties, it is undoubtedly extremely rare nowadays. Not many people could indulge in it without being discovered in a society like China's where privacy is very difficult to find. And a known bigamist would certainly be punished severely.

The Marriage Law of 1950 devotes a great deal of space to divorce. Clearly the government was anxious to give people every chance to dissolve marriages arranged under the old system. But of course divorce was also possible for those who had chosen their partners themselves but later found the union a failure. Where both parties are agreed on a divorce, the procedure is simple and involves little more than registration with the authorities, who naturally ensure that either the wife or husband will care for the children. However, where only one side wants it, the case comes before a court. The assessor will often encourage the couple to patch it up, and the government strongly discourages 'frivolous' divorces, but actual practice varies considerably according to the place, the particular court, and the concrete circumstances.

In the early days of the People's Republic divorce was very common, becoming less so as the fifties progressed. Figures given in the *People's Daily* of 13 April 1957 show the numbers declining from 1 100 000 in 1953 to 510 000 in 1956, but they probably include only those cases which came before the courts. In the first four years after 1949 the rate was about 1·3 per 1000 population (excluding divorces granted outside the courts). By way of comparison I add that the divorce rate in the United States in 1962 was about 2·2 and in Canada 0·4 per 1000 population. It is thus clear that many people were taking advantage of the new order just after 1949 to escape from unhappy arranged marriages. Unfortunately social pressures left over from before 1949 still made the situation of divorced wives far from easy and some found it difficult to find new husbands. Shame led quite a few to commit suicide. However, as the Marriage Law took effect and arranged marriages became fewer, so also the problems of divorce tended to dwindle.

It is apparent from the Marriage Law that equality between the sexes is a central goal of the Chinese Communists, and the obvious question arises whether they have achieved this objective. Although no full answer can be given, the overall conclusion must be that, while the status of women is very much higher in China today than at any time in the past, there is still a long way to go before they are truly equal to men.

Let us look at some of the signs. There has been a dramatic growth in the number of working women and mothers at all levels. In my experience doctors are more often women than men. In the institute where I worked, quite a few of the teaching staff were women. On the other hand, only about one-third of the students were female. Women take a very active part in politics, especially since the Cultural Revolution, yet men still predominate greatly in the Communist Party. One frequently finds women in leading positions in factories and communes, but not nearly as often as men. Married women retain their own surname. However this does not prove very much since they did so legally also in traditional times. The idea that the women's place is in the home is breaking down, but is very far from dead.

The notion of the working mother implies a system of public services to take care of the children. In most organizations there are crèches and kindergartens which, though not free, are within the means of most families concerned. The women take the children there before work and collect them afterwards, but there are also many cases in which the parents see their young offspring only at the weekend, which in effect means Sunday since China has a six-day and forty-eight-hour working week. Another custom is the use of a private *a-i* ('aunty'), usually a grandmother, to look after the children of working mothers at home. Any visitor to China will notice the large number of children playing in the alleys and streets. They are often supervised by their grandmothers, although of course many mothers choose not to work outside the home. Women who have taken a job get fifty-six days off on full pay after the birth of a baby. After that their hours are arranged to suit feeding times until the child is weaned.

An important problem related to giving women opportunities in the work force is that of birth control. Government policy has been somewhat inconsistent since 1949, but during most periods has been one of strong encouragement. Methods used range over the whole gamut of those followed elsewhere, the main one being late marriage. Since the Cultural Revolution special attention has been given to informing the public, especially the peasants, on the subject of contraception. The system of barefoot doctors, by which incompletely trained practitioners willing to forsake the comfort of the cities tour or live in remote areas dispensing knowledge and medical services, has been of particular help. At present China's population is nearly 900 000 000 and growing at about 2 per cent per year. It is hoped to reduce this rate to 1·5 per cent within the next few years. Recent visitors have commented favourably on Chinese efforts to keep the population down, especially in the cities, and it is likely that the 1·5 per cent growth rate will be achieved. Certainly the emphasis on birth control has been a key factor in liberating women for the work force.

The Chinese remain extremely prudish in their attitude to extramarital sexual relations. Freedom in such matters is definitely not part of their socialist programme. Although undiscovered deviations certainly occur, China's general lack of privacy makes them difficult. Known offenders find themselves targets of harsh criticism and can even be sent to the countryside for remoulding. Nevertheless it is only fair to add that condemnations are less severe than before 1949, when in rural areas adulterous couples were sometimes stoned to death and sexual freedom was largely the preserve of rich men.

Another vital change which has taken place in the Chinese family system is that the aged no longer enjoy the privileges of the past. Yet the old are still accorded great respect on all levels, certainly more than in a typical Western country. Old people usually live with their grown children, if they have any. There are also homes for the aged, where the basic principles of management are to make the inmates feel useful by keeping them busy and to impress upon them that they are an integral part of society by teaching them Maoist principles.

At the same time as the status of old age has declined, there has been a sharp rise in the social position of youth. Young people, even in their teens and before, are encouraged to criticize their teachers and elders, and frequently do so. This was particularly evident during the Cultural Revolution, when the young enjoyed unprecedented political power, certainly more than at any other time in China's history. Since the Red Guards disbanded in mid-1968, China's youth has lost much of its authority in government, and several million former Red Guards have been sent to the countryside. On the other hand, the position of youth in the administrative structure of the country probably remains stronger than it was before 1966, and it is commoner now to find people in their twenties occupying responsible posts.

The interests of the young are, in my experience, extremely idealistic, and they show very much more concern about the future of their own society than is customary in the West. They do not appear to hanker after drugs and would in any case find them virtually impossible to obtain. Comparatively few people under twenty even smoke tobacco. The social pressures are very strongly against the development of sexual potential for people still in their teens. Dancing parties are much rarer and more staid than in the West, and erotic literature unavailable. Drunkenness among the young is not a serious problem. In short, although the young play a far more vital role in society than they did under the Kuomintang, or especially the imperial dynasties, their everyday life is much more disciplined than that of their counterparts in a typical Western country.

The overall picture that emerges is of a general breaking down of the old family structure, with its rigidity, stress on filial piety, and the superiority of men and old age. Marriage reform has been much more effective than it was under the Kuomintang. The ceremonial aspects of such occasions as weddings have been greatly simplified, a trend which may be irksome to the rich but is extremely beneficial for the poor. It is not true, however, that the Communists have abolished the family as a social unit, nor is there any sign that they intend doing so. In my view, the changes made in family life since 1949 are a genuine liberation, especially for the young, and as time goes on the number of people who

Above—A workers' spare-time chemistry class

Below—A scene from the ballet *The White-Haired Girl*. The heroine, Hsi-erh, has just been made a maidservant in the house of the landlord Huang, whose wife maltreats the girl despite her adherence to the Buddhist faith

regret them will probably decline to vanishing point, just as has happened in our own society.

Education

In an earlier section I described how all-embracing was China's commitment to Maoism. One of the most important vehicles through which the government persuades the people to accept this ideology is the education system.

The Chinese see the purpose of education as the moral, intellectual, and physical development of people. The first part of this triple aim means in effect that the imparting of Maoism to students at all levels is the conscious policy of Chinese schools and institutes. This ideological or moral aspect is actually closely linked to the other two. Students should be competent professionally, but, in the view of the Maoists, good ideology assists professional expertise by instilling enthusiasm into the learner, and showing him or her the reasons why he or she should study hard. Owing to the emphasis on physical development, the Chinese authorities encourage students to take part in sport and manual labour. During the Republican period intellectuals eschewed this second kind of activity, an attitude dictated by tradition. But the Communists see manual labour as a way not merely of promoting physical development but also of preventing students from regarding themselves as an élite divorced from the masses. They see this approach as particularly necessary because there has always been a deep feeling in China that a child from a poor background was able to lift himself in the social scale through education, and hence leave the labouring masses behind him. The stress on physical development is, at least in part, aimed at breaking down this élitist tradition.

Another important philosophical basis of contemporary Chinese education is that there should be unity between theory and practice. The Maoists see no point in learning which has no application in production and everyday life. As a result of this concept, Chinese education is extremely utilitarian. It emphasizes subjects like engineering, medicine, and science, but downgrades classical studies and the pure humanities. In the institute where I taught English, the students wanted to be able to speak, read, and write the language but showed virtually no interest in English literature or its history. For the Chinese, the aim of education is not the abstract seeking and imparting of truth, but a tool to build up a backward country into a strong and advanced one.

Partly for this reason Mao's followers have always seen the eradication of illiteracy as one of their primary educational tasks. When the new government came to power in 1949, it faced formidable problems: not only were about 85 per cent of the people unable to read or write, but the population was spread over a vast area and there was a grave shortage of competent teachers.

Quantitatively the achievements of the Communists have been very impressive. The number of primary schools has risen sharply and there are now about 145 000 000 pupils attending them. Almost all children have the chance of gaining at least primary education, although it is not yet compulsory. The drive against illiteracy is seen also in the importance attached to adult and part-time education. In 1960 there were some 25 000 000 workers undertaking courses. The numbers of people who proceed beyond primary schooling are much smaller. At present about 35 000 000 students attend secondary schools, and in 1965 there were 664 universities and tertiary institutes with about 1 000 000 students.

One of the methods the government has used to facilitate its drive to increase literacy has been to simplify the Chinese script. Although many people have argued that such a measure undermines Chinese culture, it has undoubtedly made the task of the masses in learning to read and write easier. Abbreviated characters are now universal on the Chinese mainland. There are also suggestions to abolish characters altogether and use a romanized script—as done earlier in Vietnam—but this is a long-range scheme and it is doubtful that it will ever be put into effect.

Having considered some of the basic points of education in China, let us take a brief look at the concrete practice at grassroots level. Children attend primary schools for six years, from about the ages of seven to twelve. Almost all are co-educational and all state-run, the government system having absorbed the missionary and private schools not long after liberation. There are two terms per year, and forty-five minute classes run from 8 to 12 in the morning and 2 to 5 in the afternoon every day except Sunday. The children learn Chinese language, arithmetic, singing, and drawing, and later on begin subjects such as history, geography, and science. Manual work is a regular feature of the courses.

Secondary schools are similar but more advanced. They also provide six-year courses, but the subjects include mathematics, world history, politics, science, and foreign languages. Only at tertiary level do students concentrate on one or two subjects.

At the institute where I taught all the students lived on the campus in dormitories, seven to a room. They rose at 6 in winter, 5 in summer, and began the day with physical exercises. They spent the morning on their major, the afternoon on other subjects and sport. They took their meals in a communal refectory, and all stood to eat owing to the lack of chairs. Their possessions were meagre, but their idealism and enthusiasm for their work were higher than I have seen in any other country. Close relations with members of the opposite sex were strongly discouraged.

The teachers also lived on the campus, though this was not invariable in all institutes. There were facilities for the care and education of their children. Like the students they ate in a communal dining-hall, but theirs was supplied with benches. Teachers who lived with their families could cook in their own flats if they chose. All teachers and students enjoyed free medical services at the institute clinic.

One difference between the teachers and students at the institute where I taught lay in their class background, most of the teachers being from the bourgeoisie, the students mainly from peasant or working class origin. In fact the Communists have always considered that the poorer people should be given better opportunities for higher education than the middle classes and the overall proportion of students from worker-peasant backgrounds has risen steadily. However progress was not nearly as fast as the Maoists wished and this problem was one of the issues brought out during the Cultural Revolution. The Red Guards claimed that higher education was still favouring the bourgeoisie. The accusation was certainly not valid for the organization where I worked, but was probably so in most others.

The general influence of the Cultural Revolution on education has been of two main kinds. In one sense it was very deleterious because it resulted in the total cessation of classes for several years. But, on the other hand, it has led to important and, from a Maoist viewpoint, desirable reforms. Education has become much more weighted in favour of the poor than it was before the Cultural Revolution. Adult classes have increased in number, and the theories outlined earlier have been put into practice more comprehensively. For instance, students devote much more of their energies applying their knowledge to a real situation than they used to, so that a youth undertaking an engineering course will spend a good deal of time in factories learning how to put what he knows to direct use. The emphasis on moral education, in effect the learning of Chairman Mao's works, has also increased sharply. Students spend more time on physical labour, and the period secondary school graduates devote to manual labour before proceeding to a university has lengthened. Courses have become more efficient and those at tertiary level have been shortened from three or four to two or three years.

Another change has been in the function of examinations. Before the Cultural Revolution these were a normal method of testing the students' progress, even though they were much less important than in Western countries. Since the late sixties, some institutions have considered the idea of abolishing them altogether in favour of a system of assessment by teachers and fellow-students. Others have wanted to introduce group examinations, in which several candidates discuss the questions together and are allowed to use textbooks. The theory runs that this method finds out how well qualified the students are to solve on-the-spot problems, and not merely the standard of their examination technique. At the moment of writing the situation is still fluid. It appears probable that the pre-1966 system will be partly restored, but examinations are unlikely ever to regain their former importance entirely.

Possibly the main effect of the Cultural Revolution has been an intensified effort to bring about universal literacy. Many of the former students who were sent to the countryside when the Red Guards were disbanded in 1968 are probably helping with teaching in remote areas. Literate peasants and soldiers are also assisting in this task. It may not be more than a decade or so before China achieves its goal of having all children in schools.

The Arts

Just as education should be for all, and a means of propaganda for Maoism, so the 'mass line' applies also for the arts. On the one hand, as many people as possible should be able to enjoy and take part in cultural activities, while on the other, Communist policy demands that art must be a form of ideological education for the masses.

The emphasis on universal participation has led to a spectacular growth in the importance of amateur art in China. All organizations, whether rural or urban, encourage cultural work among their members. But, like the professional, the spare-time artist must keep his products and activities within clearly defined ideological limits. To forget that art is a vehicle of propaganda for socialism and to try to make it above or devoid of class content is seen as equivalent to using it against the interests of the masses.

Of all forms of art, probably none has received stronger encouragement from the Communists than the theatre. In the early period after 1949, they saw 'healthy' influences in traditional drama and patronized it with vigour. The regional types and the Peking Opera flourished as never before since the nineteenth century or even earlier. The social status of actors rose, the number of theatres multiplied, and the 'liberal' phase of 1956–57 saw as wide a variety of classical items performed as any period in China's history.

At the same time the government's policy has always been to promote the production of modern operas and plays with directly revolutionary themes. In 1964 it changed its attitude towards the parallel development of old and new theatre and decided that the former was, after all, unsuited to a socialist society. Since then only modern operas have been encouraged, and the Cultural Revolution saw the total suspension of the classical theatre. At the moment of writing, however, its eventual revival seems likely.

Until 1966 most of the famous playwrights of the pre-1949 period occupied important administrative posts in cultural organizations. Almost all came under heavy criticism during the Cultural Revolution, but in any case had produced no outstanding work after 1949. The best known items nowadays are either group compositions or the works of newly prominent authors.

One sample of their productions is the Peking Opera *The Red Lantern*, which deals with three generations of revolutionaries and their attempt to convey a secret code to the Communist guerrillas during the war against Japan. Two of the three are killed by the Japanese general, but the youngest succeeds in contacting the patriotic forces.

The costumes and décor of *The Red Lantern* are entirely modern and realistic, and retain very little to remind the viewer of the traditional drama. However, like the other revolutionary Peking Operas, it still includes the complicated acrobatics which have thrilled audiences since the birth of the Peking Opera late in the eighteenth century, and some other highly stylized traditional actions. One very significant change is that female roles are now almost always played by women. It is in the music that the links with tradition are strongest. Although it has undergone some changes, including the addition of European orchestral instruments, the music of the revolutionary Peking Operas makes them readily identifiable as such.

Many themes are used not only in one theatre-form but in several. A single story might be found as a Peking Opera, Cantonese Opera, spoken play, and so on. *The Red Lantern* was originally a Shanghai Opera. Another example is *The White-haired*

Above—In August 1967, a platoon of the Chinese Army was taking some Red Guards over a river when a wave broke over the bow of the boat throwing all on board into the torrent. Through his presence of mind and courage, the leader of the platoon saved the Red Guards. This story was famous in China and is the subject of this painting

Below—These figures come from a series of 114 life-size clay figures called the Rent Collection Courtyard. The collection was made in 1965 by thirteen sculptors from the Szechwan Institute of Fine Arts and depicts scenes in Szechwan. Here an enraged young peasant is about to attack an oppressive landlord

Girl, which won great popularity as a Peking Opera during the Great Leap Forward, but is now most often performed as a ballet, a form in which the Chinese excel despite its European origin.

The White-haired Girl concerns a servant of a rich landlord. She is treated with great cruelty but escapes to the mountains where intense suffering causes her hair to go white. In the end she is found by the Communist army and during the land reform takes a leading role in accusing her former oppressor of his crimes. With liberation a new life begins for her.

The directly political nature of art is apparent also in the novel, and in this field also the most widely read new items are from the pens of authors who have come to prominence since 1949. Heroic themes dominate. Among the best known is *The Song of Ou-yang Hai* by Chin Ching-mai. It deals with the life and ideological development of a young soldier who is born into a poor peasant family and joins the revolution as a child. The story ends when Ou-yang Hai throws himself in front of a train to remove a horse from the line. He fulfils his aim of preventing a major accident, but is himself killed in the process. The novel claims to be based on a true story, one which my students in China found very moving. First published in 1965, *The Song of Ou-yang Hai* quickly sold about a million copies, but was then attacked during the Cultural Revolution.

Although heroic novels dominate the scene, certain classical works of the dynastic period have kept their following. They were widely read and loved through the fifties but fell into disfavour in the more fervent ideological atmosphere of the period leading up to and including the Cultural Revolution. My students, for instance, were strongly discouraged from reading them. Recent reports tell of intensified criticism being levelled against the classical novel.

In other fields of art, like music and painting, the Communist approach has been similar. New works tend to stress the heroic, the directly political, and the folk idiom, but in the fifties and early sixties due respect was paid to tradition and the revival of ancient items, even those with very little appeal to the masses. For instance, a special research committee carried out a great deal of highly scholarly work in exploring the music of the *ch'in*, a seven-stringed instrument formerly the preserve of the educated classes. Highly qualified experts also restored ancient buildings and made new and extremely valuable discoveries in archaeology.

During the Cultural Revolution China appeared headed towards an extremely uniform and stereotyped art. Very few musical pieces or paintings remained in favour, and those that did revolved directly around the worship of Mao Tse-tung's thought and the revolutionary struggle. More recently, the Chinese press has revealed that archaeologists were still at work even during the campaign and it has given much prominence to valuable and beautiful objects excavated at that time. There is a new interest in classical poetry and ancient history. Whereas during the period 1966 to 1970 China appeared to be turning its back on the cultural achievements of its feudal past, its people have now very clearly adopted a more positive attitude towards them.

Probably Chinese artists will continue to follow the propaganda line. However there are two reasons why, in my opinion, optimism over China's future artistic development is justifiable. One is that propaganda art need not necessarily be bad. After all the aim of the Christian art of the European Middle Ages and Renaissance was undoubtedly to convey a religious message, a fact which has not prevented even atheists from admiring the culture of that period. No worthwhile artistic tradition grows in a short time, and there is no reason why Chinese art should not absorb new ideas and the best from the past while still retaining its highly revolutionary themes.

The other point is the stress on amateur art and the participation of the masses. To encourage all people to develop an artistic and creative sense is a new trend in China and surely an extremely healthy one. Though most of the products of the amateurs may be stereotyped at present they need not necessarily remain so. Where vast numbers of people turn their hands to artistic creation, a fine tradition is almost certain to emerge eventually.

One of the most constant themes of Chinese publications is that all activity should cater for the interests of the poor and oppose those of the rich. The effective implementation of this doctrine has resulted in severe limits on freedom of artistic and intellectual expression, especially among the bourgeoisie. At the same time it has also led to a steady improvement in the lives of the masses, who enjoyed very little opportunity to express themselves at all in the past, whether freely or otherwise. And the Communist policies have enabled the poor to shake off the restrictions imposed by the family system, by their economic subjection, and by their backward condition. It is worth emphasizing strongly that in China the poor are the vast majority, the wealthy but a small minority. If the Communists retain the support of the formerly oppressed classes, they can claim success for their administration, whatever the attitude of the rich.

Select Bibliography

Fraser, Stewart E. (ed.) *Education and Communism in China, An Anthology of Commentary and Documents*, International Studies Group, Hong Kong, 1969. This book contains articles covering different aspects of education in China today, some of them being extremely valuable.

Mackerras, Colin and **Hunter, Neale** *China Observed 1964/1967*, Sphere Books, London, 1968. A first-hand account based on the years the authors spent as teachers in Peking and Shanghai.

Meijer, M.J. *Marriage Law and Policy in the Chinese People's Republic*, Hong Kong University Press, Hong Kong, 1971. An excellent and readable book on all aspects of marriage law in China. It includes a section on the liberated zones before 1949.

Price, R.F. *Education in Communist China*, World Education Series, Routledge and Kegan Paul, London, 1970. The author taught in a foreign language institute in Peking, and has combined his experiences with a great deal of other material to make a readable and reliable book.

Yang, C.K. *Chinese Communist Society: The Family and the Village*, The Massachusetts Institute of Technology Press, Cambridge Mass., 1965. This work contains in one volume two of Dr Yang's books, *The Chinese Family in the Communist Revolution* and *A Chinese Village in Early Communist Transition*, both originally published in 1959 by The Massachusetts Institute of Technology Press. The second is based on field work in China from 1948 to 1951.

Part 5
China's international relations
Chapter 10
China's foreign policy, 1912-49

Edmund S.K. Fung

With the demise of the Manchu dynasty in 1911, the Chinese had cause to believe that China was on her way to becoming a strong, modern nation-state. The alien rule had been corrupt, effete, and, as the Chinese revolutionaries charged, the cause of China's repeated humiliations and defeats at foreign hands. The new republic was a Chinese regime, in the making of which certain modern Western ideas had been catalysts at one stage or another. Representing a new concept in Chinese political thought, the republic seemed to promise a bright future able to adopt a new approach to foreign affairs that would lead China to a respected position among the nations.

Modern China's foreign policy was in large measure conditioned by her past history, cultural traditions, domestic problems, and existing relations with the foreign powers. China in 1912 was a weak, backward, underdeveloped 'semi-colonial state', exploited by the powers through a series of 'unequal treaties', concessions and settlements which stripped the Chinese government of many of its sovereign rights. It was a common desire of all Chinese regimes and political groups to vindicate the battered pride of a great civilization and to rehabilitate their country's power position. They wanted modern armies, an adequate transportation system, national industrialization, and a strong economy—in short modernization that would enable China to emerge as a world power. An end should be put to foreign exploitation and encroachment and adjustments be made to existing relations with the powers accordingly.

The principal objectives of new China's foreign policy were thus to achieve effective equality in her relations with the powers, to uphold her independence in fact as well as in name, and to maintain her territorial integrity. The abolition of the 'unequal treaties' was given first priority, being the dominant theme of

China's international activities and of its anti-imperialism.

During the period under review, 1912–49, certain historical trends seem to stand out clearly in China's foreign relations. We find a weak China struggling with the powers, all of which evinced a pronounced reluctance to let the Chinese off the hook as quickly as the latter desired, but were never hesitant in increasing their privileges whenever possible. This period also witnessed an increasingly aggressive Japan bent on establishing control over the Chinese mainland. Until 1941 this aggression was largely unchecked from outside the East Asian scene because of a favourable (to Japan) international situation marked by the onset of Stalinism in the Soviet Union, the Great Depression in the United States, nazism in Germany, and finally the Western powers' preoccupation with affairs in Europe.

Another trend was the Soviet Union's expansion into Central and Northeast Asia. The problem facing China was that she had to deal with potential enemies on two fronts. To solve it, the Chinese government fell back on the traditional policy of playing off one power against the other. But this failed to check the advance of either power and instead provided the Soviet Union with opportunities to extend its influence to the Far East and to involve itself in China's political developments to its advantage.

The last years of this period were characterized by American involvement in China's internal and external policies. An advocate of the Open Door, the United States respected the administrative and territorial integrity of China and was sympathetic to the Chinese cause. But she was not prepared until the Japanese attack on Pearl Harbour in 1941 to sustain her policy by any means other than diplomatic. Even then national interests, as well as ideological motivations, were important determinants in the American China policy.

China experienced the trauma of two world wars. She participated in the first one voluntarily, with high hopes that she would be justly rewarded at the peace table. The second one, which virtually began with the Japanese invasion of north China in July 1937, was imposed on the Chinese who fought it as a matter of national preservation. From neither of the wars did China emerge as a respected member of the world community.

The limitations to China's foreign achievements can be attributed to various factors. Obviously the countries China was dealing with were either too powerful or too aggressive, or both. As in the past, China was unable to back up her diplomacy with military power. The internecine wars that plagued the country from the warlord years down to the struggle between the Nationalists and the Communists had prevented the establishment of an effective, central government which would have been in a better position to cope with the international situation. Internal dissensions among the rival regimes encouraged the powers either to deal officially with the faction which happened to control Peking (before 1928) or Nanking (after 1928) which they recognized, or to fall in with Chinese intrigues and to strengthen their own positions by supporting the regimes that controlled the areas of their special interests. The powers were inclined to work in both ways whenever it suited their purposes to do so. The Soviet Union, for one, dealt with Sun Yat-sen and other military regimes while making friendly overtures to the Peking government, and later with the Chinese Communists while at the same time maintaining proper relations with Nanking. It was China's administrative fragmentation and military inadequacy that made possible this two-level approach of foreign diplomacy in China.

The Early Republic 1912-16

When the Chinese believed that the new era following the collapse of the Manchus would usher in a strong government capable of warding off foreign encroachment, they were engaging in wishful thinking. From the very beginning the republic fared no better, and probably even worse, than the regime preceding it. The advent of the new government was received by the foreign powers with anything but enthusiasm. The United States was probably the only Western nation that really showed sympathy to the republican cause. The European powers cast doubts on the viability of the republic and, out of national self-interest, feared that the emergence of a strong and modern China would threaten their established positions and privileges there. If the republican cause meant throwing off the trammels of the 'unequal treaties', none of the powers wished to see a strong military power in China. If, on the other hand, the Chinese were unable to maintain order at home, the chaos that ensued would equally prejudice the commercial interests of the powers in East Asia.

Japan, in particular, watched developments in China with hostility. Her appetite for continental expansion having been whetted by victories over China and Russia in the previous decades, Japan could not help viewing the rise of a modern China as a formidable obstacle to her imperialist aspirations, and would have helped the Manchus to stay in power had it not been for the disagreement of the Western powers. The republic could indeed have been strangled at birth.

International approval of the republic was slow in coming. In May 1913 the United States, acting independently, was the first power to grant recognition. Russia, Britain, France, and Japan did not follow suit until Yüan Shih-k'ai was formally installed as president five months later.

It is ironic that no sooner had it been established than the republic lost control over the outlying regions of the Ch'ing empire. In its last years the Manchu dynasty had pursued a forward policy in Mongolia, Tibet, and Manchuria with remarkable success. But as soon as the Chinese revolution got under way, Outer Mongolia, in December 1911, declared its independence and gradually moved into the Russian sphere. By a bilateral agreement of November 1912, Russia committed herself to help the Mongols to 'maintain their autonomous region'. Subsequent Sino-Russian negotiations resulted in an agreement in November 1913 recognizing China's suzerainty and Outer Mongolia's autonomy, while the signatory parties jointly pledged themselves to abstain from intervention in the internal affairs of Outer Mongolia. This was a defeat for the Chinese government, as Outer Mongolia had now virtually become a joint Sino-Russian protectorate.

Meanwhile Peking received a similar setback in Tibet, over which the Manchu dynasty had reasserted its suzerainty in 1906. After forcing the Chinese troops to withdraw from Lhasa, the Dalai Lama, in January 1913, declared the independence of its country and became oriented to the British who were taking an active interest in Tibet out of fear of Russia. Eventually China reached an agreement with Britain recognizing Chinese suzerainty and Tibetan autonomy. Just as Russia gained a controlling influence in Outer Mongolia, so Britain was given a special position in Tibet.

Political instability caused the infant republic to be exploited by the powers in other ways. The foreigners gained further control over China's maritime customs revenues which were now fully pledged to meet China's foreign loans and indemnity payments. This was paralleled by further expansion of foreign influence in Shanghai, the hub of foreign trade, where the Mixed Court came under foreign control late in 1911. The Chinese efforts to elevate themselves from a position of international inferiority had scarcely begun when they met with further infringement upon their sovereignty.

The worst was yet to come. On 18 January 1915 Japan presented Peking with Twenty-One demands, divided into five groups, which, if accepted, would have virtually made China a Japanese protectorate. Yüan Shih-k'ai, hoping to win foreign support, leaked the news to the foreign press and legations, thus forcing the Japanese to make some concessions. But no foreign aid materialized. The allied powers, preoccupied with the European war, were reluctant to stop Japan who had shortly before declared war on Germany. The Americans could have acted alone, but Washington was not the least disposed to be entangled in international difficulties in the distant Far East. In these circumstances Yüan, realizing China's military weakness and probably anticipating Japanese support for his monarchical movement, complied with the first four groups of demands, thereby giving Japan a dominant position in Shantung, south Manchuria, and eastern Inner Mongolia, as well as special interests in the industrial base in central China. This did great harm to the republic's standing. When Yüan died in June 1916, he left the legacy of a divided nation, exposed to foreign encroachment as of old.

The Warlord Era 1917–27

The warlord era opened a complex chapter in the history of modern China, one fraught with internecine wars, political instability, social and economic dislocations, and considerable human suffering. It saw the ferment of an intellectual revolution and the rapid growth of Chinese nationalism that featured the May Fourth Movement, the founding of the Chinese Communist Party, the reorganization of the Kuomintang, and the Northern Expedition. In foreign affairs, it witnessed China's entry into the First World War, the Soviet Union's early activities in China, and China's early efforts at rights recovery.

In 1917 the First World War was entering its fourth year. Peking's earlier attitude of neutrality, favoured by Yüan Shih-k'ai, had begun to change since Japan declared war on Germany on 23 August 1914 and moved her troops into Kiaochow and Shantung, the German spheres of interest. Despite Chinese protests, Japan managed to secure the agreement of the allied powers to her succession to Germany's rights, privileges, and property in Shantung and the Pacific islands. The powers placed China low in their scales of values and paid for Japan's participation in the war at China's expense.

The desire to sit as an equal and independent partner with the victorious nations at the peace table where Chinese grievances could be aired must have weighed heavily on Peking's decision to lead the country to war against Germany which it had no more cause to fight than it did the other powers exploiting China. Britain and France welcomed the Chinese declaration of war on 14 August 1917, their main concern being the elimination of German interests and competition in China. Japan, prepared for the Chinese decision, lost no time in securing a blanket American acknowledgment of her 'special interests' in the 'contiguous' parts of China.

Most Chinese intellectuals, especially the radicals, approved of the government's policy, as they interpreted the war as 'a struggle between the Anglo-French forces of progress and democracy against German militarism and monarchism'. They assumed that the allies were fighting for the cause of justice and that their victory would have a salutory influence on political conditions in China. Added to this assumption was the feeling that Chinese participation in the war was a matter of national prestige and a step towards improving China's international standing.

Blasted hopes easily turn into bitter resentment. The Versailles decision at the end of the war to turn over to Japan the former German concessions in Shantung immediately set off a storm of protest and student demonstrations in Peking, on 4 May 1919, against Japanese aggression. The demonstrations rapidly spread to all the major cities in China, manifesting a seething nationalism and a long buildup of patriotic indignation shared by people from all walks of life. The peace treaty, the Chinese were convinced, was a blatant violation of the much celebrated principle of national self-determination and a naked betrayal of Chinese interests. Through concessions to Japan, it also posed a serious threat to China's security.

The May Fourth Incident was not an isolated phenomenon; it must be seen in the context of the intellectual revolution which demanded an independent foreign policy for China aimed at the maintenance of Chinese interests as well as justice and world peace. While essentially directed against Japanese militarism, it reflected a tremendous disillusionment with Western humanism and democracy on the part of the radical intellectuals. As one writer has put it, 'For many of the students and young intellectuals of the May Fourth era the image of a liberal and progressive West that would instruct China in the principles of democracy and science had been forever submerged under a wave of nationalism and anti-imperialism'.[1] This disillusionment served to create a ready receptivity to the anti-imperialist appeals of Lenin, preparing the ground for the founding of the Chinese Communist Party two years later.

It was against this background that the newly established Communist regime in Moscow made friendly gestures to the Chinese. In an endeavour to discredit the Versailles powers, to contribute to the surge of Chinese nationalism, and to endear itself to the Peking regime, the Soviet Foreign Office announced the famous Karakhan Manifesto of 25 July 1919, repudiating the 'unequal treaties' and renouncing all the conquest of Chinese territory made by the Czarist regime. But when the Manifesto was communicated to Peking in March 1920, China gave no official reply because she realized that the Soviet proposals concerned not only herself but also her relations with the other powers. For some years China had been co-operating with the allied powers—fighting the World War, supporting the intervention in Siberia against the Bolsheviks, blockading Bolshevik areas in Manchuria, and withholding recognition of the Communist regime—and now felt that, in spite of the Versailles settlement, it would be too hasty to enter into official relations with the Soviet Union before others did. But the Manifesto could not be simply ignored for fear of 'hurting Soviet feelings'. Thus caught in a dilemma, Peking acted with circumspection, not replying officially but secretly making informal responses to the proposals. Representatives from both countries met informally at Copenhagen and Vladivostok, followed by a Chinese mission to Russia. However the negotiations, or exchange of views, came to nothing apparently because of the question of the Chinese Eastern Railway in Manchuria.

The Soviet gestures should not suggest that Russian interests in the Chinese borderlands and encroachment on Chinese territorial integrity lessened with the ascendency to power of the Bolsheviks. In fact they were just as expansionist and predatory as the Czarist regime had been. In July 1921 the Soviet Red Army invaded Outer Mongolia on the pretext of expelling the White Russian forces which had earlier seized the capital of Urga. In 1924 the Mongolian People's Republic was set up and became a virtual Soviet satellite. Meanwhile the Russians developed an interest in Central Asia after subjugating the Kazakhs, Kirghiz, and other minority races, thus bringing its influence to bear upon Chinese Sinkiang. Commercial relations were maintained between the two regions.

It took Peking some years to enter into official relations with

Moscow, as it was still looking to the capitalist West for support. It was not until the Washington Conference brought home a combination of enlightenment and disappointment that Peking felt compelled to reorient its foreign policy.

The aim of the Washington Conference (12 November 1921— 2 February 1922) was to find solutions to the current problems of the Pacific and East Asia. The Chinese representatives went there in the belief that the mistakes of Versailles would be corrected and that the 'unequal treaties' would be discussed at length and specifically revised. But before long they were disappointed, as their grievances were dealt with in a rather evasive manner. The Western powers seemed more interested in the limitation of naval armament, which was achieved on the basis of a five-five-three ratio for Britain, the United States, and Japan, their policy being to *counter* Japan's postwar expansion, not to *check* it. Given an assurance of her naval domination of the western Pacific, Japan agreed to give up her wartime territorial gains by withdrawing from Shantung and the northeast Asian continent (except from Korea).

True, the Chinese received some attention from the conference and some minor concessions regarding foreign privileges in China, but the key problem of the 'unequal treaties' remained unsolved. The lesson they learned was that the powers, whatever they professed in principle, would not proceed fast enough to allow them to recover their national sovereign rights. The capitalist West had once again ignored their aspirations, thereby causing them to turn to the Soviet Union.

At this time Soviet representatives were actively dealing with Sun Yat-sen's Kuomintang and the infant Chinese Communist Party, in an effort to forge a united front to overthrow the warlord government in Peking as a first step towards fighting imperialism in China. The Kuomintang-Communist alliance was achieved in 1923, followed by Soviet aid in the reorganization of the Kuomintang and in the training of a revolutionary army which was to unify the country in 1928.

Motivated by national self-interest, Moscow was, in the meantime, eager to formalize relations with Peking. A friendly Peking would constitute a buffer zone protecting the Soviet Far Eastern flank against Japanese attacks. The Soviet Union was not party to the Washington Conference and appeared most sympathetic with the Chinese. On 31 May 1924 official relations were re-established by an agreement which declared null and void, at least on paper, all previous Chinese treaties with Czarist Russia.

Peking agreed to joint Sino-Soviet operation of the Chinese Eastern Railway while Moscow agreed to surrender its extra-territoriality in China. The Russians also recognized Outer Mongolia as 'a component part of the Chinese Republic', while the Chinese acknowledged the Russian *de facto* dominance there. (Future developments show, however, that Chinese sovereignty remained in the shadow until Outer Mongolia declared its independence in October 1945.) Finally a new delimitation of the Sino-Soviet boundary was agreed upon, but it was never implemented.

The improvement of Sino-Soviet relations was contrasted by a cooling of China's relations with the Western powers. The crux of the matter was still the 'unequal treaties'. The powers' reluctance to renounce their rights added fuel to the burgeoning Chinese nationalism. Anti-foreign feeling ran high, reaching an apex on 30 May 1925 when the police of Shanghai's foreign settlement fired into a crowd of students demonstrating against the arrest of strikers from a Japanese mill, and on 23 June when a Chinese crowd in Canton protesting against the Shanghai incident was likewise fired upon by British troops. The ensuing violence and nationwide boycotts of Japanese and British goods and firms illustrate the frustration of the Chinese people as well as the rising tide of anti-imperialism.

Generally the warlord regimes could ill afford to antagonize the powers and foreign interest groups on which they relied heavily for financial support and the supply of arms, and they therefore often appeared to be instruments of foreign imperialism. The Peking regime of Tuan Ch'i-jui, who had emerged as a strong military man since 1917, was accused of pro-Japanese tendencies. By contrast, the Canton regime of the Nationalists was rapidly gaining popularity because of its avowed aim of anti-imperialism. However it is unfair to charge the Peking regime with apathy towards foreign encroachment. In spite of their rivalries, Peking and Canton were in genuine agreement on the need to recover the country's sovereign rights. This is evidenced by their joint memorandum of 24 June 1925 to the powers demanding modification of the treaties.

The Chinese determination, coupled with the anti-foreign disturbances following the May Thirtieth Incident, helped to soften the foreign attitudes towards treaty revision. The powers had agreed in Washington in 1922 to move towards *gradual* liquidation of the treaty system by calling for conferences on the Chinese customs tariff and on extraterritoriality, and now felt obliged to live up to their promises. On 26 October 1925 the Special Conference on the Chinese Customs Tariff was held in Peking. But, owing to internal strife which led to the collapse of Tuan Ch'i-jui's government, and the divergent interests of the powers, the conference achieved nothing except for a resolution that tariff autonomy should be returned to China by 1929. In early 1926 the Commission on Extraterritoriality opened in Peking. However the subsequent report on the political conditions in China was unfavourable, and the powers therefore opposed the abolition of extraterritoriality at that time.

Nevertheless the powers realized that China's demands for concessions could be temporized but not entirely ignored. There could be no doubt that the demands represented the wishes of all sections of the Chinese population which would support any party working diligently towards the unification of the country and the elimination of foreign imperialism. The Chinese were convinced that the foreigners would be more agreeable if the political conditions at home improved and if they stood firm. The smaller nations were less intransigent. For example, in 1926 Peking advised Belgium that their treaties would not be renewed, but that a new equal one could be negotiated. The same was done to Spain and France with partial success. It did not work of course with stronger nations such as Japan which found the Chinese measures unjustifiable and arbitrary.

Had there been internal peace, a modern military system, and an effective central government in China, the Chinese would have been more successful in their quest for respectability, and the powers, or at least some of them, would have been convinced that the Chinese were able to run their own country properly. What was necessary for China to become a respected member of the world community was to put her house in order and to modernize her administration. Indeed it was this popular desire for unity which gave the Northern Expedition the strength it needed to eliminate worlordism and to establish the Kuomintang government in 1928.

The Nanking Decade 1928-37

The Kuomintang under Chiang Kai-shek began as a revolutionary party committed to a programme of modernization internally and anti-imperialism externally. It was Chiang's conviction that all China's national humiliations and socio-economic problems were caused almost entirely by foreign imperialism. The treaty system was viewed as an instrument of exploitation, and its liquidation was essential for national revival and moral regeneration. In this respect Chiang seems to have been influenced in some measure by Lenin's interpretation of imperialism. At the same time there was a distinct Chinese strain in Chiang's thought. Chiang was a conservative nationalist who showed considerable reverence for Tseng Kuo-fan (1811–72), the scholar-official who had vigorously defended Confucian values and the Manchu dynasty during the Taiping uprising. Like Tseng, Chiang was in the grip of China's past. He wanted to revive the idea of a great Chinese empire not only by abolishing all the 'unequal treaties' but also by recovering and claiming all territories which had once been parts of the empire. His assumption was that lost territories were merely concessions to force and that they should be brought back into the Chinese fold when China was able to do so diplomatically or militarily. Hence his government, as soon as it was established, pursued a twofold vigorous foreign policy: the recovery of sovereign rights, which was synonymous with the re-establishment of full national independence, and the restoration of China's 'traditional' frontiers, which was synonymous with the maintenance of territorial integrity. There was of course a third area where attention was due and that was national defence; but, as we shall see, this received a lower priority than internal security.

Nanking achieved some remarkable successes through negotiation. In 1929 it recovered the British concessions at Kiukiang, Amoy, and Weihaiwei, the Belgian concession at Tientsin, and abolished extraterritoriality for the nationals of Belgium and Denmark. In the following year it regained tariff autonomy and secured the agreement of the powers to make available Boxer indemnity payments for educational use. By then the foreign community in Shanghai had given up their control of the Mixed Court, although extraterritorial rights were still retained by Britain, the United States, France, and Japan.

China succeeded where negotiations were based on appeals to reasoning, but failed where she resorted to the application of force. This can be illustrated by her clash with the Soviet Union in 1929 when Chinese troops raided Soviet consular offices at Harbin, arrested some Soviet citizens, and seized control of the Chinese Eastern Railway. The border skirmishes that followed served as a warning to the Chinese that unilateral, arbitrary measures could not succeed.

The Japanese invasion of Manchuria on 18 September 1931 put

a temporary halt to Nanking's drive in rights recovery. The Japanese were advancing very rapidly in their conquest. On 1 March 1932 they turned Manchuria into the puppet state of Manchukuo with P'u-i, the last Ch'ing emperor, as regent. In the following year they seized Jehol Province and established a demilitarized zone between the Great Wall and Peiping (Peking). Before the end of 1935 north China was declared a neutral zone.

The Chinese people reacted to the Japanese aggression by demanding firm military resistance. The Chinese Communists, riding on the wave of nationalism, started organizing resistance forces behind the Japanese lines, in a process of mass mobilization. Non-communist groups, politicians, and intellectuals expressed equal concern over the national crisis, all calling for action. They organized national salvation associations, strikes, and demonstrations to bring pressure to bear on the government.

Nanking, however, adopted a policy of appeasement and non-military resistance. The Kuomintang leadership was fully aware of the popular demand at home, but the nationalism which it had manifested in earlier years was submerged by a partisan concern over the growing threat of the Chinese Communists. To Chiang, the Japanese invasion was 'a disease of the skin', the Communist threat 'a disease of the heart'. Instead of mobilizing the Nationalist troops against the foreign enemy, Chiang was first of all determined to eliminate the internal foe through a series of extermination campaigns which forced the Communists onto the Long March in 1934. The Kuomintang slogan, 'unification before resistance' meant simply 'to trade space for time'; in other words, the Nationalist government gave top priority to fighting the Communists even at the risk of losing some territory to the Japanese.

Chiang needed time not only to build up his German-trained army but also to invoke foreign intervention against Japan. He proceeded from the premise that if the Chinese themselves could not stop the Japanese, he might as well ask the Western powers to do so. Had the powers not pledged themselves to respect China's territorial integrity? Chiang therefore placed the Chinese problem before the League of Nations. The League responded by demanding a Japanese withdrawal of the occupied Chinese territory and by setting up a commission to look into the Manchurian situation. But Japan ignored this and made further advances in north China. None of the Western powers was willing to risk war with Japan, and they all confined their actions to diplomatic representations. Even the United States, Japan's competitor in the Pacific, was not inclined to come to China's aid. Without the United States, which was not a party to the League, any collective security system could hardly succeed.

Adding insult to injury, Japan declared, in April 1934, that it was her responsibility to maintain peace in the Far East. The implication was clear: Japan was to be the policeman in the region, and other nations should not interfere with Chinese affairs or intervene in the conflict. Japan even objected to Western assistance to China, whether in financial, technical, military, or political forms. Despite Chinese protests, the Western powers reacted to the declaration with relative calm. Once again they wanted to avoid antagonizing Japan when their attention was being drawn to Europe.

From the beginning of the conflict Chiang Kai-shek had hoped that the Soviet Union, on account of its rivalry with Tokyo, would support the Chinese militarily. Accordingly he tried to make a deal with the Russians while at the same time appealing to the League. The price he was willing to pay was the restoration of regular diplomatic relations which had been interrupted since 1929. He calculated that the resumption of Sino-Soviet relations would confer certain political leverage on Nanking, in that it was a good-neighbour policy playing on Japan's fears of a Sino-Soviet military pact as well as on the Western powers' fears of communism in the Far East.

Moscow was delighted to resume relations in 1932, but gave Nanking no prospects of Soviet aid. Knowing precisely what was on Chiang's mind, Moscow, while declaring Japan an aggressor, let it be known in both Nanking and Tokyo that it had no intention of being entangled in the Sino-Japanese conflict. What remained of Chiang's hopes was dashed on 23 March 1935, when Moscow settled its differences with Tokyo over Manchuria by an agreement for the sale of the Chinese Eastern Railway to Manchukuo, which was now firmly under Japanese control.

There could be no doubt that Chiang's diplomacy was unrealistic. The centuries-old device of luring one barbarian into fighting another had lost its effectiveness. There was no reason why any of the powers should rush gallantly to China's defence if the Chinese government did not resist the enemy itself. The failure of Chiang's diplomacy made it clear that the Chinese themselves had to save their own country. All Chinese patriots were critical of Nanking's policy and called for immediate resistance and a united front. But Chiang still turned a deaf ear to the popular demand. It was not until the Sian Incident of December 1936 that he complied with the wish of his people to end the civil war, if only temporarily, and to collaborate with the Chinese Communists in a war of attrition.

The Sino-Japanese War 1937–45

The full-fledged Japanese invasion of China began on 7 July 1937. The Japanese troops took possession of north China in no time and then forced their way to Shanghai, which they captured after meeting with very stubborn resistance from Kuomintang troops. At the end of 1937 they succeeded in driving the Nationalist troops from Nanking to Wuhan in central China, which also fell in the autumn of 1938. With the loss of the rich, populous, eastern coastal regions, the Nationalists retreated to the western mountainous provinces where they set up a wartime government in Chungking.

Before the end of 1938 the Japanese wanted to enter into negotiations with Chiang Kai-shek with a view to dictating terms for a peace settlement. But the war had not yet reached a stage where the Chinese would concede defeat. When the Chinese rejected the terms, the Japanese set up a host of 'puppet regimes' to help run the occupied areas. Wang Ching-wei, a veteran Kuomintang opponent of Chiang, was lured to Nanking to head another national government.

The years from 1939 to August 1945 formed a period of relative peace and stalemate, with neither belligerent undertaking any spectacular military operations except for the Japanese offensive in the summer of 1944. The Kuomintang troops made no attempt to regain lost territory or to organize guerrilla resistance in the way that the Chinese Communists were doing. Now somewhat relieved from Japanese pressure, the Nationalists turned their attention to the Communists with whom they clashed from time to time. After 1941 the united front had become, to all intents and purposes, defunct.

Another reason that the Nationalists took no major initiative against the Japanese was Chiang's conviction that sooner or later a Western power would clash with Japan and virtually fight the war for him. There seemed to be some basis for such thinking. In August 1937 China had concluded a non-aggression pact with Russia which caused a stir in Tokyo, and since then the Russians had been supplying the Chinese with arms and funds. In 1938 and 1939 Soviet-Japanese relations were strained by border clashes between their respective troops in Northeast and Central

Asia, and it looked as if war were imminent. However Moscow, preoccupied with the European crisis, had no intention of risking war with Tokyo. After some tough negotiations, a non-aggression pact was reached between the two countries on 13 April 1941, after which Soviet aid to China diminished to a trickle.

A second possible source of foreign aid to China was the United States, which had been watching the Japanese aggression with discomfort. The initial American reaction was within the bounds of moral condemnation of the aggressor and diplomatic protests. But developments in the Asian scene since 1940 had begun to compel the Americans to review their relations with the Japanese. In early 1940, somewhat belatedly, Washington started to restrict the shipment of certain war materials to Japan. The following year when Japan moved into Southeast Asia to secure the supply of raw materials and to establish a Greater East Asia Co-Prosperity Sphere, Washington felt obliged to take some strong action. On 24 July 1941 Japanese assets in the United States were frozen and an embargo was placed on petroleum exports to Japan. The world waited for another five months to witness the outbreak of the Pacific War following the Japanese attack on Pearl Harbour on 7 December 1941. At last China had become an ally of the United States.

By then the Second World War had gone far enough to warrant full concentration of the allies on the struggle against Germany. This meant that the Chinese, now with massive American aid, had to bear the brunt of the war in Asia. Chiang Kai-shek was made Commander-in-Chief of the China area of the China-Burma-India Theatre, created in January 1942 in co-operation with Lieutenant General Joseph W. Stilwell, the American commander. It was the United States strategy to build up the Chinese (Nationalist) Army and to confer a power status on China so that she 'might exact a constantly growing price from the Japanese invader'. In October 1943 China was recognized, thanks to the United States, as one of the 'big four' that would shape the postwar world. In December of the same year China, again on American insistence, obtained promises from her allies that Manchuria, Formosa (Taiwan), and the Pescadores (Penghu Islands), which were under Japanese occupation, would be returned to China. Besides this, the United States and Britain also agreed to relinquish their extraterritorial rights in China.

Although he desired the making of a China war theatre in order to get the Americans more deeply involved, Chiang did not set himself to combat the Japanese troops to any significant extent.

He was in fact not fighting in concert with the Chinese Communists against their common enemy and gave little attention to recommendations from his American advisers on the ways in which the Japanese should be fought. Not surprisingly, he quarrelled with General Stilwell, who was later relieved of his command. Basically his strategy was to bleed the United States of as much military equipment and funds as possible on the grounds of fighting the Japanese, while preserving the strength of his armies for a showdown with the Communists, particularly in the postwar period.

The United States realized that military aid to Chiang's government would unavoidably strengthen the Nationalist position in relation to the Communists. A civil war in China at this time was most undesirable as it would, firstly, induce the Soviet Union to support the Communists and, secondly, disrupt the operations against the Japanese. President Roosevelt therefore hoped to bring about a political settlement and accordingly, in November 1944, sent his special envoy, Major General Patrick Hurley, to China to confer with Mao Tse-tung in Yenan. But the mediation failed as neither the Communists nor the Nationalists were satisfied with the terms on which a workable union between them was to be forged.

Meanwhile the international situation was not very favourable to China. The Soviet Union had indicated to the United States its intention of entering the war against Japan when the European war was over. President Roosevelt welcomed the Soviet move, with the consequence that the importance of China in the Asian war situation was considerably reduced. The 'great power' status China obtained with American help was artificial. Her inferior position in the ranks of the allies was never mistaken. Whatever concessions and help she had obtained from them had been given out of national self-interest rather than genuine sympathy with the Chinese plight. It was this same consideration that was to betray China's interests in the Yalta Agreement.

The Yalta Agreement of 11 February 1945, signed by Roosevelt, Churchill, and Stalin, set forth the conditions on which the Soviet Union would enter the war against Japan. It provided for the preservation of the *status quo* in Outer Mongolia, the restoration of 'the former rights of Russia violated by the treacherous attack of Japan in 1904', and Russian possession of the Kurile Islands. In conceding such privileges to the Soviet Union in China, the United States overlooked the fact that the repudiation of the Russo-Japanese peace settlement of 1905 was precisely a reversal of the American stand on Japanese rivalries with the Russians. In allowing the Russians to enjoy 'pre-eminent interests' in southern Manchuria, with the internationalization of Dairen, the lease of Port Arthur as a Russian naval base, and joint operation by China and the Soviet Union of the Chinese Eastern and South Manchurian Railways, the Americans showed no regard for Chinese interests. The Yalta decision was made without prior consultation with China, and was presented to the Chinese as a *fait accompli*. Chiang Kai-shek was compelled to accept it by a country which claimed to have been fighting for justice. Political expediency dictated American policy, and little consideration seems to have been given to long-term postwar consequences.

Chiang reacted to the secret agreement with indignation, but there was nothing he could do, except to negotiate with the Russians for better terms. The negotiations, watched closely by Washington as if the Chinese were not under enough pressure, led to the signing of the Treaty of Friendship and Alliance, under which both countries were committed to extended war against Japan. The National government was recognized as the central government of China, to which Soviet aid would be supplied. Russia agreed to refrain from interfering in the internal affairs of Sinkiang, and to recognize Chinese sovereignty over Manchuria in return for the concessions there. A set of notes supplementary to the treaty was also drawn up concerning Dairen, Port Arthur, and the railways in Manchuria. On Outer Mongolia, the agreement was that a plebiscite was to be taken there when the war with Japan was over to find out whether the population desired independence.[2] After all this, Chiang contented himself with assurances of Soviet 'goodwill'.

The Soviet Union entered the Pacific War on 8 August 1945, two days after the American bombing of Hiroshima and one day before the bombing of Nagasaki. The war ended only six days later.

The Postwar Period 1946–49

At the end of the war China recovered from Japan the lost territories of Taiwan, the Pescadores, and Manchuria. Inside China there was widespread hatred for the Japanese and many people, including government officials, who had lost their homes, families, and property, would have liked the war culprits to pay dearly for their guilt. But Chiang Kai-shek chose to take a magnanimous attitude towards the Japanese and did not wish for revenge. The reason for this was that he wished to restore good relations with Japan in order to counter the Russian influence in the Far East and, more importantly, to maintain cordial relations with Washington which was planning to contribute in large measure to Japan's postwar rehabilitation. What he wanted, as far as his policy on Japan was concerned, was to have some say in the United States' formulation of policies on Japan, whereby he could be assured that the economic rehabilitation of Japan and the development of an American military base there would have no adverse effects on the rehabilitation of China's economy and power position.

Postwar Sino-Japanese relations proved to be proper. The Japanese were somehow grateful for Chiang's 'soft' peace. Besides that, they were not in a position to threaten China's security for many years to come. Although Chiang did not in fact play any significant role in the rehabilitation of Japan, he was assured of a friendly neighbour which had been his enemy for over a decade.

Internally, postwar China saw a period of fierce civil war that ultimately led to the Communist accession to power in October 1949. The civil war had wide external complications and could hardly fail to affect China's foreign relations. The Nationalists were fighting against an internal enemy which seemed to have Soviet backing, and this inevitably brought into play the interests of the United States and the Soviet Union as a logical development of the growing polarization of power in the international situation that began the Cold War. Both powers, for ideological reasons and national interests, were entangled in China's internal developments, and this could not but help to deepen and widen the Nationalist-Communist breach which it was the American policy to heal. Naturally the Chinese were split, largely along partisan lines, between the American and the Russian camp.

Of course the picture is not as simple as that. The Soviet Union, having regained much of the privileged position Czarist Russia had once enjoyed in Manchuria, seemed initially interested in some sort of collaboration with China in the latter's postwar rehabilitation, promising to refrain from interfering in the Chinese civil war and to honour its commitment of supporting the central government. However the two countries soon found themselves in dispute over Manchuria with regard to economic co-operation, the withdrawal of Soviet troops, and the recovery of Manchuria by the Nationalist troops from the surrendered Japanese forces. The first issue was settled, after much hard bargaining, to Russia's advantage. The last two issues touched upon the relative positions of the Nationalists and the Chinese Communists. The Russians completed their evacuation by May 1946, but before that they had dismantled and removed the 'war booty' of key elements of the rich industrial plants built by the Japanese and stripped Manchuria of most of its valuable industrial components. Meanwhile Stalin was still interested in co-operating with Chiang, only to be rejected once again. With American backing, the Nationalists were now in renewed armed struggle with the Communists for the control of Manchuria. They captured the major cities and railways in the south, while the Communists, who won sympathy but no material support from Moscow, were firmly established in the rural areas and all of northern Manchuria. Incidentally, the Russians were still in control of Dairen and Port Arthur and of the greater part of the vital Chinese Changchun Railway (formerly the Chinese Eastern Railway).

Chiang was also perturbed by developments in Sinkiang, where the Soviet Union appeared to be supporting, at least morally, a revolt in the Ili region against Chinese control. After reaching an agreement with the Chinese government in 1946, the rebel group gradually moved into the Russian sphere, through which it maintained communications with the outside world. This pro-Russian trend proved to the advantage of the Chinese Communists, and in 1949 Sinkiang went over to them smoothly.

While trying to maintain proper relations with Moscow, thereby, as it were, weakening the position of the Chinese Communists, the Nationalists had no trust in the Soviet leadership. Past experience had shown that the Russians were not easy to deal with, and Chiang was opposed to any Soviet co-operation that would necessitate Nationalist collaboration with the Chinese Communists—specifically, the establishment of a coalition government in China. Even if his relations with the Soviet leadership should be strained, Chiang believed that he could rely on the United States to counteract the Russians, as well as to help defeat communism at home.

Chiang's policy of committing China to alignment with the United States was built largely on American fears of a Communist victory in China, particularly a victory achieved with Soviet aid. The Americans had continued to supply the Nationalists with massive aid. They had airlifted thousands of Nationalist troops back to the coastal regions at the conclusion of war with Japan, and were never slow in pouring money and arms into Nationalist hands.

Washington's support for the Nationalists stemmed, for a start, from President Roosevelt's belief that China under Chiang, and given a 'power status', would contribute to postwar stability. The president was also confident that the National government could be induced to reform itself, thus winning the support of the Chinese population. Hence he did not consider the advice of some of his Foreign Service Asian specialists that Washington should adjust itself to possible realignment in China. Yet he did not wish to lead his country to fight another war in East Asia. It seemed to him that the best strategy was to prevent the Chinese, Communists or not, from falling under the Stalinist-Moscow umbrella by bringing about a political settlement in which Chiang would still maintain his position or even probably gain the upper hand. In December 1945, therefore, General George C. Marshall was sent on a peace mission to Chungking, but he proved no more successful than Patrick Hurley had been a year before. When the Nationalists refused to collaborate with their opponents on Communist conditions, the civil war was fought to the end in Chinese terms.

Money and arms alone were not sufficient for the Nationalists to defeat their opponents who enjoyed the confidence and support of the Chinese masses that they lacked. Chiang and his government knew at heart where their weaknesses lay, but for political reasons they blamed outsiders rather than themselves for their ultimate collapse—the Americans for withholding adequate help and the Russians for supporting the Communists wholeheartedly.

Conclusion

When the People's Republic was established, China had recovered all the special privileges and concessions from the powers, except for Hong Kong, Macao, and some Russian rights in southern Manchuria. The long efforts at rights recovery, which assumed a new dimension in the Nanking decade, had finally paid off. The 'unequal treaties' would have been abolished much earlier had it not been for China's military weakness and internal disunity. The outbreak of the Sino-Japanese War in 1937 had hamstrung the Chinese efforts initially, but ironically the Western powers were later obliged to relinquish their rights in 1943, as the Japanese occupation armies paid no attention to other foreign interests and privileges in China.

By 1949 all foreign troops had evacuated China. At long last, it would appear, Chinese independence was achieved in substance as well as in form. Yet there was still the problem of Taiwan, where

Chiang and his remnant Nationalist forces took shelter under the protective umbrella of the United States. From the Chinese Communist point of view, the United States had become the dominant imperialist power in East Asia preventing Peking from unifying the country by military means.

To what extent had the Chinese achieved equality with the powers in international relations? By 1949 the 'semi-colonial' era in China was past. No powers seemed to dispute this, and none would have hoped to deal with China again on terms and in a manner they had formerly used. 'The Chinese people have stood up!' as Mao exclaimed with pride on his rise to power. However there was another side to the picture, and a gloomy side. China was still a poor, underdeveloped country, with an enormous population and a host of social, political, and economic problems which only an exceptional leadership could deal with. The birth of the People's Republic was, not surprisingly, seen by the capitalist West at best with suspicion and at worst with hostility and contempt. The number of Western countries quickly granting Peking recognition was small; the Scandinavian countries, the Netherlands, Switzerland, and the United Kingdom. For many years China's relations with Britain were somewhat ambiguous at the *chargé d'affaires* level. Not until January 1964 did France become the second major Western nation to establish diplomatic relations with Peking.

The most important lesson the Chinese had learned from their experiences with the powers since the nineteenth century was that military strength determined the position a country occupied in the world community. China had always been unsuccessful in her foreign relations because of an inferiority in arms. The rule of the international game was that diplomacy, if it were to be effective, must be supplemented with military force. This being so, China could not inspire awe and respect from the rest of the world until she was in possession of a powerful military system.

China's history, cultural traditions, and experiences with foreigners had entered into the consideration of all Chinese governments in the formulation of their foreign policies. It will be shown in the following chapter that these factors continue to influence the behaviour of the Communist leadership in international relations.

Notes

1 Maurice Meisner *Li Ta-chao and the Origins of Chinese Marxism*, Harvard University Press, Cambridge Mass., 1967, p. 99.
2 This plebiscite was held on 20 October 1945. The Mongols voted 'unanimously' for independence. Three months later the National government formally recognized the Mongolian People's Republic. No one doubted, however, that in practice Outer Mongolia had become a Soviet satellite.

Select Bibliography

Clubb, O. Edmund *20th Century China*, 2nd edn, Columbia University Press, New York, 1972. A good, readable book, dealing with both the internal and external developments in modern China.

Fairbank, John King *The United States and China*, 3rd edn, Harvard University Press, Cambridge Mass., 1971. An indispensable book for anyone with an interest in the perplexing problem of American relations with China.

FitzGerald, C.P. *The Birth of Communist China*, a Pelican book, Harmondsworth, 1964. An interesting account of modern China from the fall of the Manchus to the rise to power of the Communists, assessing the varying influences of Confucianism and Christianity, of East and West, and of the Japanese and Russians on the Chinese revolutionary movement.

Levi, W. *Modern China's Foreign Policy*, University of Minnesota Press, Minneapolis, 1953. A standard work on the subject.

North, Robert C. *Moscow and Chinese Communists*, 2nd edn, Stanford University Press, Stanford, 1963. Highly scholarly, but readable, offering much insight into the course of Sino-Soviet relations.

Chapter 11
Foreign relations, 1949-74

Colin Mackerras and Edmund S.K. Fung

The accession to power of the Communist Party has resulted in a stronger and more self-assured China than the world has seen since before the British shook the Manchu dynasty's confidence by launching and winning the First Anglo-Chinese war of 1839–42. As he proclaimed the People's Republic on 1 October 1949, Mao Tse-tung foreshadowed this new posture in the world when he declared that China had stood up and would never again be a humiliated nation. Certainly the great powers, both of the West and of the East, have taken far more notice of China's foreign policy attitudes since 1949 than they were ever used to doing in the past.

The Bases of China's Foreign Relations

The reassertion of China's position of strength as well as the pictures of Chairman Mao shaking hands with some foreign leader or other so constantly published in the Chinese press have led many observers to equate the contemporary Chinese attitude to foreign policy with that which prevailed in traditional times. Do not the Chinese still regard themselves as the 'central kingdom', to which the 'barbarians' of the rest of the world still send tribute? Are there any real signs that the Chinese really think of other nations as equals and not inferiors?

It is tempting to see replicas of the past in the present, and certainly there is much in what happens today which would have appealed to the emperors of old: the sense of China's ideological superiority and even uniqueness, the pride with which China feels able to display herself to admiring, even adulating, foreigners, the knowledge that the Chinese government is at all times in complete control of foreign policy and is not being unduly influenced by pressures from abroad. Yet it would be superficial to see Chinese attitudes to foreign policy as mere continuations of the past. There are basic differences which are more important than the similarities.

One is that China has accepted the techniques and to some extent the theory of international law, originally a Western concept. For instance, China has nowadays adopted the Western practice which dictates that each country should send representatives to reside permanently in the capitals of other states. In the dynastic past China received ministers who visited her capital for specific purposes, but they certainly did not live there for long periods of time as the representatives of foreign powers. An example of China's acceptance of the ideals of international law is the extreme emphasis she lays on concepts such as national sovereignty.

Another difference between past and present is that China is now well aware that she is technologically much inferior to several of the nations with which she deals. In fact the unquestioned assumption that China can deal *only* with inferiors is gone forever.

Perhaps more important is the fact that official policy is hostile to the lingering chauvinism individual Chinese might feel or display. Mao is on record as saying 'we Chinese people should get rid of great-power chauvinism resolutely, thoroughly, wholly and completely'.[1] Of course, the very strength of the statement's wording indicates that the reality does not correspond fully to the ideal, but it is surely important to note that a Confucian attitude would be to encourage feelings of superiority, not to stifle them.

On one point, contemporary Chinese approaches to foreign policy resemble those of the past and indeed all other states at virtually all times. No matter how important ideology may be to the framers of foreign policy, national interest will take precedence when the two conflict. Although there may have been short periods during the Cultural Revolution when ideology was paramount, such times are very much the exception, not the rule.

The most important aspect of national interest is security. This is a question which has obsessed the Chinese government since it came to power in 1949, and with good reason. At the very time the Communists were trying to consolidate their government, the United States as the most powerful nation on earth remained formally and openly committed to its overthrow. More recently the Soviet Union has sent over 1 000 000 troops to its border with

China and although they claim to be defensive, they must look very threatening from China's angle.

To say that national security and interests weigh more heavily than ideology is not to deny the importance of the latter. In China's case this is based on Marxist internationalism which demands support for the proletariat all over the world but rejects intervention and hegemonism. China should support progressive causes everywhere, including guerrilla liberation struggles, but it must never 'export revolution'. As Mao put the general principle in 1963: 'In the fight for complete liberation the oppressed people rely first of all on their own struggle and then, and only then, on international assistance.'[2] The Chinese government has made innumerable statements denouncing the hegemonism and aggressive policies of the superpowers, declaring that it will never join their ranks. It claims that to practise intervention and aggression are features of a capitalist power (either the Soviet Union or the United States) but that a genuine socialist state will never commit such a crime.

One prime example showing China's dual approach to foreign relations is her attitude to nuclear weapons. Ever since China's first atomic bomb was exploded in October 1964—and even before—China has made it clear that she regards her own nuclear arms as protectors of her own national security, a deterrent to the vast nuclear armoury arrayed against her both from the United States and the Soviet Union. But there is an ideological aspect as well. As an opponent of hegemonism, China has constantly stated that treaties to limit nuclear weapons serve merely to preserve the nuclear monopoly of the superpowers and should hence be opposed. The correct policy in China's eyes is the total destruction of nuclear arms. This would make the world safe from such weapons and also leave all countries equal as far as their possession is concerned. But until both the United States and the Soviet Union agree to this proposal, China will not abandon her own nuclear armoury.

It is the expectation of the Chinese government that the revolution will triumph all over the world in the long term. However its policies are posited on two assumptions: first, that this will be the result of an irreversible historical trend and will happen irrespective of what the Chinese themselves do; and second, that the ultimate victory of the world revolution lies in the dim, distant future.

The whole dilemma of a socialist foreign policy in a still predominantly capitalist world rests in the question of class. As

Marxists the Chinese should support the proletariat of all countries against the capitalists; they should defend the poor nations against the rich. These ideals are realized to a great extent. One can cite the example of China's attitude in the United Nations debate on the seabed. In his speech to the General Assembly on 2 October 1973, the Chairman of the Chinese delegation, Ch'iao Kuan-hua, strongly supported the claim of the small and medium-sized countries to establish national jurisdiction over a strip in the seabed of two hundred nautical miles from their coast. The grounds for this position were simply that it is the rich powers who gain most when the coastal limits of smaller countries are only three or twelve nautical miles.

But how should a socialist country deal with capitalist powers? In fact the Chinese have opted for conducting relations with capitalist or even feudal governments with great propriety and respect, provided that the government concerned is prepared to be friendly to China and that China's national interests have nothing to lose. We see here again the paramount place of national interests.

China's Relations with the West

The pre-eminent role of national security and interests is a striking feature of China's relations with Western countries, above all the United States. Actions which successive American governments condemned as aggression are susceptible also to the interpretation that a new and relatively weak nation militarily was merely defending itself against what it perceived as threats to its own security. Of course the stark contrast between the prevailing ideologies of China and the United States served to intensify their mutual bitterness.

Right from the start, the Chinese People's Republic (CPR) fared badly in its relations with the West. Although there had been some friendly contacts between US liaison officials and the Communists during the war against Japan, the Americans had done a great deal to prevent the Communists from winning the civil war which had broken out in 1946. Small wonder that Mao felt the Chinese Communist Party would have to 'lean to one side' in its foreign policy, and adopt a pro-Soviet and anti-American posture. Not long after Mao made his famous statement in his article 'On the People's Democratic Dictatorship' issued on 30 June 1949, the US administration under President Truman withdrew its support from the already obviously defeated

Chiang Kai-shek and there was even the possibility that it might recognize the new Communist government.

The Western nations considered their attitudes to the CPR. On 6 January 1950 Britain recognized the new government and some other small European countries followed suit. France, upset by Chinese support for the Vietminh in Indochina, refused to do so while Italy awaited the American lead. Australia and Canada seriously considered recognition. In the end it was the outbreak of war in Korea which froze relations with the United States and many other Western countries into hostility for over two decades.

The Korean War began with an attack by North Korea on the South on 25 June 1950 to which the United States responded, not only by sending troops to Korea at the head of a United Nations army, but also by ordering the Seventh Fleet to defend Taiwan from any attack by the Communists. To the Chinese this was direct intervention in the still uncompleted civil war. As the UN forces under General Douglas MacArthur moved closer to Manchuria, the Chinese became increasingly concerned lest the United States should actually attack China and attempt to reinstall Chiang Kai-shek. In mid-October 1950 Chinese troops, officially known as the 'Chinese People's Volunteers', entered Korea and pushed back the UN forces.

The war dragged on to a bloody stalemate, ending with an armistice signed on 27 July 1953. The net result was, as the United States saw it, that Communist aggression against South Korea had failed; and, in the Chinese view, that an imperialist attempt to overthrow her own fledgling socialist government had been thwarted. But one thing was clear: it was now obvious that the United States would do all within its power to prevent Taiwan from reverting to its (for the Chinese) rightful place in the CPR.

United States attitudes to China had become harder than ever with the election of Dwight Eisenhower as United States President in November 1952 and his subsequent appointment of John Foster Dulles as Secretary of State. No sooner had Eisenhower assumed the presidency than he formalized what the Chinese had feared from the start, by ordering on 2 February 1953 that the Seventh Fleet would no longer have to prevent Nationalist attacks from Taiwan on the CPR. To the Chinese this was a serious threat to national security, because it was tantamount to supporting invasion by Chiang Kai-shek.

The end of the Korean War failed to dampen Sino-Western hostility. It is true that the Geneva Conference of mid-1954, which ended the Indochina War, gave some promise of improved relations with France and Great Britain, because one result of the conference was that both the French and British prime ministers met and got on well with Chou En-lai. One positive outcome for Sino-US relations was that, through the good offices of Great Britain, the two countries agreed to regular discussions at consular level. These were raised to ambassadorial level in mid-1955, but unfortunately achieved very little indeed. On the whole, the United States was very unhappy about the Geneva Agreements and regarded them as giving away too much to the Communists in Vietnam. It was as a direct result of the agreements that the United States arranged the formation of the Southeast Asia Treaty Organization (SEATO) on 8 September 1954, one of the aims of which was to 'contain' China. Not unnaturally, the Chinese saw SEATO as a threat to their security. Hopes for a substantial improvement in relations with Britain and France were also dashed, among other factors, by the fact that both nations joined SEATO.

The year 1957 marked a change in direction in the CPR's attitude to the West. Up till that point it had been as conciliatory as its national interests would allow in the face of what seemed unreasonable hostility. In 1957 the Soviet Union launched the first sputnik. This achievement signalled to China the superiority of the technology of the socialist countries over that of the imperialist powers and led Mao Tse-tung to declare in Moscow that 'the east wind is prevailing over the west wind'. He also believed that this superiority could be used to push diplomatic advantage, although it was to appear later that Khrushchev did not share this view.

Trouble had been brewing for some time over possession of certain islands off the southeast coast of China which were still occupied by Nationalist troops, the most important being Quemoy and Matsu, both very much closer to China's Fukien Province than to Taiwan. However it was only in 1958 that a serious crisis erupted over the offshore islands.

Late in August the Chinese harassed and blockaded the islands making clear their intention to capture them from the Nationalist troops. Dulles made known the US view that this was the beginning of an attempt to take Taiwan and would be resisted. By the end of September it was clear that the blockade of Quemoy had failed and soon after the harassment ceased. In effect, the final result of the offshore islands crisis was to tie Chiang Kai-shek and the United States closer than ever before. The fact that the

Russians made no attempt to support the Chinese position was also a factor leading to the split between the two nations.

With the resignation of Dulles in April 1959 and the accession of John Kennedy of liberal reputation as the US president in January 1961, there seemed some hope that the ice of Sino-Western relations might begin to thaw. Such was not to be. Whereas Dulles had followed a consistent one-China policy, Kennedy seemed prepared to think in terms of a 'two-China' formula, in other words Taiwan and the mainland would be recognized as being ruled by different governments and each would give up all ideas of conquering the other. Both to Mao Tse-tung and Chiang Kai-shek such an idea was utterly an anathema.

China's suspicions of Kennedy proved well founded when in 1961 he devised a new scheme for keeping China out of the United Nations. Since 1951 the majority in favour of keeping the China seat occupied by the Republic of China (the Chiang Kai-shek regime on Taiwan) and not by the CPR had been getting smaller and smaller. Faced with the strong possibility of defeat in 1961, the United States under Kennedy successfully pushed for a vote to make Chinese representation an 'important question' requiring a two-third's majority. By this means the CPR was denied a place in the United Nations until 1971.

Nevertheless the first few years of the 1960s did bring some gains for the Chinese in their relations with the West. Kennedy's approach did at least signal to the Chinese that the United States no longer expected the imminent collapse of Mao's government, as had been the case in the Dulles era.

But more important was China's diplomatic advance in Europe. In December 1958 Charles de Gaulle was elected as French president. Although the early years of his rule were most noted (from China's point of view) for his attempt to suppress Algerian independence through war, he began to steer France in a quite different direction from 1962 on. In the first place he granted Algeria its independence. More important was the increasingly independent stance he adopted from the United States. In 1963 China and France were among the few major countries to reject the Moscow partial test-ban treaty. With this confluence of views, it was natural that France and China should establish diplomatic relations. This they did in January 1964, to the extreme annoyance of the Americans under Lyndon Johnson (Kennedy had been assassinated on 22 November 1963).

The follow-up to the *détente* with France, however, was disappointing for China. No other European countries moved in the same direction and China suffered several serious foreign policy reversals, in particular the *coup* against Sukarno in Indonesia in September 1965. Moreover the Cultural Revolution, which began at about the same time as the setbacks, more or less paralyzed Chinese foreign policy for over a year. The Foreign Office came under the control of Red Guard groups, as a result of which extreme insistence on ideological purity in the conduct of foreign affairs led to a deterioration of relations with almost every country in the world. In addition Red Guards attacked some foreign diplomats in Peking. The most serious example was the sack of the British *chargé d'affaires* office on 22 August 1967.

As far as the Americans were concerned, the onset of the Vietnam War in 1965 and the Cultural Revolution the following year both served to make each side forget about *détente* on a government-to-government level. At the same time, the fact that the Chinese did not see their national security threatened seriously enough to send troops to Vietnam made the war quite different in kind from the Korean War which had created such a devastating impact on Sino-US relations. Moreover the intense opposition the US war effort in Vietnam aroused among its own people seemed to herald an imminent end to the era of American paranoia against communism in Asia.

One authority on China's foreign policy has written of Sino-American relations up to 1969 that 'When the Chinese were ready for gradualism, America was totalistic. When America adopted gradualism, the Chinese had swung to totalism.'[3] It was not until the 1970s when China and the United States were emerging respectively from the Cultural Revolution and the Vietnam War that there was a confluence of the 'gradualist' approach in both countries and when for the first time real progress was made towards a Sino-Western *détente*.

Because it hinged on the repudiation of revision, the Cultural Revolution brought the Chinese to the conclusion that their principal enemy was the revisionist Soviet Union rather than the capitalist United States. Because of such events as the Soviet invasion of Czechoslovakia in August 1968 and the clashes on the Sino-Soviet border the following March, the Chinese came to regard the Soviet Union as a serious threat to their national security. The leadership therefore determined to form links with the Western powers, especially the United States. The justification for so drastic a reversal of policy was that it is both legitimate and wise to form a united front with a secondary enemy against the

This is a Chinese cartoon commenting on US intervention in Vietnam. The words
on the oven are 'aggressive war in Vietnam', on the wood 'anti-US struggle', and on
the sleeve 'South Vietnamese people'

principal one. This was, after all, what the Communists had done in 1936 when they formed a united front with the Nationalists against Japan.

The first major Western countries to react to China's new posture were Canada and Italy, both of which recognized the CPR in 1970. France had earlier occupied a very special place in China's Western relations and continued to do so after the Cultural Revolution. Mao Tse-tung is reported to have a special affection for France and to have told Maurice Schumann, the French foreign minister who visited Peking in 1972, 'I cannot receive Foreign Ministers who visit China, but with you, Monsieur Schumann, it is not the same thing. You are not just a Foreign Minister. You are a Minister of France'.[4] The French also played a significant liaison role between Peking and Washington in the early stages of their bilateral negotiations.

The United States began making conciliatory gestures in 1969 by taking a few minor measures towards relaxing bans on United States trade with China and travel there. These were increased and strengthened especially in 1971. In April 1971 a group of American table-tennis players visited China, the first United States delegation to visit the CPR. Then came the real breakthrough when the United States president, Richard Nixon, announced on 15 July that his chief adviser on foreign affairs, Dr Henry Kissinger, had visited Peking secretly and secured from Chou En-lai a favourable answer to Nixon's request for an invitation to visit China.

Both China and the United States presented the initiative as having come from Nixon. China claimed, with some justice, that the turnabout showed the failure of America's 'containment of China and communism' policy, while Nixon claimed credit for bringing China out of its isolation. Actually both sides were active in bringing about the new relationship. Both stood to gain in terms of playing off the other against the Soviet Union while America hoped to use China's help to get it off the hook in Indochina.

The first United States president ever to visit China landed in Peking on 21 February 1972. He stayed exactly one week, and the day before leaving he issued with Chou En-lai the famous Shanghai *communiqué*, which outlined the results of the bilateral talks.

The *communiqué* specified that the United States recognized that there was but one China and that Taiwan was one of its provinces. Moreover the United States promised to withdraw its forces and military installations from Taiwan as tension in the area decreased However it undertook no guarantee to withdraw its recognition from the 'Republic of China' on Taiwan.

Although the Nixon visit thus did not solve the basic problem, there has been considerable flow-on for both countries. The United States did obtain help from China to reach a settlement in Indochina which left the anti-communist Nguyen Van Thieu administration in place. On 22 February 1973 the United States and China announced that they would set up 'liaison offices' in each other's capitals. These are embassies in effect although not in name; and the United States has at the same time kept its ambassador in Taipei. Trade and cultural exchanges of various kinds have expanded considerably. This last factor is of course useful both to China and the United States. But much more important for China has been the increase in international recognition of it which the Nixon visit was at least one major factor in causing.

Among the most important of these factors was the CPR's entry into the United Nations on 25 October 1971. Although the United States fought against Taiwan's expulsion and consequently, in effect, against changing the occupation of the Chinese seat, the fact that Nixon had announced his intention to visit Peking may well have swayed some vital votes against the 'important question' resolution, thus assuring China a substantial majority when the vote to exclude the 'Republic of China' (Taiwan) from the world body and include the CPR was eventually put.

Since October 1971 the number of countries with full diplomatic relations with China has risen steeply from just over fifty to about a hundred at the end of 1974. These include all countries in Europe, including the most anti-communist of them, Spain, which recognized China in mid-1973. Australia and New Zealand established diplomatic relations with the CPR in December 1972 following Labor electoral victories in the two countries. Just as the United Nations had to exclude Taipei in order to include Peking, so ambassadorial relations with the CPR in all cases excluded any possibility of diplomatic links with Taiwan. Despite this, the CPR's recognition by the countries of the Western world is now almost complete.

China's acceptance by the Western world in general and the United States in particular has been accompanied by deterioration in relations with the other power of supreme importance to China, the Soviet Union. It will therefore be worthwhile to consider the progress of Sino-Soviet relations since 1949.

Sino-Soviet Relations

As soon as the CPR was established, it pledged to 'examine' all treaties that had been concluded by the previous Chinese government and to 'recognize, abrogate, revise, or renegotiate them according to their respective contents'. The objectives were to roll back the wave of imperialism, which was not yet dead in Chinese eyes, and to attain full equality for China in the international community; in other words a resumption, after the interruption of the Japanese and civil wars, of the rights recovery movement which had begun decades before. The imperialist nations headed by the United States were to be fought against and, in spite of Peking's decision to 'lean to one side', the Soviet Union's long record of expansionism in China was to be remembered.

While most of what remained of the 'unequal treaties' had actually lapsed, in February 1950 the CPR concluded with Moscow the Treaty of Friendship, Alliance, and Mutual Assistance. Ironically it did not come off much better than the Nationalist government had in 1945. It was difficult to deal with the Russians, as evidenced by the unusually long time Mao Tse-tung had spent in Moscow negotiating the treaty. Mao, whose rise to power owed very little to Soviet support, was obliged to acquiesce in the Soviet Union's maintenance of its special interests in Manchuria, even though he was committed to terminating the old pattern of concessions. It appeared apparent to him that Stalin had no inclination to treat China on an equitable basis.

At a time when the new Peking government was faced with an array of domestic problems on the one hand and considerable external hostility on the other, the alliance provided the military and political backing it badly needed. The Chinese leadership, however, was fully aware of the Russian intention to turn the alliance into an instrument for creating and controlling a Soviet satellite. While the military, economic, and technological aid arriving from the Soviet Union contributed significantly to China's reconstruction, it appeared to be enabling the Russians to tighten their control over Peking on all major international affairs.

In September 1952 Chou En-lai visited Moscow with a view to modifying the terms of the treaty. He succeeded in recovering the rights and property of the Changchun Railway, but the Russians, on the pretext of the Chinese intervention in the Korean war and the threat of American troops stationed in Japan, refused to withdraw their troops from Manchuria which, according to the treaty of 1950, they should have evacuated by the end of 1952. Furthermore the Chinese were extremely embittered by the fact that the Russians not only avoided involvement in the Korean war but also asked Peking to pay for the Soviet arms with which the Chinese troops fighting in Korea were equipped.

On the economic front, the Chinese were disappointed with the amount of Soviet credit extended to Peking in 1950 (US $300 million at 1 per cent interest), which was barely sufficient for the reconstruction of a country of China's size. They felt the Russians were niggardly, even though they were grateful to the Russians for their valuable technical know-how, expertise, and assistance in installing factory plants and, in short, in giving China's economic reconstruction a good start.

In any case, signs of conflict between Peking and Moscow were already discernible in the early years of the CPR. What lay at the roots of the conflict, from the Chinese point of view, appeared to have been Stalin's unwillingness to abandon the Russian special positions in China. Added to this was the mutual dislike which Stalin and Mao showed for each other. It was only their common interests which prevented the Chinese leadership from disrupting the friendship and unity with its Soviet ally, particularly after the Korean war when the CPR's political isolation forced it to move closer to the Soviet camp.

The death of Stalin in March 1953 saw Nikita Khrushchev emerging to a position of power in the Soviet Union. In a drive for leadership in the world Communist movement, Khrushchev was committed to a *rapprochement* with Tito of Yugoslavia and wished to cultivate Mao at the same time. In October 1954 he led a Soviet delegation to visit Peking for the celebration of the fifth anniversary of the CPR. At the end of the visit he reached an agreement with the Chinese, under which the Soviet Union undertook to increase the scale of economic aid to China and, more significantly, to withdraw the Soviet troops from Manchuria by May 1955, which it did as scheduled. Plans were drawn up for technological and scientific co-operation between the two countries, with the possibility of Soviet assistance in the development of a Chinese nuclear capability. Above all, Khrushchev's pledge to consult and co-ordinate with the CPR on matters of common concern was seen as promising the Chinese an equal place in world affairs.

The CPR welcomed the 'sincere co-operation' and 'indestructible friendship' of the Soviet Union, and seemingly enjoyed the cordial relations that marked the so-called 'honeymoon period' from 1953 to 1956. But the strength of the Moscow-Peking axis was yet to be tested. While the Soviet Union in fact continued to treat the CPR as a subordinate partner, the Chinese were increasingly bent on furthering their national interests. During those same years the CPR sought to enhance its prestige and influence in Asia and set about restoring its position as a great power in world affairs. Its admission to the Geneva Conference on Korea and Indochina in 1954 accorded it an opportunity to recapture a rightful position on the international stage quite independent of the Russians.

The development of close Sino-Indian relations in the summer of 1954 was also indicative of the CPR's attempt to assert its influence in Asia with the intention, as the Russians suspected, of developing an 'Asia for the Asians' policy. What probably was more disturbing to Moscow was the Chinese desire to assume leadership in Asia in the Conference of Asian and African states held in Bandung in April 1955 (see next section) in which the Soviet Union played no part. It was on that occasion that Chou En-lai, who put forward the celebrated Five Principles of Peaceful Coexistence, made a deep impression on many of the under-developed countries which were represented. This caused the Soviet leadership so much concern that in June 1955 it invited Nehru to visit Moscow and, several months later, sent Khrushchev on a long Asian tour which included visits to India, Burma, and Afghanistan, with promises of extensive Soviet aid. The race for influence in Asia had begun before the Sino-Soviet dispute came into the open.

The origin of this dispute, the Chinese claimed, lay in the Twentieth Congress of the Communist Party of the Soviet Union in February 1956, when the process of 'de-Stalinization' was initiated by Khrushchev in a secret speech to the Congress attacking Stalin. Khrushchev advocated 'peaceful coexistence' as the new line of Soviet foreign policy and the 'parliamentary road' as a viable means of transition to socialism. His idea was that the Soviet Union, while opposed to capitalism and interested in the ultimate victory of world communism, had no intention of interfering militarily in the internal affairs of capitalist countries. The idea was not new, but Khrushchev carried it further by saying that countries with different systems could not only coexist peacefully but also improve their relations and strengthen their mutual trust and collaboration. He saw only two paths in the world situation: either peaceful coexistence or a third world war which would be the most devastating in the history of mankind. Even if 'sharp class, revolutionary struggles' might still be necessary in some countries, it was now possible to achieve peaceful transition to socialism by parliamentary means.

In Peking's view, Khrushchev's 'new line' added up to a revision of Marxism-Leninism. The Chinese understanding of peaceful coexistence was that it should not impede opposition to colonialism and imperialism or inhibit the struggle for national independence. The stage was not yet set for peaceful transition to socialism.

In 1956, it must be noted, the CPR was intensifying its efforts to establish itself as an equal to the Soviet Union in the Communist bloc. During the Hungarian crisis of that year the CPR charged Moscow with 'big-nation chauvinism', demanding full equality between socialist countries and non-interference in internal affairs.

The quarrels were, however, not serious until some time later. One main turning-point was China's diplomatic switch in 1957 following the launching of the sputnik (see previous section). Mao's position on war, which amounted to a policy of settling the differences between socialism and capitalism by military means if necessary, worried the Soviet Union, which was seeking to improve relations with the United States. As borne out by its attitude towards the offshore islands crisis of 1958, Moscow was not inclined to support Peking's military initiatives which involved the risk of clashing with the Americans.

Meanwhile the Great Leap Forward was being implemented in China, reflecting the CPR's desire to work out an independent economic strategy. Already in 1956 it was felt that the Soviet experience did not suit Chinese circumstances and that it was necessary to reorient China's economic policy. The new strategy of the Great Leap was a challenge to Soviet influence and naturally led the Russians to dismiss it as 'a road of dangerous experiments, a road of disregard for economic laws and for the experience of other socialist states'.

The situation was compounded by the issue of Chinese national defence. The Soviet Union had promised in October 1957 to supply samples of the atomic bomb to the CPR, but such aid was withheld the following year because of the CPR's objections to placing its nuclear weapons, when fully developed, under Soviet veto, as well as to joint command of their naval forces in the Pacific. Meanwhile Khrushchev was seeking a summit meeting with the US president and was eager to impress the Americans with his efforts at prevention of the spread of nuclear weapons. This caused considerable apprehensions in Peking in the face of what it called the US-Soviet collusion. The military aspect of the treaty of 1950 had lost its importance thus forcing the CPR to develop its nuclear capabilities from its own resources.

The year 1960 saw a further escalation of the Sino-Soviet dispute leading to more exchanges of polemics and attempts by both sides to lobby for support within the Communist bloc. It was in this year that Khrushchev withdrew over one thousand Soviet specialists from China, and terminated a large number of contracts and projects and various other forms of economic aid.

In 1961 the quarrels between the Soviet Union and Albania made the latter gravitate to the Chinese side. The situation in the following year was even more explosive when the Chinese accused Khrushchev of 'adventurism' for putting nuclear weapons in Cuba and of 'capitulationism' for withdrawing them later before United States nuclear 'blackmail'.

There were, of course, ideological considerations in the rift between the two giant Communist countries. Each accused the other of 'revisionism', that is breaking with Marxism-Leninism. The Chinese polemics were directed at Moscow's new policies on imperialism, war and peace, proletarian revolution, and the dictatorship of the proletariat. The Soviet Union, on the other hand, poured scorn on the Chinese methods of building socialism which it saw as a harmful departure from Marxism. It did not matter who was the 'revisionist'. What really mattered was that Peking was raising its ideological stature within the Communist bloc.

Any increase in Chinese influence in bloc affairs would force the Soviet Union to treat the CPR as an equal. But Moscow thought that the CPR, being both economically and militarily weaker, had no grounds for claiming equality. Furthermore the Russians believed that China would eventually seek not only equality but superiority.

Once the dispute came into the open, it could be explained further in terms of historical hostility and deep-seated grievances. The Chinese experience with the Russians had been an unpleasant one. The Czarist regime had been as imperialist as any of the Western powers Chinese nationalists had been fighting against. The Soviet Union, despite its endeavours, had failed to endear itself to either the Nationalist government or the Chinese Communists under Mao's leadership before 1949. Apart from ideological differences, a very real issue was the common boundaries between the two countries which were too long to be delimited to the satisfaction of both parties.

Over the last two centuries or so the Chinese had lost considerable territory to Russia. The CPR, which was as much a nationalist regime as communist, felt an urge to reclaim part of the lost territory. This desire inevitably led to border problems, especially following the deterioration of relations towards the end of the fifties. One case in point was Sinkiang, where the Chinese Communists had been attempting to Sinicize the Kazakhs, Uighurs, and other national minorities, a large number of whom fled across the border, allegedly under Soviet instigation, early in 1962. Peking's subsequent decision to close the Soviet consulates in Sinkiang, at Urumchi and Kuldja, showed the gravity of the problems.

Early in 1963 the CPR laid historical claims to some parts of Siberia, and Soviet Central Asia, areas which had been wrested from the Chinese empire by force. The Chinese intention was to renegotiate the 'unequal treaties' on an equal basis. Moscow, however, refused to enter into comprehensive boundary negotiations, convinced as it was that the old treaties had sufficient legal foundations. Consequently, since that year, border incidents have taken place, particularly after the Cultural Revolution.

Actually there was a strong anti-Russian element in the Cultural Revolution, the roots of which can be found in the aftermath of the Great Leap Forward. The floundering of the Leap had led P'eng Te-huai, the Minister of Defence, to launch an attack on Mao's policies in mid-1959, and to advance instead programmes featuring Soviet military, economic, and technical aid. The subsequent dismissal of P'eng made it clear that Mao still persisted in his anti-Russian policy. The domestic struggle culminating in the Cultural Revolution represented a conflict between 'experts' and 'reds'. The 'experts', who were technicians and professionals within the bureaucracy, favoured more liberal and pragmatic policies and advocated learning from and uniting with the Soviet Union, while the 'reds' were more ideological and idealistic, advocating a return to an economic programme based on 'self-reliance' and rejecting a pro-Russian foreign policy. The group surrounding Liu Shao-ch'i was denounced for collaboration with Soviet revisionism.

The Russians vehemently attacked the Cultural Revolution, portraying Mao as a lunatic with great personal egotism and a xenophobic mentality. More important was the fact that they were worried about the threat the Cultural Revolution posed to the principle of Party rule. Mao did not believe in party infallibility and found that his Party had erred, so he directed a revolution against it by bringing non-party elements into the scene. The Soviet leadership believed in the supremacy of Party rule and felt that an attack on it was an open defiance of Soviet leadership which would have adverse effects on the socialist countries.

During the Cultural Revolution border incidents in Sinkiang, and along the Amur and the Ussuri Rivers between Manchuria and the Soviet Far East, were frequently reported. The Soviet Union, meanwhile, was hastening the development of Siberia for political as well as economic purposes. It started to explore the possibilities of co-operation with Japan in the development of natural resources, including an oil pipeline to the Sea of Japan. In August 1968 a Soviet-Japanese agreement for joint development of Siberia was concluded, causing tremendous discomfort in Peking on account of its political implications.

Coinciding with this was the Soviet invasion of Czechoslovakia, followed by Moscow's enunciation of the Brezhnev Doctrine, which gave the Soviet Union a self-proclaimed right to judge when the common interests of communism were in jeopardy and, thereby, to prevent this danger by military intervention. This added to the Chinese feeling of national insecurity, particularly in view of the possibility of a Soviet pre-emptive nuclear strike.

Such a strike did not take place, but the frontier was never quiet. In March 1969 hostilities broke out following a heated dispute over the island of Damansky, or Chenpao in Chinese, in the Ussuri River. In August heavy fighting occurred along the Sinkiang border, after which the Kremlin warned that a war with China, very likely a nuclear one, was a real possibility. Taking the warning seriously, the Chinese made every effort to prepare for the eventuality and were reported to have secretly moved their nuclear installations in Sinkiang to some safe place. In October the two countries entered into some high-level border talks, which failed to yield any satisfactory results. The situation continued to be tense and explosive, with both sides massing troops along the borders.

Since then the CPR has singled out the Soviet Union as China's chief and most dangerous enemy. It was precisely the fear of Russia that led the Chinese leadership to a reappraisal of its relations with the United States, which in turn caused a significant change in the world's international relations.

With China's recognition by a growing number of countries, her entry into the United Nations, and the development of Sino-US relations at a 'liaison office' level, China is now in a stronger position, at least diplomatically, to deal with the Russians.

Because of this political leverage, the threat of a major Sino-Soviet conflict seems to have receded, despite some foreign reports to the contrary. Genuinely or not, the Russians appeared more conciliatory. In October 1974 they proposed to the CPR the revival of their defunct mutual defence treaty. Their offers included a treaty on refraining from the use of force, either conventional or nuclear; a non-aggressive treaty based on a final border settlement; and development of relations 'in various spheres'. The Chinese did not respond with enthusiasm, demanding that Moscow should first of all review their disputed borders and pull back from along their frontier their powerful forces estimated to exceed 1 000 000 men equipped with jet planes, tanks, and rockets. Disappointed with the total inactivity of the Sino-Soviet border talks in Peking, the Chinese saw no indications of a change in Soviet hostility and remained highly suspicious of the Kremlin leadership.

It will still be a long time before relations between Peking and Moscow can be 'normalized'. Nevertheless the likelihood of a large-scale war between them in the near future appears very remote. Both countries seem to realize that such a war would do more harm than good to the victor as well as to the defeated.

China and Asia

An interesting aspect of China's relations with the world's two superpowers is the dimension of their antagonisms in Asia. The American containment of China has been based on the assumption that a Communist China in Asia was a challenge to American policy. This containment seems to have broken down since the thaw in Sino-US relations and the American disentanglement from Vietnam. Yet it is also since then that the CPR has insinuated a desire for some form of continued United States presence in Southeast Asia, in order to counter the growing influence of the Soviet Union on the Asian subcontinent.

There can be no doubt about the CPR's desire to establish its influence in Asia. But to suggest that the Chinese are attempting to revive the idea of the Chinese empire, with its tributary system, through the creation of a ring of subordinate Communist states, is not only to exaggerate the CPR's capacity, but also to generate unwarranted fears of China. It would be nearer the mark to say that the CPR's objective in Asia, particularly in Southeast Asia, is the promotion of a non-hostile and/or friendly region without the controlling influence of any extraregional powers. China has no fears from weaker neighbours, but she is fully aware of the possibility that those neighbours could be used by a hostile power to threaten her security.

Peking sees non-hostile neighbours as those which reject any provocative or antagonistic associations with countries or organizations that are openly hostile to it. It is unnecessary, though desirable, for those countries to have diplomatic ties with Peking, and they may receive foreign aid from China's 'enemies' if they so wish. What is important to Peking is that they should neither allow a foreign military presence on their soil, nor be a party to military alliances directed against the CPR.

Friendly states which recognize the CPR are sympathetic with the Chinese and likely to support, or at least not oppose, China's foreign policies. Because of this, the CPR regards them as a foil to hostile third parties in international disputes, or encourages them to adopt a neutral attitude. Neutral countries, which are aligned neither with the United States nor the Soviet Union, are generally opposed to imperialism, colonialism, and the establishment of foreign military bases on their territories, even though they are in receipt of American or Soviet aid. They are also politically accessible to the CPR through aid programmes, propaganda, and, in some cases, diplomatic agencies. The neutrals have very different social systems from the Chinese, but the CPR can coexist with them peacefully until they start to drift away in another direction to its disadvantage.

The development of Sino-Japanese relations from 1949 to 1970 showed how an Asian neighbour allied to the United States figured in the CPR's quest for security. At first the CPR was apprehensive about a resurgence of Japanese militarism, and later it saw an even greater threat in the United States military presence in Japan. The Korean War proved that the Chinese fears were well founded. For over two decades China and Japan were still at war officially, since they had never signed a peace treaty to conclude the war, even though it had in fact already ended in 1945. Indeed it was Japan's alignment with the United States, as well as its recognition of Taiwan, that inhibited the growth of normal diplomatic relations between Peking and Tokyo, despite the maintenance of trade relations. When the government of Tanaka Kakuei set up an embassy in Peking at long last, in September 1972, it was only a few months after President Nixon's historic visit to China.

Since the US-Japanese security treaty has lost its anti-Peking character, both Peking and Tokyo have been attempting to use each other as a political lever against the Russians through increasing trade and economic co-operation. In 1974 Peking was worried about Japanese involvement in the development of Siberia, particularly in the exploration of crude oil reserves at Tjumen in western Siberia, a project which involved, among other things, the construction of a 400-kilometre pipeline between Irkutsk, on the southern tip of Lake Baikal, and the Sea of Japan for the shipment of crude oil to Japan. The CPR saw the proposed pipeline, which was to run under paved highways, as a direct military threat from the Soviet Union. Japan later gave up the pipeline idea in return for China's agreement to provide her with large supplies of crude oil, reported to be 10 per cent of China's total annual output. The amount of supplies will probably reach 400 000 000 tonnes annually by 1980. Future developments in Sino-Japanese relations will depend largely on China's relations with the Soviet Union as well as with the United States.

In Southeast Asia the CPR is ideologically committed to the concept of struggle and 'people's war'. However its support for revolutionary wars is limited by two important factors: the 'practicality' of Mao's thought, as distinct from the 'purity' of Marxism-Leninism, and the principle of self-reliance. The Chinese road to success may be followed, but it must be adapted to local circumstances. Revolution, as the CPR sees it, is a protracted struggle, the success of which depends not so much on foreign support as on the insurgents' ability to win the support of local masses and to develop their own resources. It has not been the CPR's policy to lend unlimited support to insurgents seeking to establish communist governments in their own countries.

The Chinese leadership is undoubtedly serious about 'peaceful coexistence' and made its position clear at the Bandung Conference of 1954 by espousing the famous Five Principles—mutual respect for territorial integrity and sovereignty, mutual non-aggression, mutual non-interference in internal affairs, equality, and mutual benefit. Under these principles the CPR has been prepared to establish normal relations with virtually every country in the world, especially Asian and African nations. It has sought to promote Asian (or Asian-African) solidarity in order to reduce Western influence in the underdeveloped countries. By acting as a sponsor of neutralism and non-alignment, it has been able to develop good relations with such Southeast Asian countries as Burma, Indonesia, and Cambodia. However, until the recent Sino-US thaw, China has been very chary about developing good relations with Southeast Asian countries committed to the West, such as the Philippines, Thailand, and Malaysia.

In 1965 there occurred considerable hostility between Peking and Bangkok. This, from Bangkok's angle, was because of China's open support of the uprising of the Thai Communists. But what really upset the CPR was Thailand's growing role in the United States involvement in Laos and Vietnam. Thailand, the Chinese believed, was becoming increasingly 'subservient' to United States neocolonialism.

In the same year the CPR received a setback in Indonesia after the massive dismemberment of the Indonesian Communist Party, following the *coup d'état* of 30 September and the subsequent rise to power of the right-wing military dictatorship under Suharto. The Chinese were suspected of being involved in the *coup*, as a result of which Peking's cordial relations with Jakarta, carefully cultivated in the past years, were seriously damaged.

With Burma, which was among the first nations to recognize Peking in the fifties, the CPR's relations deteriorated from mid-1967, owing to the Cultural Revolution in China and anti-Chinese riots in Burma. In 1970 relations between the CPR and Cambodia also ran into trouble because of the latter's co-operation with the United States military operations in the region.

The American involvement in Vietnam popularized the domino theory, which presupposed that when one country in Southeast Asia fell into Communist hands, other countries in the region would follow suit, as in a game of dominoes. This theory, coupled with China's support for the Communist parties there, added to the suspicion, apprehension, and hostility which Southeast Asian nations felt towards the giant Communist neighbour.

The Sino-US *détente* naturally led the Southeast Asian countries to reappraise their relations with the CPR. It seems only a matter of time before they all come to terms with Peking. In June 1974 Malaysia in fact became the first member of the Association of Southeast Asian Nations to extend recognition to Peking. The First Lady of the Philippines, Imelda Marcos, was warmly received in Peking in September 1974, and the Philippines is likely to extend recognition before too long. In 1971 Thailand also resumed contacts with the CPR through and in third world countries. The visit to China of Deputy Foreign Minister Chatichai Choonhavan in December 1973 cleared the ground on many subjects of mutual concern. Bangkok was obviously pleased with the contract signed with the Chinese for the delivery of 50 000 tonnes of diesel oil at a price well below the world market. The pace of *détente* seems to have gained momentum.

Indonesia and Singapore will probably be the last countries in the Association of Southeast Asian Nations to establish diplomatic ties with the CPR. The Chinese population in Indonesia, which has soured Peking-Jakarta relations in the past, remains a major hurdle in the way of friendship. Singapore is not prepared to recognize China until all its immediate neighbours of Malay stock have done so. Lee Kuan Yew has always been suspicious of China's ultimate objective in Southeast Asia, and he also takes offence at the assumption in some quarters that Singapore is a 'third China'.

The CPR's relations with Burma have gradually returned to normal since President Ne Win's goodwill visit to China in 1971. Meanwhile the Chinese are eager to cultivate Laos, where the Soviet Union is also developing an interest. In June 1974 Sino-Laos relations were upgraded to ambassadorial level, followed by an increase in the scale of Chinese aid.

Another area of vital concern to China is South Asia. India recognized China shortly after the Chinese Communists came to power, and the two countries enjoyed good relations until 1959 when trouble over their mutual borders, among other factors, turned their friendship to hostility and led the Soviet Union to attempt to build up India as a counterweight to the CPR. In March 1959 the Dalai Lama fled to India, following the Chinese suppression of an uprising in Tibet. Some months later fighting occurred between Chinese and Indian troops and again, on a larger scale, in October 1962.

The rivalry with India forced the CPR to woo Pakistan, which was even more resentful than China about a threatening Indian neighbour supported by the Soviet Union. From the Chinese point of view, a friendly Pakistan was useful in diverting much of India's attention from Tibet and the Himalayan area. Sino-Pakistan relations developed rapidly in the sixties. The fact that Pakistan was one of the very few foreign countries to establish civil air links with Peking is excellent testimony to the importance China attached to their friendship. Karachi was also the site of various secret meetings between Chinese and foreign officials intending to improve relations with China.

The CPR was undoubtedly embarrassed by Pakistan's suppression of the Bengali nationalist movement which led to the India-Pakistan war of December 1971. Had it not been for its good relations with Karachi, and the involvement of India and the Soviet Union in the Bengali cause, the CPR would probably have supported the struggle led by Sheikh Mujibur Rahman. The

CPR refrained from intervention, not only because of its adherence to 'non-interference', but also because the war did not really threaten China's security. Moreover the Chinese suspected the ulterior motives of India and the Soviet Union in the Bangladesh movement.

In August 1972 China vetoed Bangladesh's United Nations membership on the grounds of the non-withdrawal of foreign (Indian) troops from Bangladesh and the threatened trial of the prisoners of war. In April 1974 Bangladesh guaranteed the repatriation of the Pakistani prisoners, which obliged China to accept, in June, the Security Council's recommendation that Bangladesh be granted membership of the United Nations. Relations between Peking and Dacca are improving, especially given the latest reports of anti-Indian feelings in some sections of the Bangladesh population.

On the other hand, China's rivalry with India seems to be on the increase. India's alignment with the Soviet Union, her growing influence on the Asian subcontinent since the dismemberment of Pakistan, and her successful nuclear test in May 1974 all add to China's uneasiness. Another incident that has provoked the CPR is India's 'annexation' of the Himalayan kingdom of Sikkim, in September 1974, which poses problems to China's security in the Himalayan region where the Indians, backed by the Soviet Union, are staking out an active interest. It looks as if the Moscow-New Delhi axis has replaced the US-Japanese alliance as the most worrying factor in Peking's Asia policy.

* * *

This is indeed a spectacular change. It is very clear that the balance of power in the Asian region is subject to alteration at an extraordinarily rapid rate. In one sense this is fairly surprising, because the ideological basis of Chinese foreign policy has been reasonably constant in the quarter of a century since the Communist Party came to power there. Although one can discern changes in direction here and there, they have not been very radical seen from the general viewpoint of overall ideology. It appears, in fact, that the basic changes in power balance in the Asian region are due primarily to the *perception* of each country of its own national interests and of how other nations interact with them. This is a point of the utmost importance, because it is fairly clear that nations devise their foreign policy largely according to how they *see* their national interests. And China, an active participant in the region's affairs, is no exception to this rule.

There are many topics connected with China's foreign relations which have not been mentioned in this chapter, let alone discussed in detail. Some of these play a fairly significant role in China's foreign relations if one can judge from the amount of space devoted to them in the Chinese press. Examples are China's attitude towards the Middle East and towards developments in Africa. Not many countries took as keen an interest in the process towards independence of Mozambique as China did. The material in this chapter is thus highly selective and merely presents some of the factors and areas which stand out as most important in Chinese contemporary foreign relations.

The same strictures could be made about this book as a whole. There are many subjects a discussion of which the reader will seek in vain in this book. They include Chinese law, science and technology, and the national minorities. However, if the reader's curiosity has been excited, and if he or she has become more aware of the problems related to China, then the book will have achieved its purpose.

Notes

1 'In Commemoration of Dr Sun Yat-sen' (November 1956), quoted in *Quotations from Chairman Mao Tse-tung*, Foreign Languages Press, Peking, 1967, p. 180.
2 'Talk with African Friends' (8 August 1963), quoted in *Quotations*, p. 177.
3 Ishwer C. Ojha *Chinese Foreign Policy in an Age of Transition: The Diplomacy of Cultural Despair*, Beacon Press, Boston, 1969, p. 95.
4 Quoted in Giovanni Bressi, 'China and Western Europe', *Asian Survey*, xii, no. 10 (October 1972), p. 839.

Select Bibliography

Barnett, A. Doak *Communist China and Asia*, Vintage book, New York, 1960. An early work on the subject, it analyzes the salient features of the CPR, its domestic and foreign policies, and the impact on Asia. The author sees a Communist China in Asia as a challenge to American policy.

Clark, Gregory *In Fear of China*, Lansdowne Press, Melbourne, 1967. Written by an Australian scholar, this book argues forcefully against the thesis that China is an aggressive nation in its foreign policy.

Gittings, J. *Survey of the Sino-Soviet Dispute 1963–1967*, Oxford University Press, London, 1968. A scholarly work, with a collection of documents tracing the developments in Sino-Soviet relations up to 1967, it throws useful light on the subject.

Hinton, Harold C. *China's Turbulent Quest*, The Macmillan Company, London, 1970. This is a comprehensive account of China's foreign policy from 1949 to 1968. The author is highly critical of the CPR and is provocative in some of his analysis.

MacFarquhar, Roderick *Sino-American Relations, 1949–71*, Wren Publishing Pty Ltd, Melbourne, 1972. Contains numerous basic documents on Sino-US relations, together with perceptive introductions by MacFarquhar. There are also three introductory essays by American scholars.

Ojha, Ishwer C. *Chinese Foreign Policy in an Age of Transition: The Diplomacy of Cultural Despair*, Beacon Press, Boston, 1969. Takes up general themes in China's foreign policy, relations with the West, with the United States, and the Soviet Union. Concentrates much more on original analyses, brilliantly put forward and defended, than on well known facts.

Chronology, 1911-73

1911: Republic of China formed with fall of Manchu Dynasty.

1913: Yüan Shih-k'ai replaces Sun Yat-sen as President of China and begins to suppress republican movement.

1915: Japan makes its Twenty-one Demands on China in an attempt to subject China to Japan's will.

1916: Yüan Shih-k'ai dies after proclaiming himself emperor; political power falls to regional military commanders and provincial governors, leading to disunity and warlordism.

1919: China betrayed at Versailles Peace Conference and former German concessions in China pass to Japan instead of reverting to Chinese people. Strong anti-Japanese demonstrations and boycotts in cities with May Fourth Movement.

1921: Sun Yat-sen leads a government in Kwangtung and opens contacts with Comintern representatives. Chinese Communist Party (CCP) founded.

1922: Sun Yat-sen rebuilds Kuomintang (KMT) but is forced to flee Kwangtung.

1923: Sun Yat-sen returns and period of KMT-Comintern collaboration begins; Third Congress of CCP agrees to co-operate with KMT and members join it on individual basis, following Comintern advice.

1924: KMT seizes Canton and Northern Expedition to unite China planned.

1925: Sun Yat-sen dies; Chiang Kai-shek assumes leadership of KMT; CCP begins to expand membership.

1926: Mao Tse-tung and P'eng Pai organize peasantry in Kwangtung and Hunan on behalf of KMT and CCP: Chiang Kai-shek leads Northern Expedition and stages *coup* against Communists in Canton but alliance preserved on Comintern advice.

1927: Communist movement shattered by Chiang's *coup* in Shanghai; Autumn Harvest Uprising under Mao in Hunan and Kiangsi fails; Canton commune broken; CCP driven underground.

1928: Northern Expedition succeeds in uniting China under Nanking government led by Chiang Kai-shek; remnants of Red Army under Chu Te and Mao establish rural guerrilla base at Chingkangshan in Kiangsi; Li Li-san controls urban headquarters of CCP Central Committee.

1929: Chu and Mao expand rural bases and establish Party control over army at Kutien Conference.

1930: First 'Bandit Extermination Campaign' against CCP launched by Chiang.

1931: Japanese invade Manchuria; Chinese Soviet Republic founded in Kiangsi by Mao; two further KMT 'extermination' campaigns fail; Li Li-san replaced by 'Returned Student' leadership from Moscow.

1932: KMT forms Blue Shirts; Kiangsi Soviet declares war against Japan.

1934: KMT launches New Life Movement; Fifth 'Extermination' Campaign under von Seekt encircles Soviet region and Long March commences following breakout.

1935: CCP conference at Tsunyi establishes Mao's predominance over Returned Student leadership; Long March survivors reach northern Shensi and establish base; CCP calls for united front against Japan.

1936: Sian Incident.

1937: Second United Front between KMT and CCP; Marco Polo Bridge Incident opens Sino-Japanese War.

1938: Mao overcomes challenge from Chang Kuo-t'ao to his leadership and writes extensively on strategy of anti-Japanese war.

1940: Mao writes 'On New Democracy'.

1941: KMT attacks CCP's New Fourth Route Army in southern Anhwei; Pearl Harbour attack brings United States into war against Japan.

1942: CCP launches rectification campaign to eradicate hostile influence and in Yenan develops mass mobilization campaigns around rent reduction, co-operatives, production drives, and the reduction of bureaucracy by sending cadres to the villages.

1943: Chiang Kai-shek writes *China's Destiny*; United States, Soviet Union, and Britain accept China as a major power; Cairo Declaration restores China's rights to Taiwan.

1944: United States attempts to bring KMT and CCP together; coalition government discussed.

1945: Japan surrenders; Soviet Union and China sign Treaty of Friendship and Alliance; CCP membership reaches 1 000 000.

1946: Soviet troops leave Manchuria; civil war between KMT and CCP; KMT troops flown into cities but Lin Piao's forces take countryside; armistice broken again.

1947: KMT crushes Taiwan rebellion, eliminates liberal democratic opponents, and takes Yenan but civil war begins to turn against it; United States critical of KMT rule and prepares to cut assistance.

1948: CCP forces win north China and carry out land reform; United States resumes aid to KMT following domestic pressure.

1949: Peking taken; KMT moves to Canton and Chiang resigns presidency; KMT government under Li Tsung-jen flees to Taiwan; Chinese People's Republic (CPR) is proclaimed 1 October; Mao travels to Moscow to negotiate treaty and aid.

1950: *February* Sino-Soviet Treaty of Friendship, Alliance, and Mutual Assistance.
April Marriage Law promulgated.
June Agrarian Reform Law; Korean War commences.
October China enters Korean War.

1951: Mutual-aid teams popularized in countryside. Campaigns launched to remove corruption and disloyalty from bureaucracy and national bourgeoisie.

1952: Private business brought under state control by joint ownership arrangements.

1953: CCP membership 6 500 000 and organization of agricultural producers' co-operatives begins. First Five Year Plan commenced but not announced until 1955.

1954: Conflict between Peking and Northeast under Kao Kang leads to purge of Kao and greater centralization of political and economic control.
July Geneva Conference reaches agreement on Indochina.
September Constitution of CPR proclaimed at First National People's Congress. Southeast Asia Treaty Organization (SEATO) treaty signed.
October Khrushchev visits Peking.

1955: *April* Chou En-lai continues to develop 'Five People's Principles' and theme of peaceful co-existence at Bandung Conference following his initial moves at Geneva in 1954.
July Mao urges acceleration of agrarian co-operativization drive.

1956: *February* Twentieth Congress of the Communist Party of the Soviet Union (CPSU) denounces Stalin and cult of the individual.
April China rejects extreme criticism of Stalin by Khrushchev. Mao gives 'Ten Great Relationships' speech on China's economic strategy.
May Mao gives speech on 'Hundred Flowers' and Lu Ting-i launches campaign.
September Eighth National Congress of CCP meets in atmosphere of confidence and stability; Mao's thought removed from new constitution and references to collective leadership made. Co-operativization largely completed.
October–November Soviet troops suppress uprising in Hungary.

1957: *February* Mao delivers speech 'On the Correct Handling of Contradictions among the People'. Strong attack on Hungarian rising of 1956.
April–May Party rectification campaign merges with Hundred Flowers Campaign and non-members criticize CCP's performance.
June Critics attacked in Anti-Rightist Campaign
September–October Third Plenum of Central Committee decides on massive decentralization of economic decision-making and adopts Mao's plan for mass mobilization for economic development. Soviet launches 'Sputnik' and agrees to share nuclear data and samples but no substantial economic aid for Second Five Year Plan.
November Mao goes to Moscow meeting and announces world balance tipped in favour of socialist world, that is 'the east wind is prevailing over the west wind'.

1958: *January* Radical shift in economic development strategy with Great Leap Forward; mass mobilization to utilize labour power; decentralization of economic control.
May Second Session of Eighth Congress of CCP ratifies Great Leap decisions; Lin Piao joins Standing Committee of Politburo.
August–September Offshore islands crisis; Soviet Union remains silent until after United States ships defy blockade.

August Mao tours Honan and endorses commune experiment; rapid movement to form communes as basic unit of imminent communist society.

November–December Wuhan meeting of Central Committee modifies extreme aspects of communes and timetable for reaching communism but accepts inflated production figures; Mao steps down as Chairman of CPR for Liu Shao-ch'i but retains Party chairmanship. Khrushchev attacks communes as 'old fashioned'.

1959: *April* Further modification of communes and doubts about Great Leap.

June Soviet Union breaks nuclear sharing arrangement.

August Lushan Plenum rejects P'eng Te-huai's criticism of Mao's policy and dismisses him as Defence Minister.

September Khrushchev goes to United States. Border incidents with India following Tibetan revolt in March and flight of Dalai Lama to India.

1960: *August* Soviet technicians withdrawn from China, taking plans.

November Communes decentralized as economic position worsens.

1961: *January* CCP reverses priorities of Great Leap by stressing agriculture over industry.

November Chou En-lai clashes with Russians at Twenty-second Congress of CPSU.

1962: General food shortage due to dislocation and poor seasons.

September Mao calls on Party 'never to forget class struggle'; Socialist Education Movement begins.

October Border war with India. Cuban missile crisis.

1963: Lin Piao restores morale in PLA and introduces study of Mao's thought; heroes from PLA publicized for emulation.

August Partial Nuclear Test Ban Treaty signed, China attacks plan. Sino-Soviet rift made public and worsens.

1964: Campaign to 'train revolutionary successors' begins through Communist Youth League, reflecting CCP concern about youth. People told to 'learn from the PLA'. Lin Piao produces *Quotations from Chairman Mao* for use first in PLA.

January China and France agree to establish diplomatic relations.

August Gulf of Tonkin Incident and United States bombs North Vietnam.

October China explodes atomic bomb. Khrushchev falls.

December National People's Congress meets; Chou En-lai hints at revisionism within CCP.

1965: United States escalates war in Vietnam throughout.

May PLA abolishes rank system.

September Lin Piao writes 'Long Live the Victory of People's War'. Communist Party of Indonesia smashed by Indonesian army.

November Yao Wen-yüan launches attack on Peking intellectuals in PLA and Shanghai press.

1966: *May* Attacks on revisionist and anti-Party leaders increase while Liu Shao-ch'i on tour and P'eng Chen falls. Schools close and Red Guards appear.

July Mao swims Yangtze after long absence.

August Eleventh Plenum meets and issues directives for Great Proletarian Cultural Revolution. Lin Piao prominent as Liu Shao-ch'i and later Teng Hsiao-p'ing fall. Red Guards active in cities.

December Workers (Revolutionary Rebels) join Cultural Revolution.

1967: *January–March* PLA intervenes in fighting and in revolutionary committees; forced to assume control where civilian administration breaks down. Emergence of Cultural Revolution Group under Chiang Ch'ing and Ch'en Po-ta.

July Wuhan Incident.

August Red Guards sack the British mission in Peking.

1968: More emphasis on unity and Party rebuilding in Mao's statements.

August Soviet Union invades Czechoslovakia.

October Remnants of Central Committee meet in Twelfth Plenum, and formally demote Liu Shao-ch'i.

1969: Cultural Revolution ends. China resumes diplomatic activity.

March Two serious armed clashes with Soviet troops on Ussuri River border. Talks to settle boundary question follow.

April Ninth Congress of CCP meets; Lin Piao gives main report; new Central Committee elected with over 40 per cent from PLA.

1970: General movement toward greater stability; government apparatus streamlined at centre under Chou En-lai; economy develops further; increasing diplomatic activity.

1971: *May* Ch'en Po-ta disappears.

July Henry Kissinger visits Peking. Nixon announces that he will visit China.

September Report of plane crash in Mongolia. Lin Piao and section of PLA high command disappear.

October China joins the United Nations.

December War between India and Pakistan results in Indian victory and establishment of new state of Bangladesh in East Bengal.

1972: *February* United States President Nixon's visit to Peking.

September Japanese Prime Minister Tanaka visits China. Japan and China agree to establish diplomatic relations.

1973: *January* Paris Peace Conference reaches agreement on Vietnam.

August Tenth Congress of CCP elects new Central Committee to fill gaps in leadership through old age, death, and purge. Chou En-lai prominent. PLA representation declines. Beginning of the Campaign to Criticize Lin Piao and Confucius.

1974: *January* The Campaign to Criticize Lin Piao and Confucius gathers momentum as a mass movement.

1975: *January* Fourth National People's Congress held in Peking.

April Chiang Kai-shek dies; Cambodia and South Vietnam fall to Communists.

Glossary of Technical Terms

This glossary includes only those terms relevant specifically to China which are mentioned in this book. However geographical proper names are not listed here.

a-i—Chinese 'aunty' who looks after a child not her own on behalf of his or her parents. The term is also used to mean simply 'aunty'.

Agrarian Reform Law—Also called the Land Reform Law, issued on 28 June 1950. It provided for the confiscation of land from the landlords and its equitable redistribution among the peasants.

Anti-Rightist Campaign—Movement beginning in June 1957 to struggle against critics of communism who had revealed themselves during the Hundred Flowers period. See also Hundred Flowers.

Association of Southeast Asian Nations (ASEAN)—A body formed in August 1967 to promote regional co-operation between its members, Indonesia, the Philippines, Thailand, Malaysia, and Singapore. It is more economic than political in nature.

Autumn Harvest Uprising—An uprising led by Mao Tse-tung and other Communists in Hunan and Kiangsi in September and October 1927. It aimed to take advantage of the autumn harvest to intensify class struggle in the villages. Although suppressed, it led on to the establishment of the first Communist base in Chingkangshan, Kiangsi, under the leadership of Mao Tse-tung.

bandit extermination campaigns—Term used by the Kuomintang to refer to the succession of attempts to destroy the Communist bases of south China in the early 1930s. They are also called 'encirclement' or 'annihilation' campaigns. There were five in all, launched in December 1930, February 1931, April 1931, June 1932, and October 1933. Only the fifth was successful and resulted in the embarking of the Communists on the famous Long March.

barefoot doctors—Incompletely trained medical practitioners, especially numerous and active in the rural regions of China, who give advice and treatment on common ailments and birth control. Most are young and highly motivated ideologically.

Blue Shirts—A fiercely right-wing secret organization set up to serve Chiang Kai-shek's government. It was at one time under the control of Tai Li, the head of the Kuomintang secret police.

Boxer uprising—An uprising against foreign domination and religion. It was led by a society called the Boxers and its most significant action was in Peking from June to August 1900 where it caused much destruction. It was suppressed by foreign troops with much bloodshed. After that China paid heavy indemnities to the powers for the loss of foreign lives and damage to foreign properties in China.

cadre—A political or administrative leader, especially at grass-roots level.

Cairo Declaration—In December 1943 United States President Roosevelt, British Prime Minister Churchill, and Chiang Kai-shek conferred in Cairo on the prosecution of the war then in progress. The resulting declaration promised, among other things, the return of Manchuria and Taiwan to China after the war.

Canton commune—A Communist-led uprising in Canton. It succeeded in setting up a commune on 11 December 1927, but was suppressed with much loss of life by the 13th.

ch'in—a seven-stringed zither-like Chinese musical instrument, formerly very popular among the educated classes.

China Proper—The eighteen provinces of China south of the Great Wall. They do not include the western areas of China like Sinkiang and Tibet.

Chinese Communist Party—The governing party of China since 1949. It was founded in 1921.

Chinese Eastern Railway—Built across Manchuria by the Russo-Chinese Bank in 1896 under a secret Russo-Chinese treaty of alliance directed against Japanese expansion on the continent. Subsequently Russia developed an active interest in Manchuria, establishing a naval presence in Port Arthur.

Chinese People's Political Consultative Conference—This body was formed as a result of Mao Tse-tung's and the Communist Party's desire to form a coalition government to replace the Nationalist government of Chiang Kai-shek. It consisted of eight 'democratic parties' which were minor political parties that continued to exist after 1949 because they co-operated with the Chinese Communist Party in its united front. The members of the Consultative Conference were chosen by the Communist leadership and, although the minority of its members were Party members, it would not have been possible for this body to take substantial measures of which the Party disapproved. It was a consultative body and its decisions were endorsed by a higher body, in particular the Central People's Government Council which was the highest executive body in the state in 1949 and was chaired by Mao Tse-tung.

Chinese (Kiangsi) Soviet Republic—Independent socialist republic founded by Mao Tse-tung in Kiangsi Province in October 1930. It fell in 1934 when Mao and his followers set out on the Long March.

Civil Aviation Administration of China—China's national airline, usually abbreviated as CAAC.

Comintern—Communist International, formed in March 1919 in Moscow to promote communism in the world and overthrow capitalism. It is also called the Third International. (The First International, also called the International Workingmen's Association, was set up in London in 1864 and the Second in Paris in 1889.)

commune—In China a commune is a co-operative community where most land is collectively owned, but which caters for industry, trade, education, social services, and militia, in addition to agriculture. At present there are more than 50 000 rural communes in China.

Communist Youth League—An association of young socialist activists in China which operates under the aegis of the Communist Party. It plays for the youth a political, social, cultural, and ideological role not unlike the Communist Party's role for the nation. Before 1957 it was called the New Democratic Youth League.

concessions—Because of military weakness, China was forced to grant foreign powers, like Britain, France, Belgium, Russia, Germany, and Japan, sovereignty over some of its cities, or sections of them, and other concerns like railways. The areas where foreign sovereignty operated were known as concessions.

Confucianism—System of ethics and religion based on the virtues advocated by Confucius (551–479 BC), especially filial piety. It is extremely hierarchial both in its theory and practice and was for many centuries the dominant ideology of the Chinese ruling classes.

Cultural Revolution—The largest of the rectification campaigns involving widespread action from the masses. It lasted from 1965 to 1969.

Cultural Revolution Group—A body set up in 1967 to guide the progress of the Cultural Revolution along Maoist lines. It was originally dominated by Mao Tse-tung's wife Chiang Ch'ing and his private secretary Ch'en Po-ta.

Dalai Lama—The title applied to the succession of heads of the Tibetan Buddhist church. The line stretches back to the fifteenth century, but the present Dalai Lama, the fourteenth, fled from Tibet in 1959. From the seventeenth century until very recently, the Dalai Lama was a temporal, as well as spiritual, leader.

Eighth Route Army—The name given to the Communist Army from 1937 to July 1946 when it was renamed People's Liberation Army. See also People's Liberation Army and Red Army.

extraterritoriality—The right of foreigners in China to be placed under the protection of their respective consuls' legal jurisdiction.

First Five Year Plan—An economic plan devised to raise production per person and other economic goals. It ran from 1953 to 1957 and gave priority to industry.

footbinding—An old Chinese custom whereby the feet of almost all Chinese women were tightly bound with cloth from about the age of five, causing pain and deformity. Its aim was to make women more fascinating sexually.

Fourth Five Year Plan—An economic plan devised to raise production over the years 1971–75.

Fourth Front Army—One of the units of the Red Army before the war against Japan. Its leader was Chang Kuo-t'ao, who founded a Provincial Soviet government in parts of Szechwan and Shensi. It collapsed in 1935 after which Chang took part in the Long March with his army. The latter was virtually annihilated, but Chang joined Mao Tse-tung in north Shensi late in 1936. Chang Kuo-t'ao quarrelled with Mao and went over to the Kuomintang in 1938, being expelled from the Communist Party the same year.

Great Leap Forward—A movement in 1958–60 to develop the Chinese economy rapidly along leftist lines: a heavy emphasis was placed on moral incentives, self-reliance, and decentralization of decision-making.

Great Wall—An ancient and enormous wall which stretches from Shanhaikuan on the coast just south of the Hopei-Liaoning border inland for about 6000 kilometres to western Shensi.

ho—Chinese word meaning river, sometimes specifically the Yellow River.

Hundred Flowers—Term applied to a period from May 1956 to June 1957 in China when intellectuals and others were invited to criticize openly the Chinese government, system, and Communist Party.

Hungarian uprising—A revolt in Hungary in October 1956 against the then Soviet-sponsored regime. It succeeded in re-establishing the more liberal government of Imre Nagy, but the Soviet Union sent in troops which overthrew Nagy and suppressed resistance by force.

imperial system of China—System of government found in China from the third century BC until 1911. It was headed by an emperor under whom was a hierarchy of officials and bureaucrats, chosen largely on the basis of education and grasp of Confucian ethical principles.

kiang—Chinese word meaning river, sometimes specifically the Yangtze River.

Kiangsi Soviet—See Chinese Soviet Republic.

Koran—The sacred scripture of Islam. The original is in Arabic.

kulakization—The growth of wealthy farmers in the countryside of a socialist country.

Kutien Conference—Communist conference held in December 1929 at Kutien in Fukien Province. It adopted a report by Mao Tse-tung condemning the ideas of Li Li-san, the urban Communist leader whose strategy was based on the primacy of revolution by the urban proletariat, and advocating the establishment of Party control over the army.

League of Left-wing Writers—An association of radical writers formed in 1930 in Shanghai and heavily dominated by Lu Hsün.

League of Nations—Emerging from the Versailles Peace Conference of 1919 that ended the First World War, this world organization was formed for the purpose of maintaining international peace, the independence and territorial integrity of the nations of the world. Its failure to prevent the outbreak of the Second World War caused it to be replaced by the United Nations in June 1945.

liberated areas—Regions of China controlled by the Communists before 1949.

loess—Fine yellowish silt, which is very fertile.

Long March—March of the Communist forces in 1934–35 from Kiangsi in southeast China to northern Shensi, through Hunan, Kweichow, Szechwan, and Kansu.

Lushan Plenum—The Eighth Plenum (Full Assembly) of the Central Committee of the Chinese Communist Party held at Lushan, a mountain in northern Kiangsi, from 2 to 16 August 1959. It made a number of vital decisions, including one to liberalize commune policy and one to dismiss P'eng Te-huai as Defence Minister.

Manchu dynasty—The dynasty which governed China from 1644 to 1911. It was ruled by a Manchu imperial family and its Chinese name was the Ch'ing dynasty.

Maoism—The philosophy of Mao Tse-tung. Note that this designation is not used by the Chinese themselves, who term the philosophy Mao Tsetung Thought.

Marco Polo Bridge Incident—Japanese troops fired on Chinese in July 1937 by the Marco Polo Bridge outside Peking. The incident sparked off the Sino-Japanese War of 1937–45.

Marriage Law—Law promulgated on 30 April 1950. It provided, among other things, for equal rights for women and free choice of marriage partners for all, and it outlawed concubinage.

May Fourth Movement—A movement of protest in China against certain provisions of the Treaty of Versailles, especially the failure to return to China rights formerly held by Germany in Shantung. It began with large-scale demonstrations in Peking on 4 May 1919, and resulted in China's refusal to sign the Treaty of Versailles and the resignation of the entire Chinese cabinet on 12 June. See also New Culture Movement and Treaty of Versailles.

May Thirtieth Incident—On 30 May 1925 the police of Shanghai's foreign settlement fired into a crowd of students demonstrating against the arrest of strikers from a Japanese mill.

Mixed Court—Set up in Shanghai in 1864, it was presided over by a Chinese magistrate with a foreign 'assessor' sitting as a co-judge. Both foreign and Chinese defendants had rights of trial before judges of their own nationality and by the laws of their own countries.

Nationalist Party—The Party founded by Sun Yat-sen. From 1927 to 1949 it ruled China under Chiang Kai-shek. Its Chinese name is Kuomintang (pronounced Gwormindarng), often abbreviated as KMT.

Nationalists—Adherents of the Nationalist Party.

National Revolutionary Army—The army of the Chinese Nationalists.

New Culture Movement—A progressive movement among intellectuals and literary figures lasting from about 1916 to 1925. It aimed to change the literary and social values of the Chinese away from Confucianism, and was closely related to the May Fourth Movement.

New Economic Policy—Following the Great Leap Forward, there was a return in China to rightist attitudes to economic development; these included pushing material incentives, giving greater power to managers, and laying greater emphasis on profitability than revolution. This was the New Economic Policy (abbreviated as NEP), which ran from 1961 to 1965.

New Fourth Army—A unit of the Communist army formed in January 1938 in Anhwei from various guerrilla groups left behind in the Chingkangshan area when the Red Army embarked on the Long March. Its massacre by Kuomintang forces in January 1941 virtually spelled the end of the Second United Front Period. See also united front.

New Life Movement—A campaign begun in 1934 by Chiang Kai-shek which aimed to revive Confucian virtues and promote public hygiene and honesty.

New Youth—A radical journal of the New Culture Movement, founded by Ch'en Tu-hsiu in 1915.

Northeast China—The standard term used to refer to the three northeastern provinces of China which make up Manchuria: Liaoning, Kirin, and Heilung-kiang.

Northern Expedition—Military campaign led by Chiang Kai-shek. It began from Canton in July 1926 and moved north. It sought to bring the warlords of north China under Chiang's control and by 1928 had largely succeeded in unifying China under a single government.

Open Door—In September 1899 the American Secretary of State John Hay issued the first Open Door note aimed at the preservation of equal foreign opportunity in China. In July 1900 Hay issued a second note stating the American desire for the maintenance of China's integrity, of all rights guaranteed to the treaty powers, and of the principle of equal trade opportunity in China. After that the Open Door became the traditional American policy towards China.

Partial Nuclear Test Ban Treaty—Treaty of August 1963 by which the United States, the Soviet Union, and Britain agreed to discontinue nuclear testing in the atmosphere, under water, or in outer space. However underground testing was allowed to continue. The treaty went into effect on 10 October 1963 and was ratified by more than one hundred other governments, not including France or China.

People's Liberation Army—The name given to the army of the Communists in China in July 1946 and retained since that time. It is often abbreviated to PLA. See also Red Army.

People's war—A protracted, revolutionary struggle waged by the oppressed people in demand of a just society and radical changes in the existing power structure. According to Mao Tse-tung, it is the inevitable result of the inherent class contradictions (conflict) within individual societies and between nations. It can be a civil war directed against reactionary rulers, or a national liberation movement directed against colonial rule and imperialism.

Politburo—The Political Bureau of the Chinese Communist Party is the main executive agent of the Party Central Committee, itself the highest executive body of the Party.

rectification campaigns—Periodic movements to purify the Chinese Communist Party of backward, anti-Communist, or reactionary influences. The first great rectification campaign took place in Yenan from 1941 to 1944.

Red Army—The name given to the Communist army until the outbreak of the Sino-Japanese war in 1937, when the Communist forces were reorganized as the Eighth Route Army of the National Revolutionary Army. See also People's Liberation Army.

Red Guards—Groups of young people who rebelled against the conservatism and backwardness of the Chinese Communist Party during the Cultural Revolution. There were numerous, often conflicting, factions. The Red Guards were stripped of their role as vanguard of the Cultural Revolution in July–August 1968 and disbanded from that time on.

regional opera—Opera found in one or many regions. There are about a hundred types in China, differing from each other mainly in music, dialect, and the region or regions where they are popular.

Republican period—Term usually used to refer to the years 1912–49.

Returned Students—Term applied to Chinese Communist intellectuals who studied in the Soviet Union and in 1930 returned to China where they exerted a pro-Russian influence within the Chinese Communist movement. They are also known as the Twenty-eight Bolsheviks. See also Tsunyi Conference.

Revolution of 1911—The revolution which overthrew the Manchu dynasty and set up the Republic of China.

Self-strengthening Movement—A series of efforts in the second half of the nineteenth century to strengthen China through the restoration of Chinese traditional scholarship as 'substance' and the application of the new Western learning for its usefulness in technological and scientific development.

Shanghai Opera—The form of regional folk opera found in Shanghai.

Shansi-Chahar-Hopei Border Area —The regions round the borders of the three provinces of Shansi, Chahar (comprising part of what is now Inner Mongolia), and Hopei. The Communists set up a Border government there in January 1938.

Sian Incident—From 12 to 25 December 1936 Chiang Kai-shek was held prisoner by Chang Hsüeh-liang outside Sian to force him to form a united front with the Communists against Japan. This event, called the Sian Incident, resulted in the formation of the Second United Front.

Socialist Education Movement—A campaign lasting from 1962 to 1966 aimed at educating the rural people anew towards socialism and at curbing the trend towards liberalism in the countryside.

Southeast Asia Treaty Organization (SEATO)—A body formed in September 1954 for the purpose of collective defence arrangements for Southeast Asia against 'Communist aggression', whether invasion or subversion. Its original membership consisted of the United States, Britain, France, Australia, New Zealand, Pakistan, the Philippines, and Thailand.

Taiping revolution—The largest in scale of the peasant uprisings of China before the present century. Starting in the far south in 1850, the Taiping forces took the city of Nanking in 1853, making it their capital. They later went within a hundred miles of the Manchu imperial capital Peking and almost succeeded in overthrowing the Ch'ing dynasty. However by the early 1860s the tide had turned against them and the last remnants were suppressed in 1866. Taiping ideology was very egalitarian by the standards of its time and strongly influenced by Protestant Christianity. The leader of the movement, until his death in 1864, was Hung Hsiu-ch'üan.

Taiwan rebellion—Following the shooting of an old woman by a Kuomintang policeman in February 1947, the people of Taipei became so incensed over Kuomintang oppression on the island that they seized control of almost all the city of Taipei. In the first half of March, however, KMT troops put down the rebellion with much bloodshed.

Taoism—An ancient form of Chinese philosophy and religion. The philosophical branch is traced to Lao-tzu (sixth century BC) whose doctrine is founded on the idea of 'doing nothing'. The religious branch is a later development. There is a hierarchy of priests with their own temples, rituals, and bible.

Ten Great Relationships—Maoist strategy for Chinese overall development put forward in 1956. It emphasized decentralization of decision-making, mass mobilization, and moral as opposed to material incentives.

Third International—see Comintern.

Three Principles of the People—The core ideas of the political philosophy of

Sun Yat-sen, called in Chinese *San-min-chu-i*. The three principles are nationalism, people's rule, and people's livelihood.

Treaty of Nanking—The treaty which ended the First Anglo-Chinese War or Opium War. It was signed in Nanking on 29 August 1842 between China and Britain. China gave substantial concessions to Britain, including an indemnity and the cession of the island of Hong Kong.

Treaty of Versailles—The agreement which ended the First World War. It was signed in Versailles near Paris on 28 June 1919, but had been drafted somewhat earlier.

Tsunyi Conference—Conference held in Tsunyi, Kweichow Province, by the Communists in January 1935 during their Long March. It resulted in an increase of Mao Tse-tung's control over the Communists at the expense of the influence of the returned students. See also Returned Students.

Twenty-one Demands—Demands made by Japan to China in January 1915 aimed at subordinating China to Japan's will.

unequal treaties—The series of treaties, beginning with that of Nanking, imposed on China by the powerful European nations during the nineteenth century. This system of international relations, which was extremely humiliating for China, was not formally abolished until 1943. See also Treaty of Nanking.

united front—Co-operation between groups, in China normally referring to that between the Communist and Nationalist Parties. The two main periods of united front were 1923–27 and 1936–41. They are called respectively the First and Second United Front Periods. See also New Fourth Army.

Versailles Peace Conference—The conference which arranged the peace treaty in 1919 at the end of the First World War. See also Treaty of Versailles.

walking on two legs—Term used in China to denote the promotion of two-pronged policies. In the economic field it means the simultaneous use of labour-intensive and capital-intensive technology, of large- and small-scale plants, and of Chinese and foreign methods.

warlords—regional rulers governing their own areas more or less independently of the central government and, above all, enjoying independent control over their own armies. In China the 'warlord' period is generally dated from 1917 to 1928 during which there was no government with effective control throughout China. However it is important to note that more or less independent warlords held sway in their own regions long before 1917 and after 1928.

Washington Conference—Held from 12 November 1921 to 2 February 1922, it was called mainly on American initiative to deal with the postwar settlement in the Far East.

Wuhan Incident—A mutiny against representatives of the central Chinese government which took place in Wuhan in July 1967. It was organized by the regional military commander Ch'en Tsai-tao and was the most famous challenge to Mao Tse-tung from a local leader in the Cultural Revolution.

Yalta Agreement—A secret agreement signed on 11 February 1945 between Roosevelt, Churchill, and Stalin which, among other matters, set forth the terms on which the Soviet Union would enter the war against Japan.

Index

ch'in 181, 241
Chin Ching-mai 181
China—*see* China Proper, Manchuria,
  north China, People's Republic of
  China, south China; *see also* area,
  Communist Party of China, foreigners,
  Japan, leadership, Republic of China,
  socialism, the West, *et passim*
China Proper 2, 3, 5, 9, 117, 122, 123,
  241
China's Destiny 34, 236
Chinchow 132
Chinese Alps 3
Ch'ing dynasty 243
  asserts suzerainty in Tibet 188
  collapse of (1911) 27, 162, 185, 187,
    207, 235, 246
  and foreign powers 208
  P'u-i as emperor of 196
  system of, persists into Republican
    period 82, 85, 157–8
  and Taiping revolution 195, 246
Ch'ing empire 48, 49, 188, 224
ching-t'ien 84
Chinghai 140, 152
Chinghai-Tibet Plateau 3, 5–7, 11, 18
Chingkangshan 34, 235, 240, 244
Chingkiang 12
Chingtiehshan 23
Chinling Range 5, 7, 18, 21, 22, 115,
  117, 118
Chinsi 132
Chinwangtao 140
Chiungchou Straits 2
cholera 97
Choonhavan, Chatichai 229
Chou En-lai
  career before 1949 31, 32, 41
  career post-1949 66, 74, 75, 238, 239
  in foreign policy 213, 217, 219, 221,
    237, 238
Chou Shu-jen—*see* Lu Hsün
Choushan Archipelago 2
Christianity, Christians 150–4 *passim*,
  168, 182, 207, 246
chromium 24
Chu Te 33, 35, 36, 37, 235
Chung-kuo—*see* central kingdom
Chungking 89, 90, 129, 139, 198, 204
Chungsha Islands 2
churches 168
Churchill, W. 200, 241, 247
cities
  coastal 32, 115, 135, 140, *see also* ports
  communications of 140
  and the Communist Party 31, 33, 39,
    90, 166, 172, 243

and education or educated people 29,
  31, 56, 149, 154
growth of 91, 115
industrial pattern of 83, 126, 133, 139
living standards in 97
and the Nationalist Party 29, 55, 203,
  236
population of 103, 107, 109, 112, 172
and revolution 31, 32, 235, 243
social trends in 147, 150–4 *passim*,
  158–62 *passim*, 168, 170, 238, 242
see also countryside, the West, and
  individual cities such as Canton,
  Changchun, Chengchow, Chengtu,
  Hankow, Hanyang, Harbin, Lanchow, Loyang, Patotow, Peking,
  Shanghai, Sian, St Louis, Wuchang,
  Wuhan, etc.
civil servants 93
clan 60, 61, 169
classes (school) 177
  length 156, 176
classes (social) 178
  background 177
  capitalist 79, 83
  comprador 79, 83–4
  differentiation between 105
  educated 241
  land-owning 75
  rich 85, 93, 155, 161
  ruling 49, 242
  slave-owning 75
  struggle between 29, 31, 33, 41, 66, 70,
    221, 238, 240, *see also* thought of Mao
    Tse-tung
  working 68, 90, 91, 177
  see also proletariat, workers
classics 154
climate 2, 5, 7, 18–23, 25, 112, 117,
  124, *see also* crops, Manchuria, north
  China, peasants, Shanghai, Sinkiang,
  south China, Yangtze River
clinics 177
clocks, water 80
cloth 98, 135, 146, 242
clothing 42, 117
Cloudy Peak Range 3
coal 132
  places of supply of 7, 83, 101, 127, 131,
    135
  production of 23, 87, 103, 131
  and steam locomotives 139
  transport of 88
coal, coking 131
coalition government 42, 203, 236, 241
coal mines 87
coarse grains 115–19 *passim*

regionalism 27, 34, 51, 74, 81, 82, 85–7,
  see also provincialism
registration of marriages 61, 170
Regulations, Provisional Factory 89
relations, international 47, 65, 185–234
religion 46, 145, 149–54, 155, 165, 167–8,
  240, 242, 246
  popular 149–50, 153–4, 167–8
  see also Cultural Revolution, education,
    peasants, Republic of China, thought
    of Mao Tse-tung
Renaissance 182
rents 36, 81–2, 91, 95
  reduction of 32, 36, 41, 236
repair plants 133
'Report of an Investigation into the
  Peasant Movement in Hunan' 33, 148
Republic of China 27–45 *passim*, 187–9
  and the arts 157–61 *passim*
  and education 154, 175
  and the family 61
  foundation of 27, 185, 235, 246
  ideology of 28
  and nationalism 51–4
  and religion 149–54 *passim*, 164
  territory of 193, 195, 196
  on Taiwan 212–14 *passim*, 217, 218,
    227
  see also Chiang Kai-shek, Nationalist
    Party, Sun Yat-sen
republicanism 29, 50
research 181
  scientific 97
reservoirs 15, 17, *see also* Kuanting
  reservoir, Miyun reservoir, Sanmen
  Gorge reservoir
restaurants 152
restorationism 28, 75, 151
'Returned Students' 39, 236, 245–6, 247
revenue 82, 86, 91, 97, 188
revisionism 215, 223, 224, 238
revolution 95, 145, 194, 244
  agricultural 62, *see also* land reform
  and the arts 158, 161, 179, 182
  Communist 60, 75, 76, 86, 87, 91, 93–9
    passim, 221, 223, *see also* peasants
  and Confucianism 146, 207
  and economics 96, 105
  'export' of 210, 228
  future of 210
  industrial 80
  intellectual 58, 189, 190, *see also* May
    Fourth Movement etc.
  Mao Tse-tung's views on 33, 67, 90,
    167, 210
  nationalist 30, 51, 53
  of 1911 27–9 *passim*, 50, 60, 84, 152,

158, 159, 185, 188, 246
  and the Party 224
  of the peasants 84, 91, 246
  social 55
  Russian 30, 31, 53, 95, 150
  and women 148
  see also cities, Cultural Revolution,
    Taiping revolution
rice 5, 9, 82, 86, 91, 113–22 *passim*
  total production of 115
  see also paddy rice
rice Christians 153
rights 47, 66
  sovereign 185, 189, 192–6 *passim*, 204,
    219, 245
river valleys 2, 23, 121
  Pearl 5
  Wei 137
  Yangtze—*see* Yangtze Valley
  Yellow 5, 15
rivers 3–18 *passim*, 25, 103, *see also*
  Amazon, Amur, East, Hai, Han, Hwai,
  Liao, Mekong, Min, North, Nun, Ob,
  Pai, Pearl, Salween, Sungari, Taching,
  Tarim, Tsangpo, Tzuya, Ussuri, Wei,
  West, Yangtze, Yellow, and Yungting
  Rivers
roads 80, 83, 88, 124, 139, 140
romanization of script 176
Rome 168
Roosevelt, Franklin D. 200, 204, 241,
  247
rubber 23
Russell, Bertrand 150
Russia, Russians
  before 1917 187, 188, 192, 200, 241,
    242
  post-1917—*see* Soviet Union
  White 191

sacrifices 149
St Louis 27
salinity 8, 121
salt 23
  sea 135
Salween River 9
San-min-chu-i—*see* Three Principles of the
  People
sand dunes 124
Sanmen Gorge reservoir 15
savings 62, 81, 85, 97, 98, 101
Scandinavia 205
schools 51, 56, 96, 152, 154–6 *passim*, 175,
  178, 238
  medical 156
  missionary 154, 155, 176
  primary 155, 156, 176

private 154, 176
religious 152, 168
secondary 29, 73, 154–6, 176, 178
state 154, 176
Schumann, Maurice 217
science
in China before 1949 80, 84, 150, 152, 246
in China since 1949 77, 97, 107, 175, 176, 220, 232
see also the West
Science and Civilisation in China 80
scientists 106
Sea of Japan 225, 228
seabed, jurisdiction over 211
seas 1–2, 12, 17, 123, 135
sea limit, territorial 2
see also Arctic, Pohai, South China, and Yellow Seas
secularism 149, 150, *see also* Communists
security, national 209–13 *passim*, 215, 227, 231
seeds 115, 121, 125
self-determination 29, 190
self-reliance 42, 65, 99, 101, 104, 141, 224, 228, 242
self-strengtheners 154, 246
self-sufficiency 42, 104, 133
in grain 115
in oil 131
regional 86, 98, 101, 115, 126, 127, 129, 131
sericulture 117
'Serve the People' 165–6
serving the people 42, 96
sesame seed 116
Seventh Fleet (US) 212
sex, extra-marital 172
sexuality 146, 173, 177, 242
Shanghai 85
captured by Japan 198
climate of 22
communications 17, 140
communiqué 217–18
as cultural centre, before 1949 56, 153, 157, 159, 161, 243; since 1949 169, 170, 183, 238
foreign community or settlement of 193, 195, 244
as industrial centre 55, 83, 87, 89, 90, 126–37 *passim*
massacre of (1927) 32, 90, 235
Municipal Council of 90
near mouth of Yangtze 11
as political centre 73, 74
seat of Central Committee of Communist Party 36

seized by Communists (1927) 32
site of formation of Communist Party (1921) 150
as trade centre 188
see also opera
Shanhaikuan 243
Shansi-Chahar-Hopei border area 156, 246
Shansi Province 5, 7, 13, 84, 88, 115, 158, 246
Shantung Peninsula 7, 13, 21
Shantung Province
topography 8, 17
economy 83, 115, 116, 126
as German or Japanese sphere of interest 189, 190, 192, 244
share-renting 82
shareholders 80
Shasi 12
sheep 123
Shengli 132
Shensi Province 7, 13, 37–41 *passim*, 87, 115, 116, 137, 236, 242, 243
Shenyang 133, 140
Shihchiachuang 137
shipbuilding 133, 140
shipping 133, 140
ships 18
Si Kiang—*see* West River
Sian 126, 137, 140
Sian Incident 39, 41, 197–8, 236, 246
Siberia 21, 191, 223, 225, 228
Sikkim 1, 231
silk 83, 112, 127, 135, 139
silt 9, 11, 12, 13, 15, 17, 18, 103, 273, *see also* loess
silver 24
simplification of characters 176
Singapore 230, 240
Sinkiang
climate of 18, 22
communications 140
economy of 23, 116, 132, 137
Islam in 152
politics of 191, 201, 203, 224, 225, 241
topography of 2, 3, 9, 11
sisal 23
Sisha Islands 2
smallpox 97
snow 5, 11, 22, 27
Snow, Edgar 36
soap 116
socialism, socialists 31, 67
and the arts 159, 178, 179
British 95, 150
in China since 1949 63, 64, 66, 73, 75, 105, 107, 125, 172, 212, 223, 242,

civil, general 43, 59, 62, 189, 200, 245;
  1927–36 198; 1946–49 42–3, 86–7,
  92, 202, 204, 211, 212, 219, 236
 expenditure on 84–5
 forces change 145
 hindrance or destruction caused by 36,
  59, 95
 Sino-Soviet 225, 226
 to suppress Algerian independence 214
 people's 228, 238, 245
 see also thought of Mao Tse-tung
War
 First Anglo-Chinese (Opium) 208, 247
 First Indochina 213
 First World 29, 31, 87, 129, 150, 189–
  91 *passim*, 243, 247
 India-Pakistan (1971) 230–1, 239
 Korean 65, 66, 69, 212, 215, 219, 220,
  227, 236
 Pacific 199–201
 Russo-Japanese 187
 Second World 65, 79, 127, 129, 186,
  199–201, 243
 Sino-Indian border 230, 238
 Sino-Japanese (1894–95) 48, 87, 187
 Sino-Japanese (1937–45) 92, 186, 198–
  201, 219, 227, 236, 241, 244, 247; and
  the arts 159, 179; and the
  Communists 39, 41–2, 57, 58, 149,
  196, 242; and the economy 41, 92;
  and the Nationalist Party 41, 55,
  204; period of 55, 62, 68, 148, 152,
  155, 203, 211, 245
 Vietnam 71, 215, 238
 warlords 247
  defy central government 86, 235
  Chiang Kai-shek's Northern Expedition
   fights against 31, 34, 85, 194, 245
  and the economy 84, 139
  and famine 91
  and foreigners 53, 192, 193
  and the gentry 82
  individual warlords 34, 84
  and nationalism 51
  period of 187, 189, 247
  and Yüan Shih-k'ai 27, 30, 235
 Washington 189, 193, 199, 201–4 *passim*,
  217
  Conference 192, 247
 water conservancy 8, 9–18, 119
  control 109, 115, 125
  traffic 140
 waterways 88, 139, 140, *see also*
  transportation
 weather patterns 103
 weddings 170, 173
 week, working 172

Wei River 15, 137
Weihaiwei 195
Weishan Lake 18
West River 9, 11, 17, 140
West, the, Western 85, 228
 assistance to China 197, 198
 characteristics of 92, 166, 170, 172, 173,
  178
 comment on China 101, 124, 205
 economic intervention in China 80, 82,
  83
 as economic model 34, 107, 111
 economic theory in 63, 80
 impact on China 48–52 *passim*, 153,
  154, 157, 159, 161, 185, 207
 influence on Chinese cities 56, 90
 powers of 54, 186–8 *passim*, 192–8
  passim, 204, 208, 223
 reaction against, by China 48, 54, 65,
  150, 151, 190, 193
 relations with China since 1949 208,
  211–18, 234
 as source of science and technology 28,
  125, 190, 246
 styles of painting 161
 and Sun Yat-sen 50, 53
 see also capitalism, communism, Europe,
  imperialism, industrialization
Whampoa 140
wheat 8, 82, 88, 113–19 *passim*, 122
 total production of 116
White-haired Girl, The 179–81
willows 124
Wilson, Woodrow 29
winds 5, 18, 21
winter 8, 11, 18, 19, 21, 115, 177
Wittfogel, Karl 81
wives, place of 145–8 *passim*, 171
wolfram 23
women 101
 education of 155
 membership of Chinese Communist
  Party 171
 social status of 75, 145–9 *passim*, 169,
  171, 242
 on the stage 159, 179
 workers 90, 171–2
 see also communes, Cultural Revolution,
  equality, revolution
wool 123, 135, 139
work points 63
workers
 attitudes of 96, 98, 104, 108, 154
 conditions of 89, 93, 108
 and education 176, 177
 political role of 32, 39, 51, 239
world order, Chinese 46, 47, 49